IMAGES
of America

PLAQUEMINE

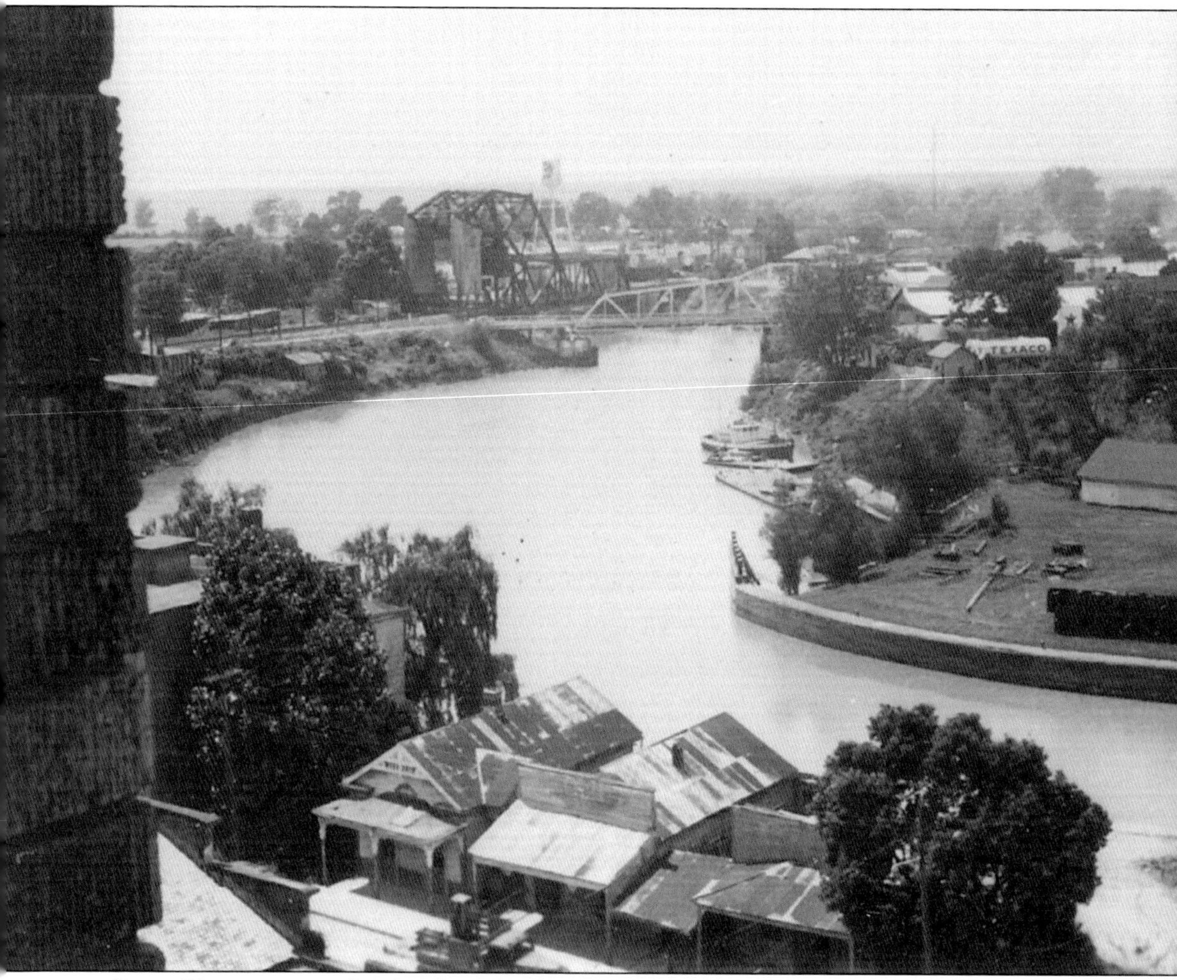

Bayou Plaquemine is what first brought the Natives and then the European and American settlers to this region, as it provided a gateway to the western half of the state. This photograph is from around 1946. (Courtesy of the Neubig Family Collection, Iberville Museum.)

On the Cover: Taken around 1922 by Philip Neubig, this photograph offers a view of Plaquemine centered on the Plaquemine Lock during high water. Also shown is the Wilbert Theatre (back center) and a view down Main Street. Neubig was born in Plaquemine in 1898 and died in 1974. He studied as an engineer at Louisiana State University but was passionate about photography. He built his family home on Church Street near Labauve Avenue. (Courtesy of the Neubig Family Collection, Iberville Museum.)

IMAGES
of America

PLAQUEMINE

Meghan C. Sylvester and Burke Devillier

ARCADIA
PUBLISHING

ISBN 978-1-4671-0714-3

Published by Arcadia Publishing
Charleston, South Carolina

Printed in the United States of America

Library of Congress Control Number: 2021945851

For all general information, please contact Arcadia Publishing:
Telephone 843-853-2070
Fax 843-853-0044
E-mail sales@arcadiapublishing.com
For customer service and orders:
Toll-Free 1-888-313-2665

Visit us on the Internet at www.arcadiapublishing.com

To the people of Plaquemine.

Contents

Acknowledgments

This book would not have been possible without the numerous people dedicated to researching and sharing the fascinating history of Plaquemine. I'd first like to thank Judy Riffel for sharing her detailed research of early navigation along Bayou Plaquemine with me. Additionally, I'd like to thank Rita Lynn Jackson, those at the law firm of Barry Marionneaux, Mary Neubig, Mercedes Dore, Linda Johnson, and Rita Mooney for sharing their private collections and knowledge of Plaquemine's history.

Unless otherwise stated, all of the images come from the Iberville Museum Association. However, I'd like to thank those at the many libraries and archives who assisted me in locating all additional photographs used in this volume: Amanda K. Hawk at Louisiana State University Libraries Special Collections, Tricia Gesnar and the researchers at the Associated Press office in New York, and Julie Simoneaux at the Iberville Parish Library (IPL) in Plaquemine. All offered their patience and expertise in the midst of a global pandemic.

I also owe a tremendous amount of thanks to those at the Iberville Museum for supporting me while I worked to complete this book. Zeena and Paul Bouy, you were always a phone call away when I needed you. James "Fry" Hymel, chairman of the Iberville Museum board, thank you for offering your leadership and counsel. And special thanks are due to Stella C. Tanoos, board historian, for her vast knowledge of Plaquemine and the years of research she has shared with me and the museum. She attended every author meeting and has read every draft of this book. Her contributions made this a richer text.

Lastly, I'd like to thank my co-author, Burke Devillier, and the Plaquemine, LA – My Home Town Facebook group community that he and Tanoos built. Your dedication to sharing the memories and stories of Plaquemine and continuing the legacy of Anthony P. Fama, Plaquemine historian, will not be forgotten.

—Meghan C. Sylvester
Director and Curator of the Iberville Museum

INTRODUCTION

Often thought of as a small, quaint town nestled behind the Mississippi River levee, Plaquemine has deep roots in Louisiana's early history. The city is believed to have been named for the wild persimmons that grew along its neighboring bayous. The word "plaquemine" is thought to have Native origins and French influence, with various other spellings such as "Piakimines" or "Pliakemine." Today, the term is also used to describe a prehistoric Native culture that populated the Mississippi River Valley. The Plaquemine people built the mounds at Manchac Point, just three miles northeast of Plaquemine, and are recognized as the ancestors of the Chitimacha Tribe of Louisiana.

When French explorers Pierre Le Moyne d'Iberville and Jean-Baptiste Le Moyne de Bienville arrived in Louisiana in 1699 with the intent of discovering the mouth of the Mississippi River and establishing the colony of Louisiana for the crown, they were led to Bayou Plaquemine by the Bayogoula Tribe. The Natives had met with the explorers as they traveled along the Mississippi River after landing in Mobile Bay and invited them to stay at their village a few miles south of Bayou Plaquemine. Iberville and his men remained there for several weeks before continuing to the site of present-day New Orleans and began preparing a way for permanent French settlement. However, despite efforts made by the French government to bring colonists to their new territory, Natives remained the only inhabitants of the Bayou Plaquemine region until the late 1700s, when Spanish land grants brought in the first European settlers. These were the families of Jean Franchebois, Jacques DeVilliers, Athanase Dardenne, and Augustin Richard.

In 1814, Thomas B. Pipkin, a native of Tennessee, came to Louisiana to defend New Orleans from the British with Gen. Andrew Jackson. He served in Capt. Jacques DeVilliers's unit in Donaldsonville, and after the war, he married DeVilliers's daughter Hyacinthe Armide. In 1817, Pipkin purchased land along Bayou Plaquemine bordering the Mississippi and began operating a ferry. He opened a tavern for travelers along the bayou between New Orleans and the Teche region. Two years later, Pipkin decided to subdivide his land into 54 lots and sell them, printing advertisements in local papers that referred to the lots as "the town of Iberville." This was one of the earliest records of the establishment of the city of Plaquemine. Pipkin's advertisement stated that buyers would gain land in a town with a "good navigable [bayou] for all kinds of boats, for nearly the whole year." Additionally, the article notes access to a great abundance of building timber and a nearby steam sawmill. However, Pipkin did not live to see the town grow. He died during a yellow fever epidemic on October 24, 1819.

By 1826, the Louisiana legislature granted the Opelousas Steamboat Company permission to open and maintain a steamboat and ferry from Bayou Plaquemine to Bayou Courtableau near Washington, Louisiana. As a result, a trade route opened between the parishes of Iberville, St. Martin, and St. Landry. The route benefited the cattle industry in Plaquemine, as drovers from the Attakapas district were able to use the ferry service to transport cattle to the market in New Orleans. Additionally, it opened business between sugar planters and loggers who floated timber down to the sawmills along Bayou Plaquemine. Ultimately, it increased the relationship between the three parishes, resulting in many marriages between families.

Iberville moved its parish seat from the small village of Point Pleasant to Plaquemine in 1835, as the town had been fast-growing in terms of population and commerce. The parish police jury purchased an old building known as the Gainne Hotel on Still Street, which shortly became known as Court Street due to the presence of the courthouse at its head. However, the police jury had plans to erect a new, official courthouse in town in the coming years and built one on a lot on Main Street in 1848. Plaquemine was incorporated in 1838, and Zenon Labauve, a member of the Louisiana senate, was elected its first mayor.

Throughout the second half of the 19th century, Plaquemine developed into "a well built, thriving and bustling town," as described by a tourist in 1860 in the *Gazette and Sentinel* newspaper. Its primary roads were Bank Street, Main Street, Church Street, Eden Street, Plaquemine Street, and Canal Street, later known as Railroad Avenue. They became home to dozens of businesses and residences that built up the community, such as Jacob McWilliams's firm, Roth and McWilliams, which was established in 1851 and was extensively involved in the sugar industry of the parish. A. Wilbert Sons Lumber and Shingle Company opened in 1868 and was influential in developing the parish's lumber industry. And James E. Dunlap's electric company erected a building on Meriam Street around 1909 that provided electricity to the community until 1923.

The introduction of the Plaquemine Lock in 1909 shaped the early part of the 20th century, once again turning Bayou Plaquemine into a commercial transport route that promoted settlement and economic prosperity, as the bayou had been closed since 1868. The lock operated for 52 years and then opened as a state historic site in the 1980s.

During the 1960s, Plaquemine became a hotbed of civil unrest as locals with the Congress of Racial Equality (CORE) began nonviolent demonstrations to protest national segregation laws and voter registration restrictions in Iberville and the surrounding parishes. Plaquemine's protests made national news when local police arrested CORE's president James Farmer in town following a night of marches on city hall and the courthouse. These events became part of the larger civil rights movement that shaped the nation and led to the signing of the Voting Rights Act of 1965. Iberville Parish was one of the three Louisiana parishes that saw a significant increase in black voter registration following the Voting Rights Act. This is undoubtedly due to the diligence of the local black leaders in town.

While much of Plaquemine would likely be unrecognizable to someone traveling through time from the past, there are still many buildings that represent Plaquemine's rich history. The town has a historic district that includes some 130 structures, and several other buildings are listed in the National Register of Historic Places.

With this photograph collection, primarily from local families who shared their collection with the late Anthony P. Fama or the Iberville Museum Association, this book aims to show how the town has changed and to preserve the stories of the people who made their home along the bayou.

One

The Bayous

Plaquemine is uniquely situated along the Mississippi River at the confluence of Bayou Plaquemine and its sister branch, Bayou Jacob. Bayou Plaquemine is a small stream, only about 11 miles long. Still, it became an important route for early travelers as it was one of the few passages that connected the Mississippi and the Atchafalaya Swamp. However, early accounts state that the bayou was not always directly connected with the river. A small strip of land covered in primeval forest and river cane once existed between the two waterways. It was commonly known as the Plaquemine Portage, or simply, "the portage."

According to old newspapers, in the mid-1700s, Joseph Sorrel of the Teche region ran a trade boat that traveled from Bayou Teche to the portage, then transferred to a vessel in the Mississippi that traveled to New Orleans. It was not until the flood of 1770 that exceptionally high floodwaters created a canal connecting the waterways. However, rough currents and continued obstruction by driftwood from the Mississippi resulted in travelers still having to pull their bateau onto the high ground and use the portage to enter the bayous. But this was only the beginning of water travel on Bayou Plaquemine. Over the next 200 years, both Bayou Plaquemine and Bayou Jacob would see significant changes that shaped the town of Plaquemine's growth.

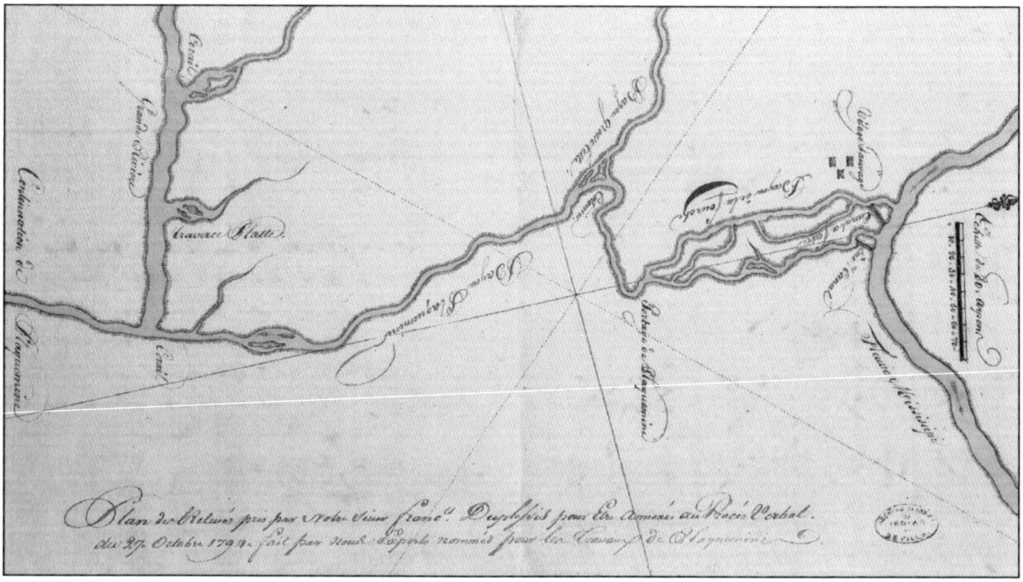

In this land survey map from 1794, Bayou Plaquemine and Bayou Jacob, then referred to as Bayou de la Fourche, were surveyed to determine which would be better suited as the route to the Mississippi River from the Atchafalaya. The four surveyors agreed that Bayou Jacob was the better choice, as it required less clearing and was preferable to navigate. (Courtesy of Archivo General de Indias, Seville, Spain.)

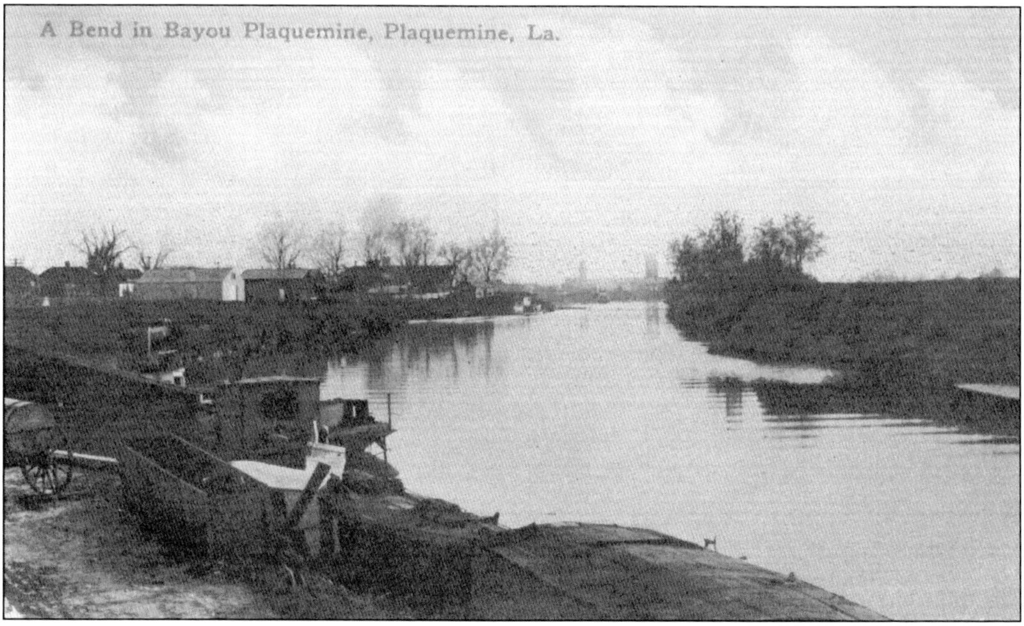

Over the next several years, residents of Attakapas and Opelousas debated over which branch would be more beneficial as a route to the Mississippi. Those in Opelousas found that the Bayou Plaquemine branch was the clearer route, determining that work on Bayou Jacob would flood too much farmland. This postcard of a bend in Bayou Plaquemine is from 1914. (Courtesy of Louisiana State University.)

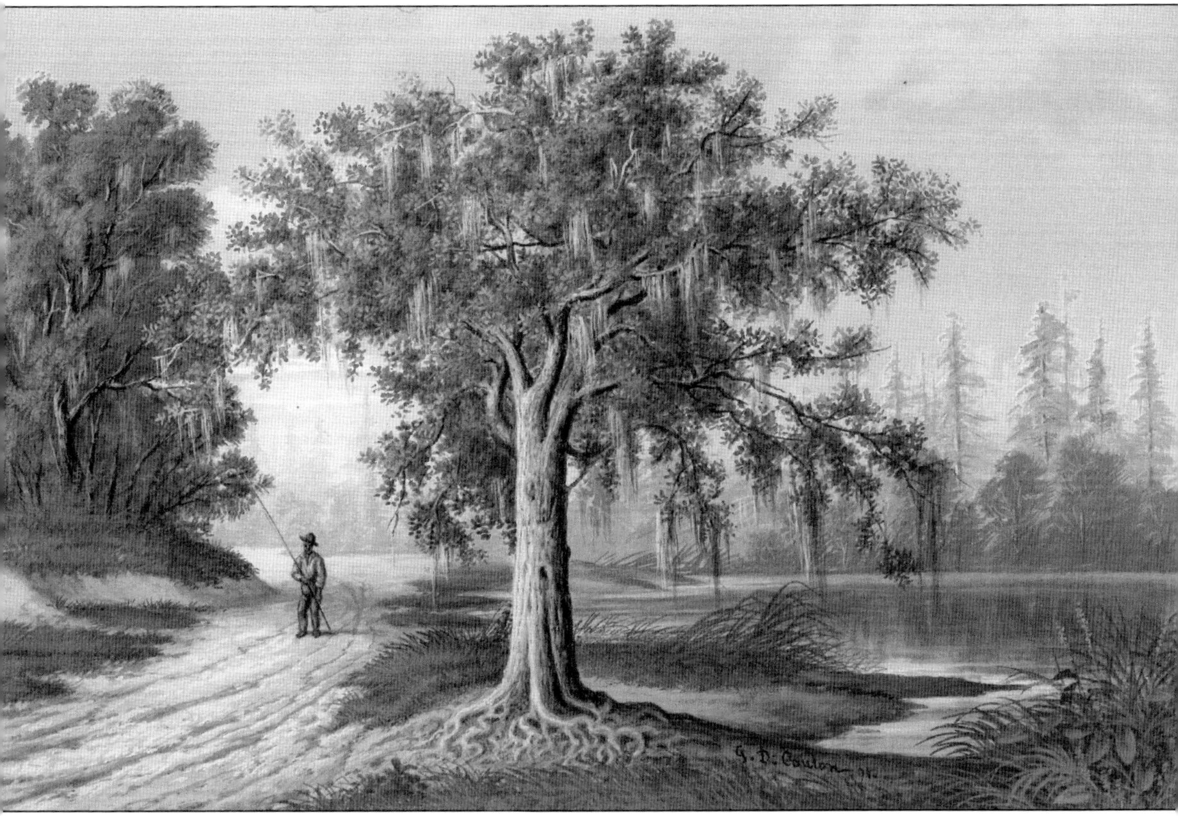

At the time of Sieur d'Iberville's arrival, the Chitimacha Tribe of Louisiana had a village on Bayou Jacob near the Mississippi River. It is uncertain when the Natives left the area, but there were reports of Chitimachas helping travelers enter the bayou in the early 1800s. Their village on Bayou Jacob was part of the bayou's appeal in becoming the main route to the river. However, in 1822, Bayou Jacob was diked, closing it to travelers. The Louisiana legislature granted Giovani Questi, a native of present-day Croatia, permission to build the dike. In turn, he was to maintain the levee and a ferry across Bayou Plaquemine. He operated the ferry until he died in 1833. This 1891 painting is by George David Coulon and is titled *Souvenir of Bayou Jacob*. It is gouache and watercolor mounted on board. (Courtesy of the Historic New Orleans Collection.)

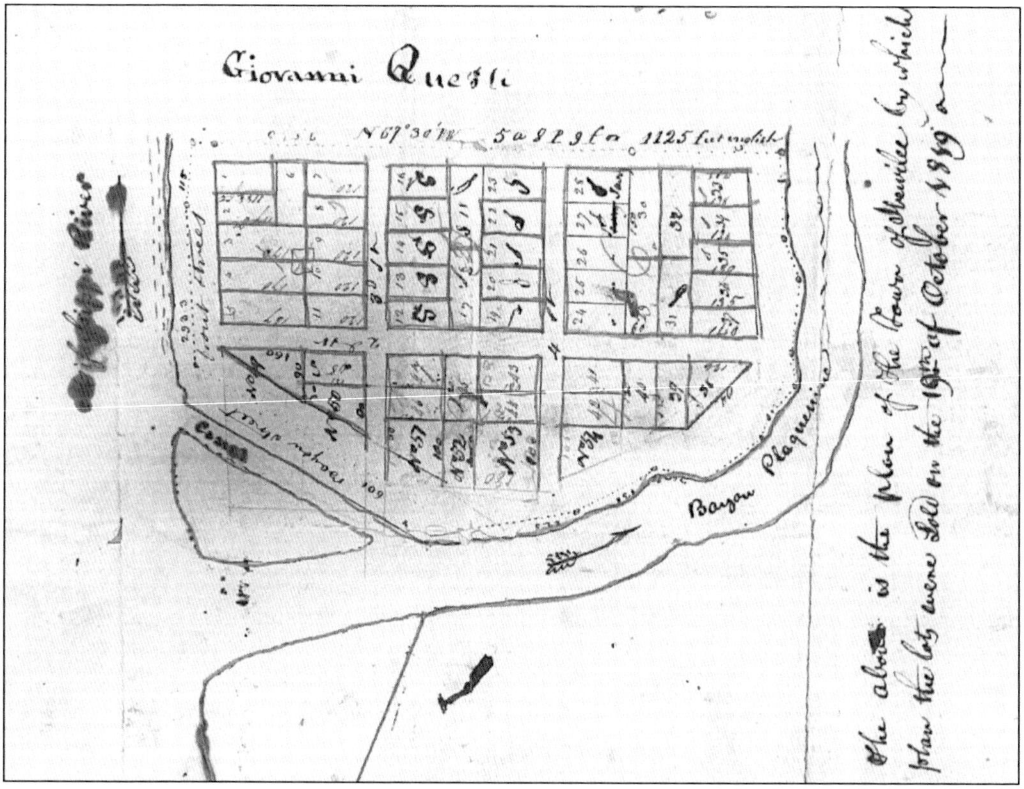

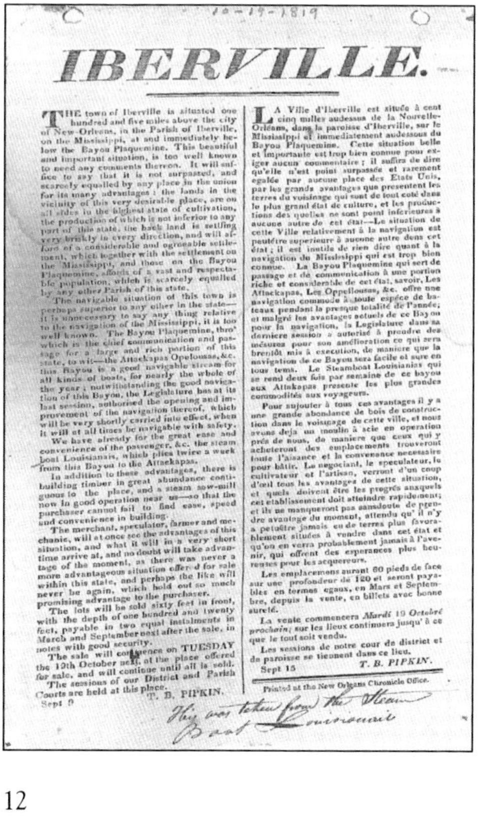

10-19-1819

IBERVILLE.

THE town of Iberville is situated one hundred and five miles above the city of New-Orleans, in the Parish of Iberville, on the Mississippi, at and immediately below the Bayou Plaquemine. This beautiful and important situation, is too well known to need any comments thereon. It will suffice to say that it is not surpassed, and scarcely equalled by any place in the union for its many advantages: the lands in the vicinity of this very desirable place, are on all sides in the highest state of cultivation, the production of which is not inferior to any part of this state, the back land is settling very briskly in every direction, and will afford of a considerable and agreeable settlement, which together with the settlement on the Mississippi, and those on the Bayou Plaquemine, affords of a vast and respectable population, which is scarcely equalled by any other Parish of this state.

The navigable situation of this town is perhaps superior to any other in the state—it is unnecessary to say any thing relative to the navigation of the Mississippi, it is too well known. The Bayou Plaquemine, thro' which is the chief communication and passage for a large and rich portion of this state, to wit—the Attackapas Opelousas, &c. this Bayou is a good navigable stream for all kinds of boats, for nearly the whole of the year; notwithstanding the good navigation of this Bayou, the Legislature has at its last session, authorised the opening and improvement of the navigation thereof, which will be very shortly carried into effect, when it will at all times be navigable with safety.

We have already for the great ease and convenience of the passenger, &c. the steam boat Louisianais, which plies twice a week from this Bayou to the Attackapas.

In addition to these advantages, there is building timber in great abundance contiguous to the place, and a steam saw-mill now in good operation near us—so that the purchaser cannot fail to find ease, speed and convenience in building.

The merchant, speculator, farmer and mechanic, will at once see the advantages of this situation, and what it will in a very short time arrive at, and no doubt will take advantage of the moment, as there was never a more advantageous situation offered for sale within this state, and perhaps the like will never be again, which hold out so much promising advantage to the purchaser.

The lots will be sold sixty feet in front, with the depth of one hundred and twenty feet, payable in two equal instalments in March and September next after the sale, in notes with good security.

The sale will commence on TUESDAY the 19th October next, at the place offered for sale, and will continue until all is sold.

The sessions of our District and Parish Courts are held at this place.

T. B. PIPKIN.

Sept 9

LA Ville d'Iberville est située à cent cinq milles audessus de la Nouvelle-Orléans, dans la paroisse d'Iberville, sur le Mississippi et immediatement audessous du Bayou Plaquemine. Cette situation belle et importante est trop bien connue pour exiger aucun commentaire; il suffira de dire qu'elle n'est point surpassée et rarement egalée par aucune place des Etats Unis, par les grands avantages que presentent les terres du voisinage qui sont de tout coté dans le plus grand état de culture, et les productions des quelles ne sont point inferieures à aucune autre de cet état—La situation de cette Ville relativement à la navigation est peutêtre superieure à aucune autre dans cet état; il est inutile de rien dire quant à la navigation du Mississippi qui est trop bien connue. La Bayou Plaquemine qui sert de passage et de communication à une portion riche et considerable de cet état, savoir, Les Attackapas, Les Oppellousas, &c. offre une navigation commode à toute espéce de bateaux pendant la presque totalité de l'année; et malgré les avantages actuels de ce Bayou pour la navigation, la Legislature dans sa derniere session a autorisé à prendre des mésures pour son amélioration ce qui sera brentôt mis à execution, de maniere que la navigation de ce Bayou sera facile et sure en tous tems. Le Steamboat Louisianias qui se rend deux fois par semaine de ce bayou aux Attakapas presente les plus grandes commodités aux voyageurs.

Pour aujouter à tous ces avantages il y a une grande abondance de bois de construction dans le voisinage de cette ville, et nous avons deja un moulin à scie en operation prés de nous, de maniere que ceux qui y acheteront des emplacements trouveront toute l'aisance et la convenance necessaire pour bâtir. Le negociant, le speculateur, le cultivateur et l'artisan, verront d'un coup d'œil tous les avantages de cette situation, et quels doivent être les progrés auxquels cet etablissement doit atteindre rapidement; et ils ne manqueront pas sansdoute de prendre avantage du moment, attendu qu' il n'y a peutêtre jamais eu de terres plus favorablement situées à vendre dans cet état et qu'on en verra probablement jamais à l'avenir, qui offrent des esperances plus heureuses pour les acquereurs.

Les emplacemens auront 60 pieds de face sur une profondeur de 120 et seront payables en termes egaux, en Mars et Septembre, depuis la vente, en billets avec bonne sureté.

La vente commencera *Mardi* 19 *Octobre prochain*; sur les lieux continuera jusqu' à ce que le tout soit vendu.

Les sessions de notre cour de district et de paroisse se tiennent dans ce lieu.

T. B. PIPKIN.

Sept 15

Printed at the New Orleans Chronicle Office.

This was taken from the Steam Boat Louisianais

In 1817, Pvt. Thomas B. Pipkin of Tennessee purchased land along Bayou Plaquemine and opened a tavern and a ferry service to assist people traveling between west Louisiana and New Orleans. Two years later, he subdivided his land into 54 lots and printed an advertisement in local papers to sell them. This was one of the earliest records of the town of Plaquemine, which was then referred to as Iberville. (Both, courtesy of the Iberville Clerk of Court Office.)

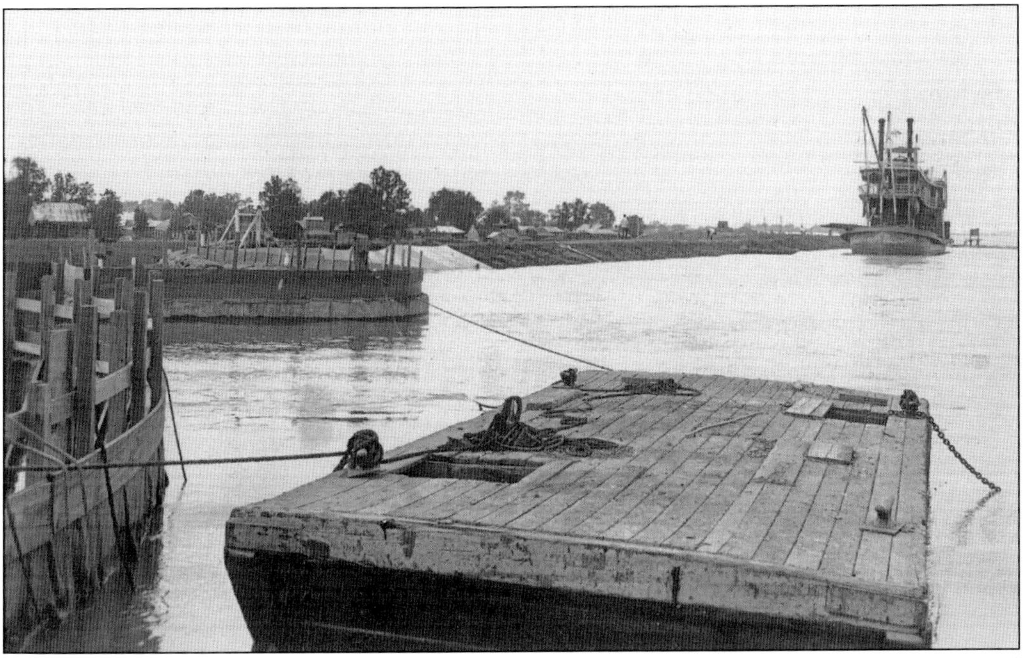

In April 1825, the steamboat *Louisville* entered Bayou Plaquemine from the Mississippi and traveled to St. Martinville. This was the first steamer to pass through the bayou. It was a relatively small boat, but it proved that steamers could use the same inland route used by smaller vessels to travel between New Orleans and the Teche region. The accomplishment signified a reduction in travel time and shipping costs and began a new era of travel for the state. The above c. 1922 photograph shows a steamer approaching the mouth of Bayou Plaquemine and the Plaquemine Lock. The photograph below is believed to be of the steamer *Carrie B. Schwing* making its first voyage in 1904 through the basin.

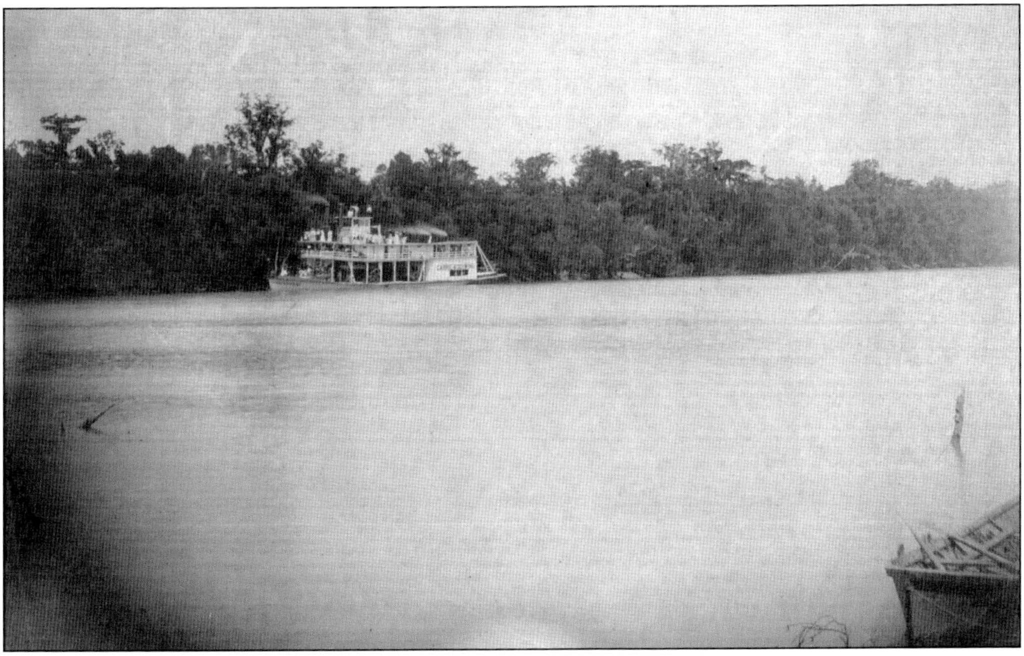

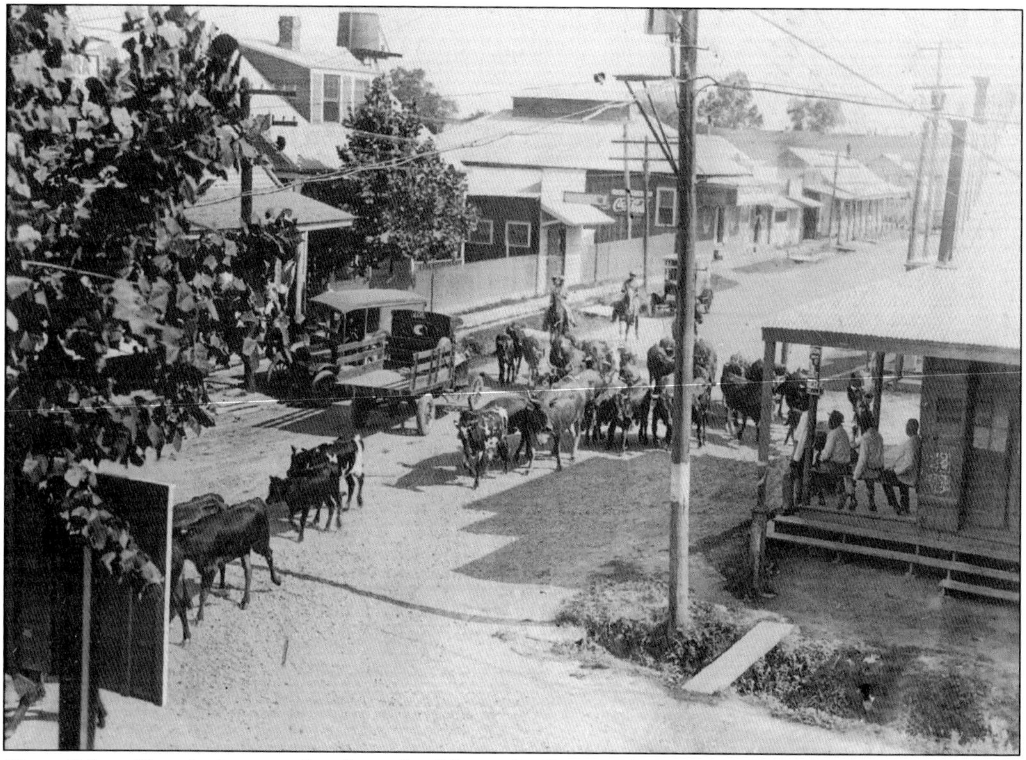

One of the oldest industries that benefited from the Bayou Plaquemine route was the cattle drives. As early as 1765, there was evidence of cattle ranchers in the Attakapas region looking to use the bayou as a quicker route to New Orleans. There was high demand for a road near the bayou because the area was susceptible to thick mud and swamp. By the 1820s, cow-boats started ferrying cattle across the basin, starting at Butte la Rose and traveling to the park at the intersection of Bayou Plaquemine and Grand River. Throughout the 19th century, Plaquemine was a stopping point for cattle drovers traveling between Texas and the Crescent City, visiting its many taverns while they waited for a steamer to take them down the Mississippi. These images are of cattle being driven to higher ground in Plaquemine during spring floods in the 1920s.

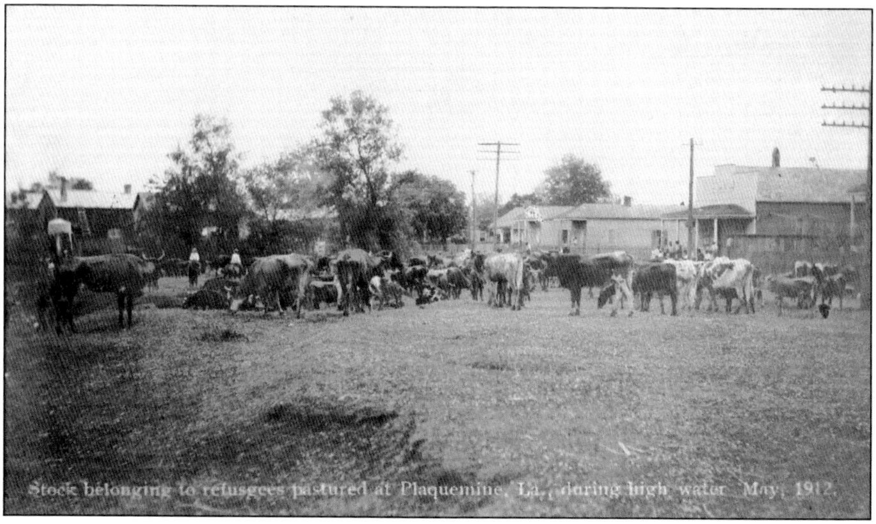

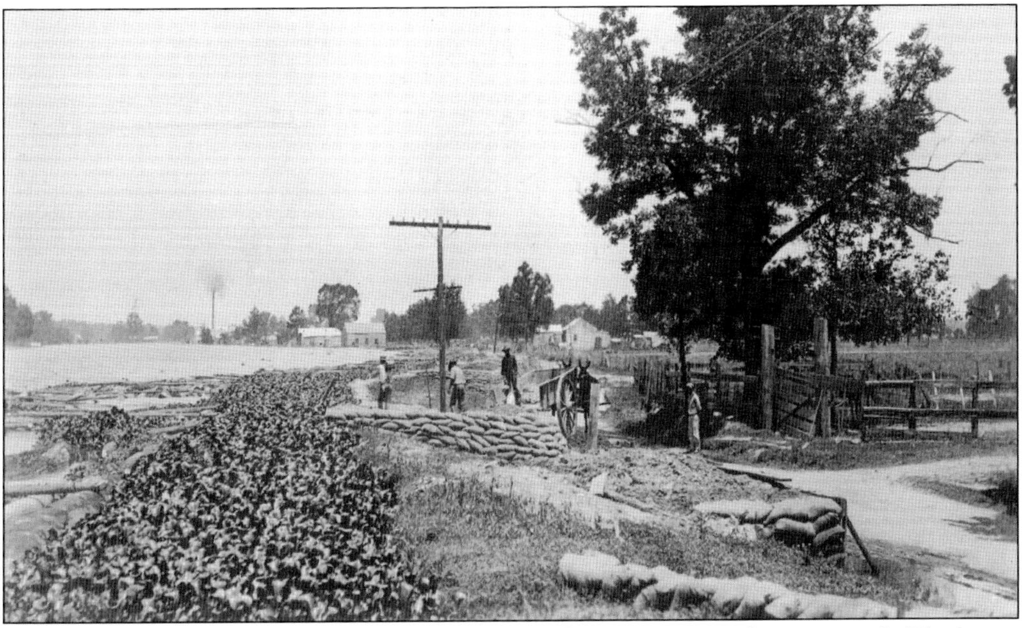

Despite being an important route, navigating Bayou Plaquemine was a dangerous task. The bayou was only passable during the river's high season, but the current was very rapid during high water. Additionally, its mouth was often blocked by driftwood from the Mississippi River and required constant maintenance or it would regularly overflow. This c. 1927 photograph shows flooded fields on Bayou Plaquemine.

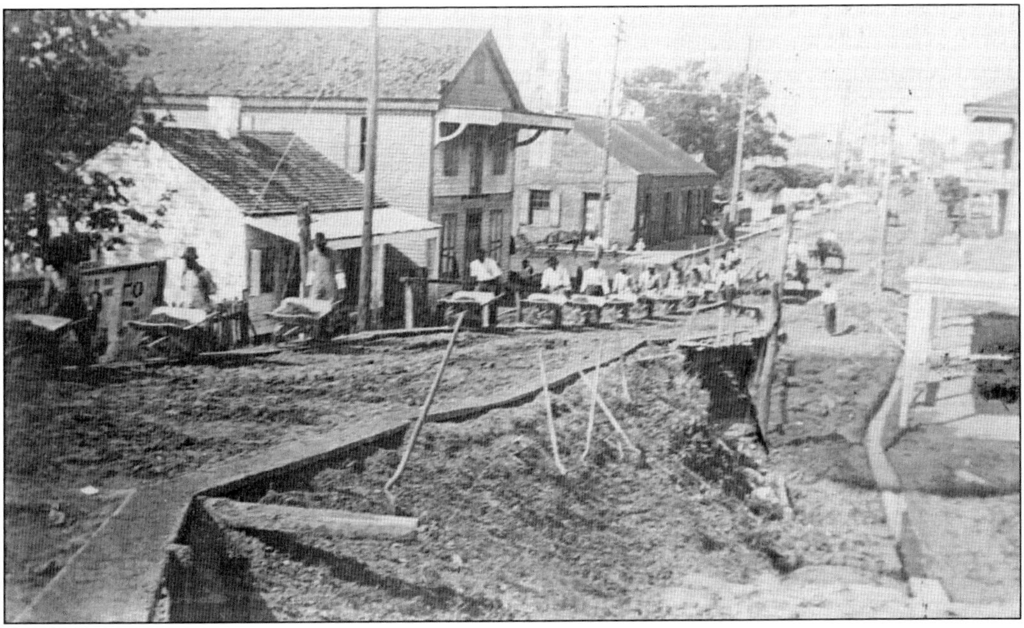

After the Civil War, local officials agreed to close Bayou Plaquemine by extending the Mississippi River levee across its mouth. Damming the bayou was a flood control measure. However, officials were aware that without enslaved people, the cost of maintenance of its levees was too expensive. This photograph is from 1912. Men are wheeling dirt up the levee on Main Street to prepare it for high water.

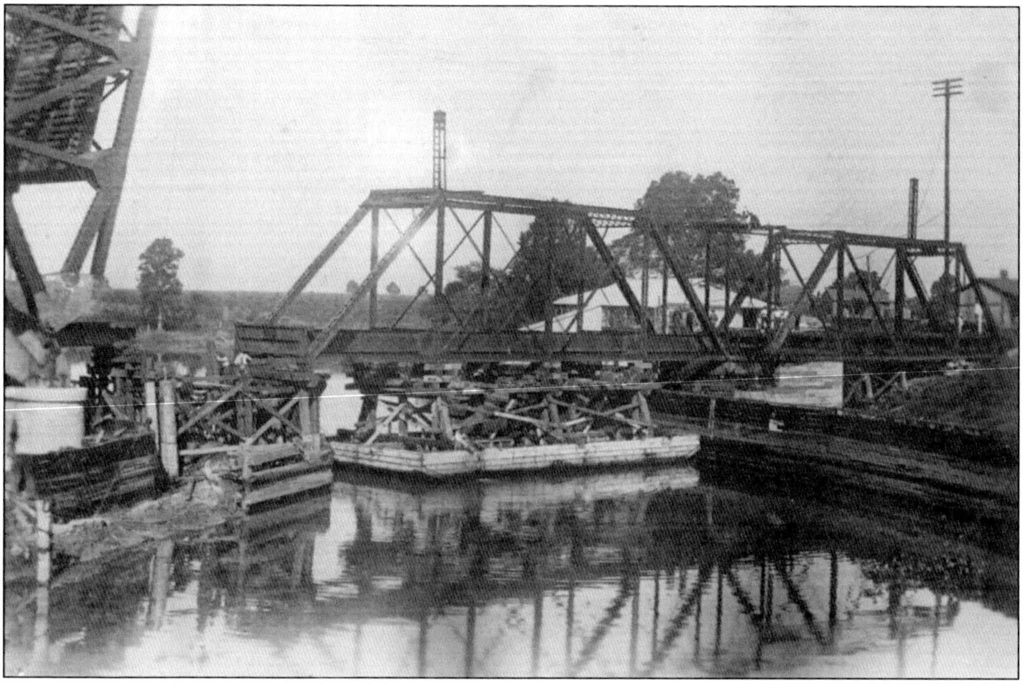

Although the bayou's closure shut off water communication between New Orleans and western Louisiana, industry along Bayou Plaquemine continued to thrive. The new levee meant less overflow into the farmland lining the bayou and the Atchafalaya's lowlands, and some areas of town were able to be developed. In 1888, the Texas & Pacific Railroad built a branch that ran some nine miles down the bayou to Indian Village near Grand River to carry supplies to the many planters and sawmills along Bayou Plaquemine. Plaquemine built good public roads that ran down either side of the bayous. Above is a c. 1923 image showing construction of a new railroad bridge over Bayou Plaquemine. Below is a trip down Bayou Plaquemine to collect palm leaves for Palm Sunday in about 1912.

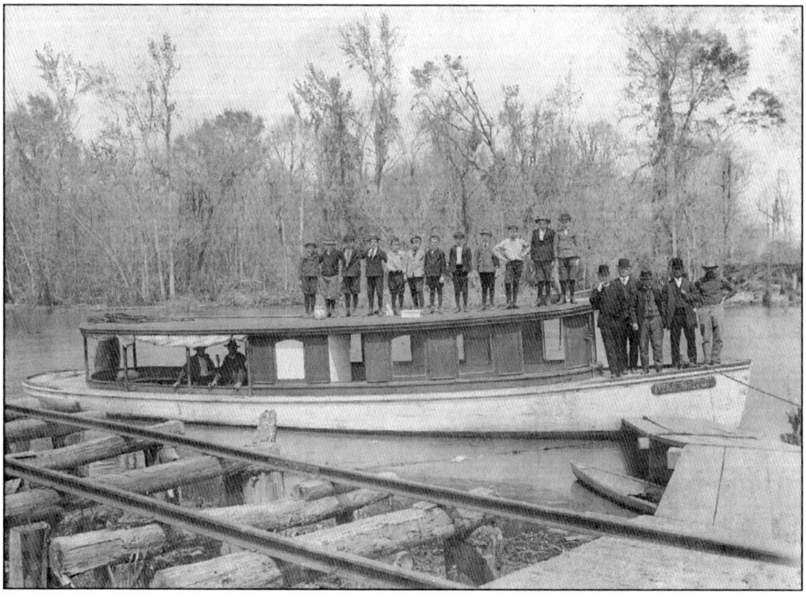

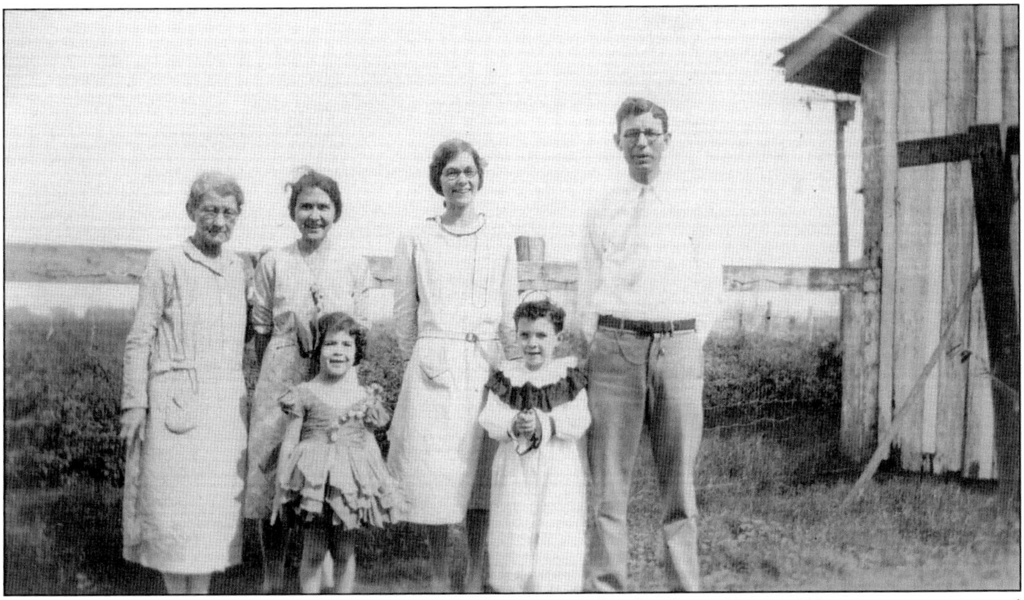

Myrtle Grove, one of the many sugarcane plantations built along Bayou Plaquemine, opened in the late 1890s on the bayou approximately five miles from town. The Hill family ran the plantation store until the 1970s, when it closed. In this c. 1923 photograph of the family, Bayou Plaquemine is seen behind them.

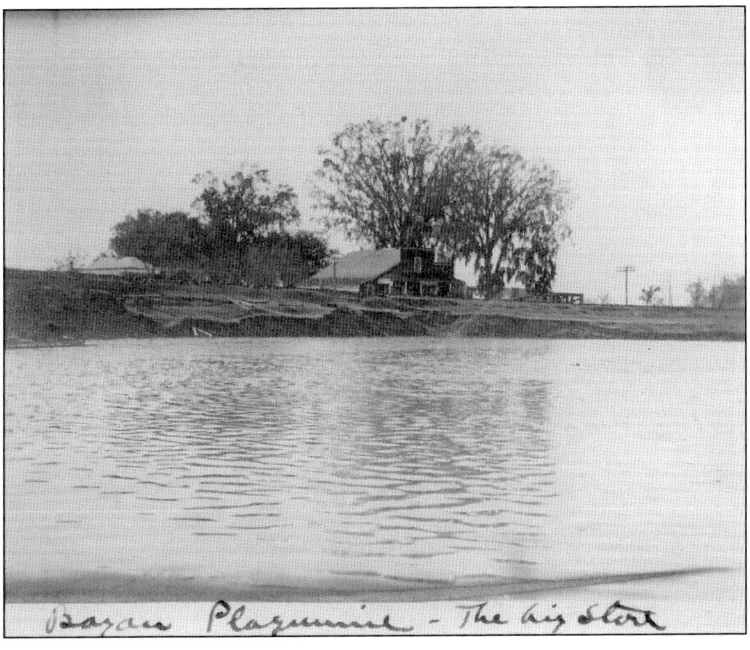

The "big store" on Bayou Plaquemine is believed to be the Milly Plantation Store. The Wilbert family owned both Myrtle Grove and Milly Plantation, and Milly's store was the bigger of the two, giving it the name. This c. 1920s photograph is from the Col. Joseph S. Tate photograph album in Louisiana State University's Special Collections Library.

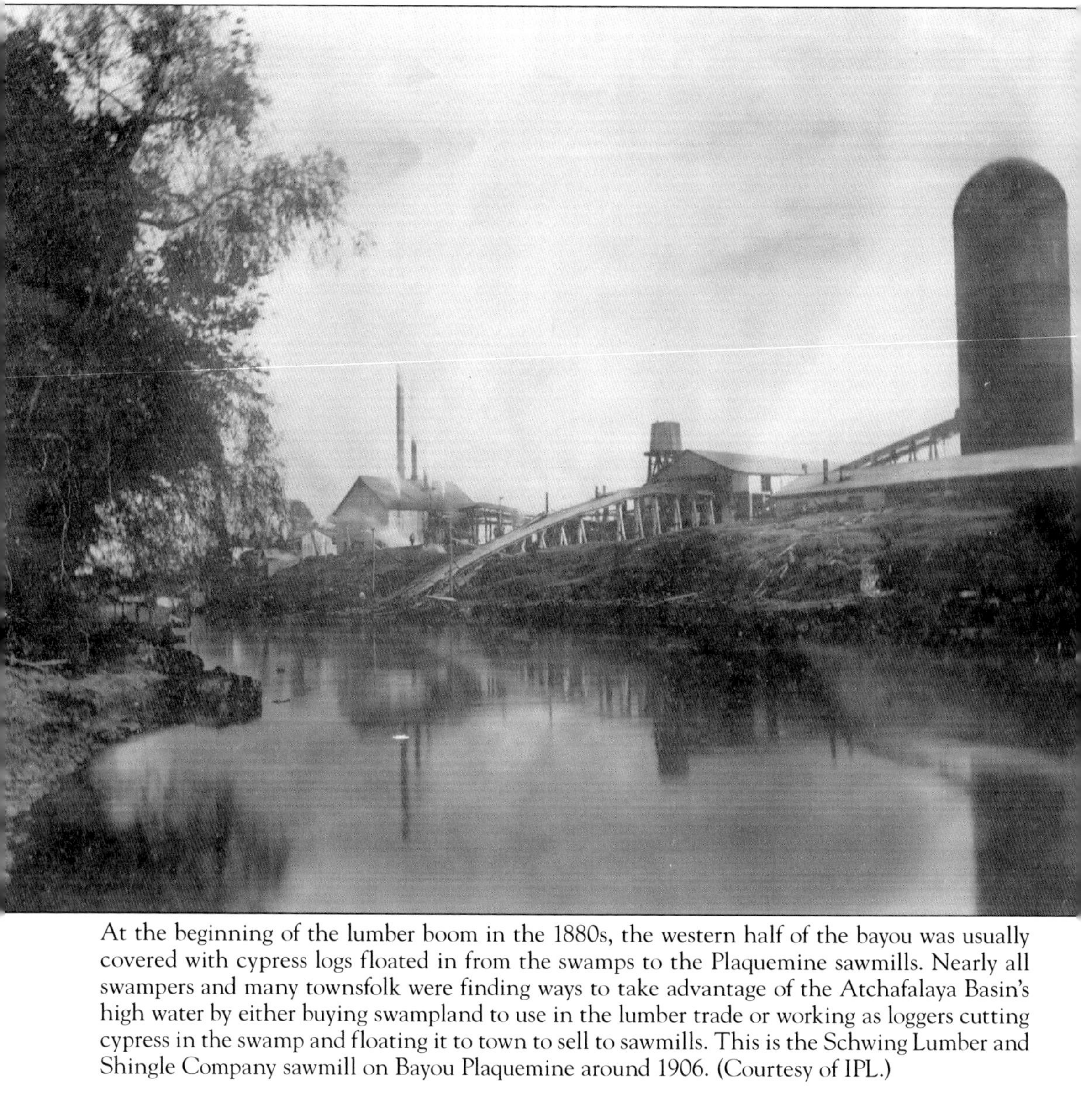

At the beginning of the lumber boom in the 1880s, the western half of the bayou was usually covered with cypress logs floated in from the swamps to the Plaquemine sawmills. Nearly all swampers and many townsfolk were finding ways to take advantage of the Atchafalaya Basin's high water by either buying swampland to use in the lumber trade or working as loggers cutting cypress in the swamp and floating it to town to sell to sawmills. This is the Schwing Lumber and Shingle Company sawmill on Bayou Plaquemine around 1906. (Courtesy of IPL.)

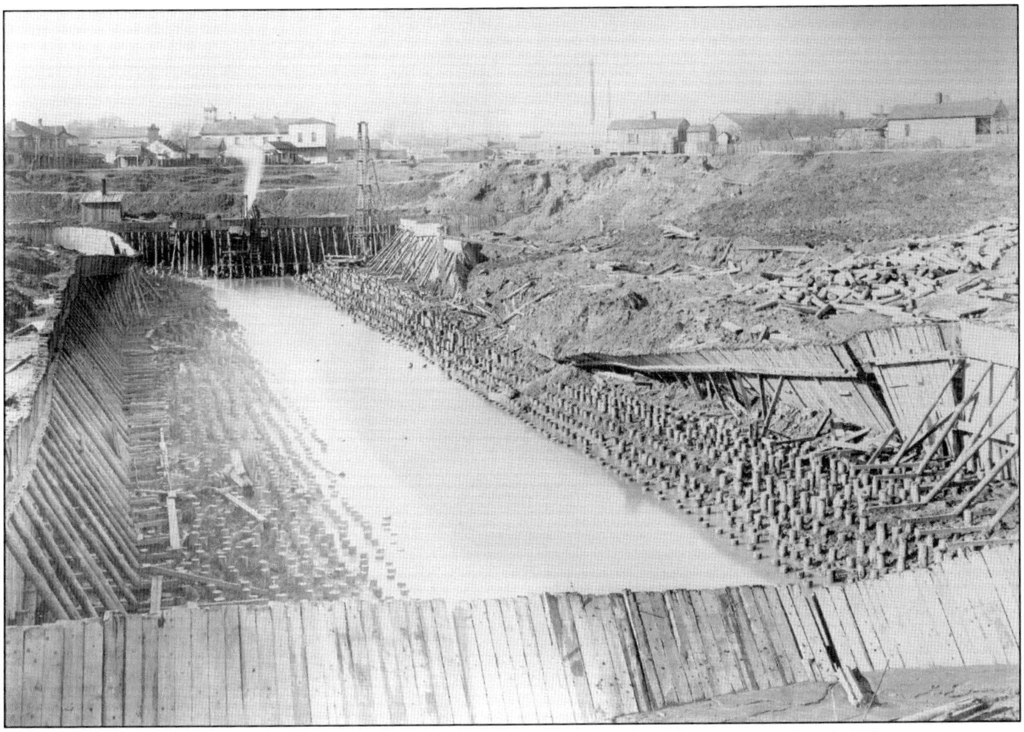

In September 1895, the government began construction on the Plaquemine Lock. The project was first submitted to Congress in 1885 after decades of discussion on reopening Bayou Plaquemine. Locals demanded the project also include Mississippi River bank protection and improvements to the interior streams that would make up the new route through the Atchafalaya Basin. Pictured is construction on the foundation for the lock around 1895. (Courtesy of the Library of Congress.)

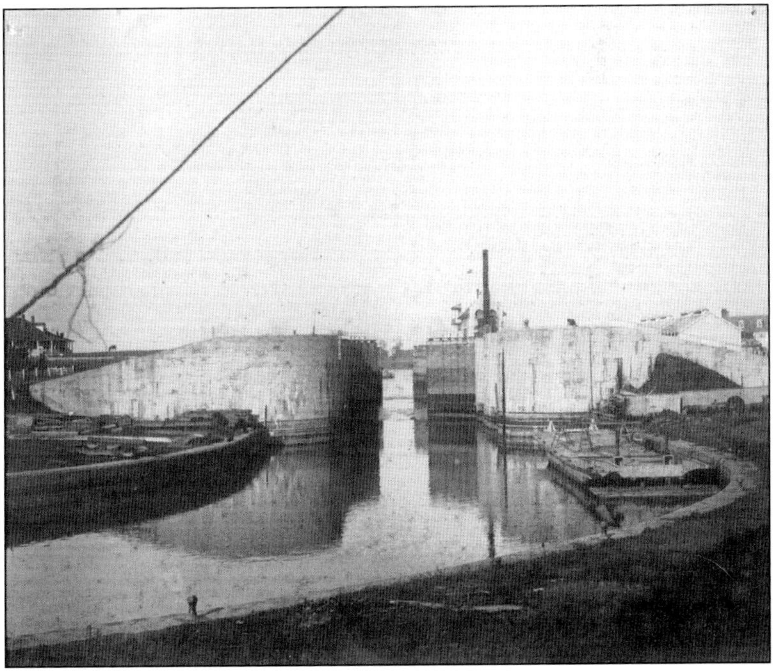

The Plaquemine Lock opened in 1909, and with it came big industrial developments to the surrounding area. This c. 1922 photograph shows the lock with its gates open to Bayou Plaquemine.

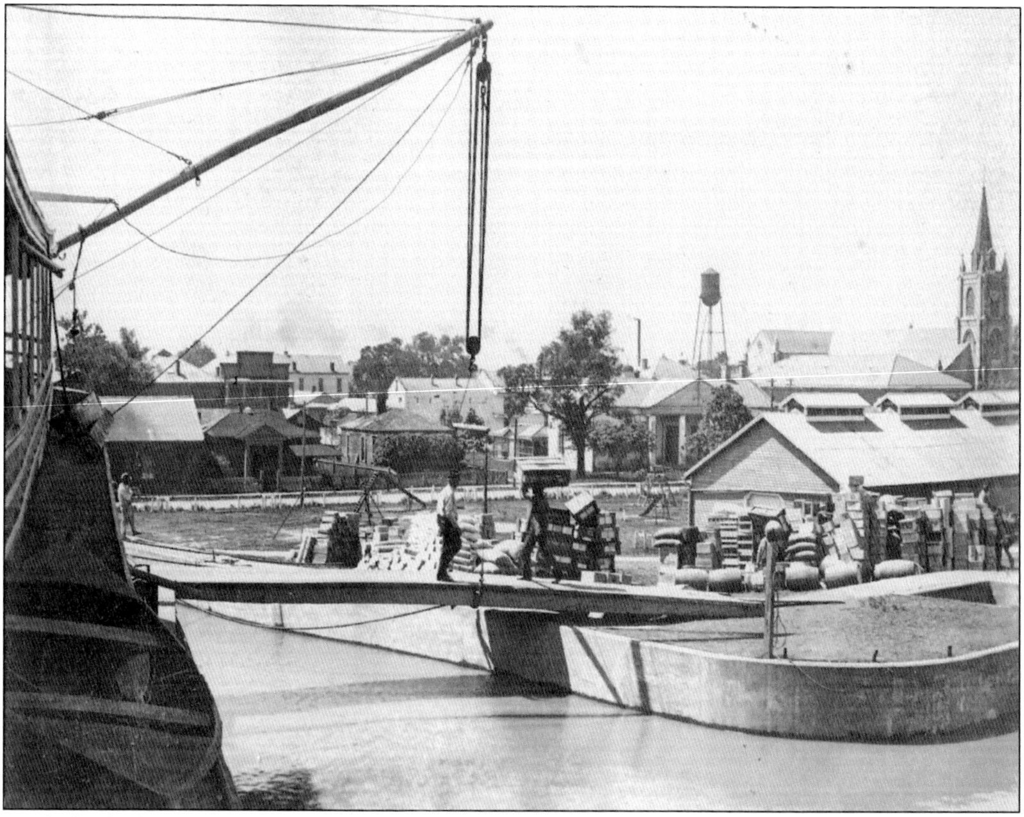

With the lock's opening, the bayou once again served as a commercial transport route, promoting settlement and new industry in southwest and north Louisiana. The lockhouse oversaw the passage of thousands of rivercraft, from wood-burning steamers to modern tugboats and barges. The above c. 1922 photograph shows the steamer *Loraine K.* docked at the Plaquemine Lock. Men are loading crates and cargo onto the steamboat. Below is a c. 1951 photograph of a tugboat pulling a barge up Bayou Plaquemine toward Grand River. (Below, courtesy of IPL.)

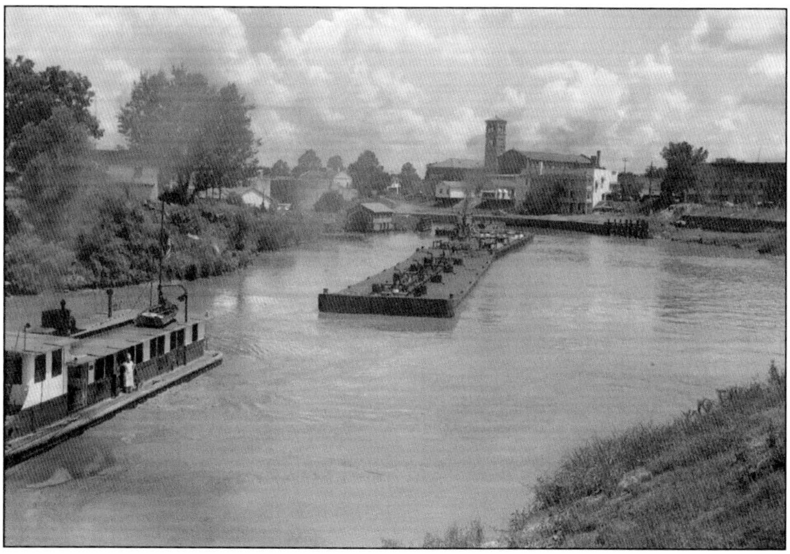

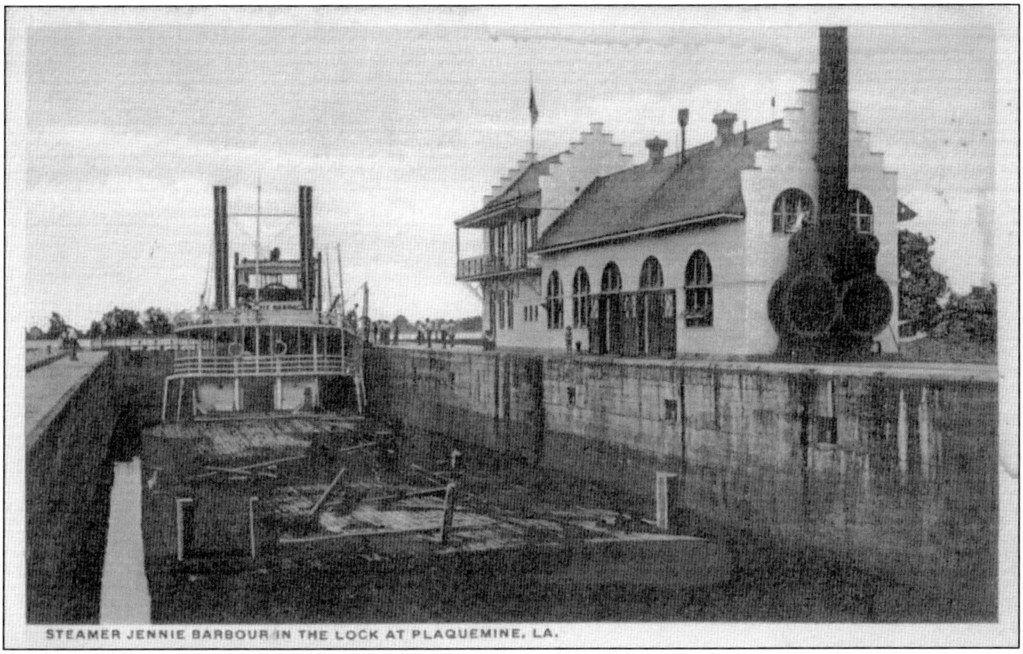

After 52 years of service, the Plaquemine Lock closed in 1961 due to the opening of the Port Allen Lock up the river. In the 1940s, discussion of building a new channel and lock at Port Allen emerged as Plaquemine's traffic jams increased. This is a postcard of the steamer *Jennie Barbour* in the lock.

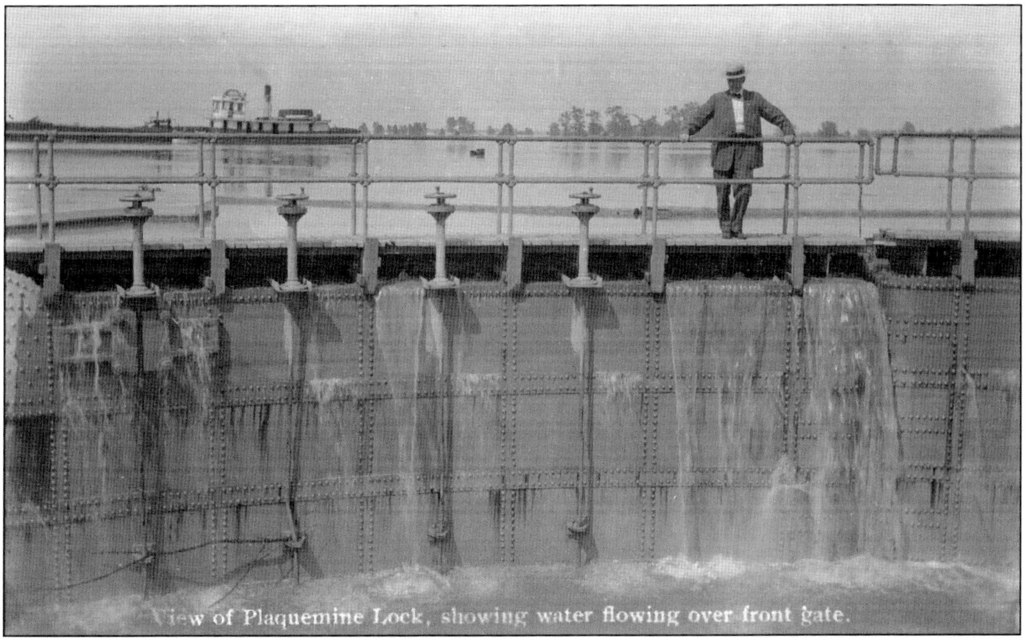

After the lock closed, the mouth of Bayou Plaquemine was once again dammed by extending the levee, ending an era of water travel in the historic bayou. This postcard shows the lock's front gates to the Mississippi River.

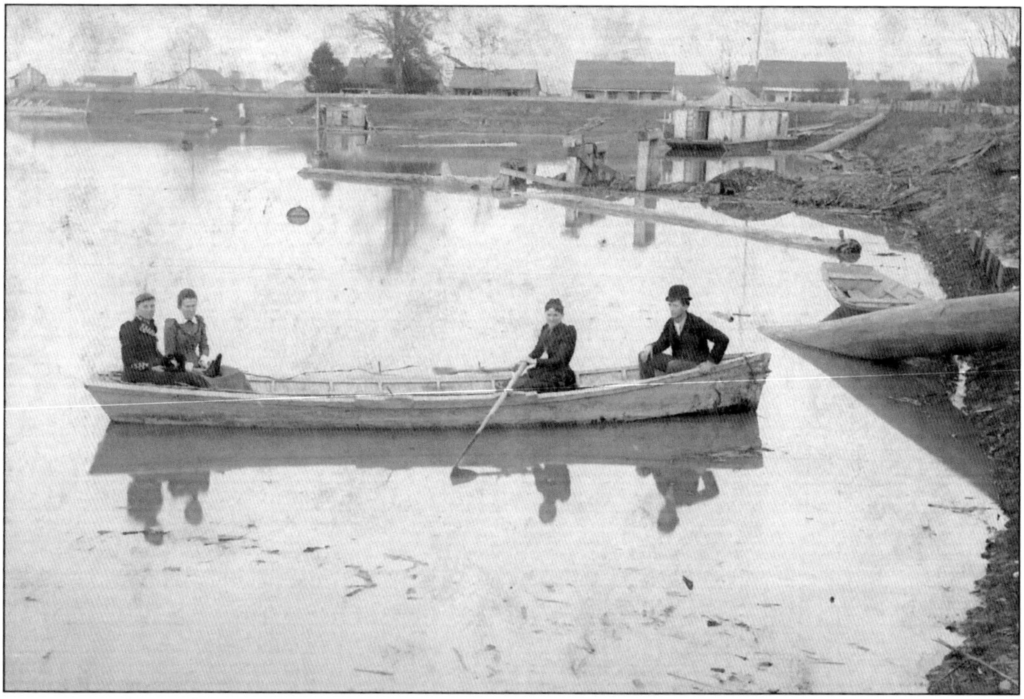

Henry Wadsworth Longfellow mentions the bayou in his epic poem *Evangeline*, published in 1847. The story follows the heroine as she journeys through the Atchafalaya swamp to reach her new home in Louisiana: "They, too, swerved from their course; and, entering the Bayou of Plaquemine / Soon were lost in a maze of sluggish and devious waters." This c. 1912 photograph is of the Neubig family and friends on the bayou.

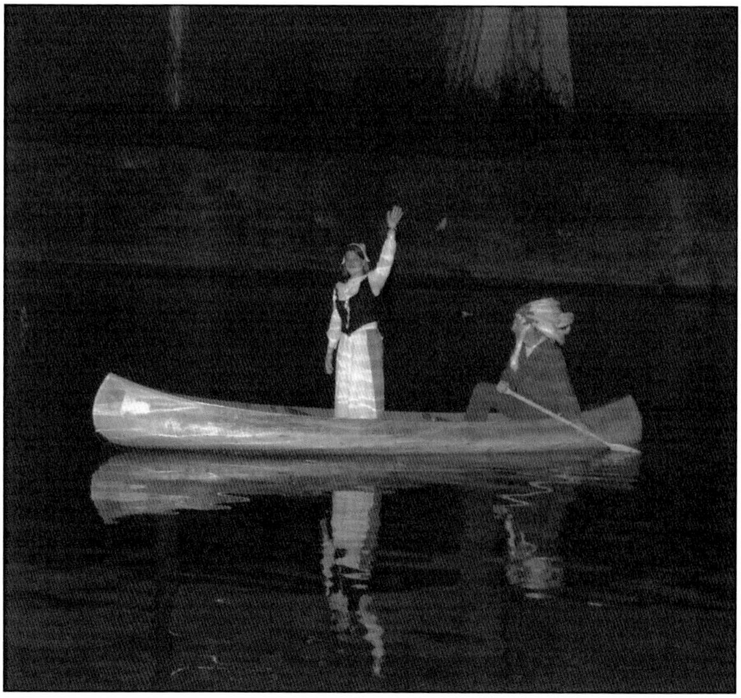

Inspired by the story, the local Knights of Columbus chapter started a festival in 1969 to highlight Iberville's Cajun heritage. The Acadian Festival annually reenacts Evangeline's passage through Bayou Plaquemine. In this c. 2002 photograph, Leigh Ann Kirkland plays the role of Evangeline on Bayou Plaquemine during the reenactment. (Courtesy of Paul Bouy.)

Two

Old Town

Throughout the latter half of the 19th century, Plaquemine became known as a prosperous river town. By 1900, it boasted many brick stores, several hotels and churches, a substantial sidewalk system, a steamboat landing, and a stop on the Texas & Pacific Railroad. In 1886, the town's population was around 4,000, split relatively evenly between white and African American. However, Plaquemine was consistently faced with a recurring issue—the Mississippi River.

Plaquemine was settled in a curve in the river, and when water was high, the current would increase as it traveled around the bend. Additionally, a sandbar across the river on the east bank pushed all the fast-moving water to the west side. The swift current would then eat away the soil under the levee, and when the water level dropped, nothing was left to hold the levee up, causing it and some of the surrounding area to collapse, taking Plaquemine's oldest homes and businesses with it and requiring residents to move the levee further and further inland. In 1897, after one of the final major cave-ins, the *Iberville South* printed, "All the landmarks of the original town of Plaquemine will disappear with the new levee. What was once called by the early settlers, 'the woods,' will henceforth bear the name of the old town."

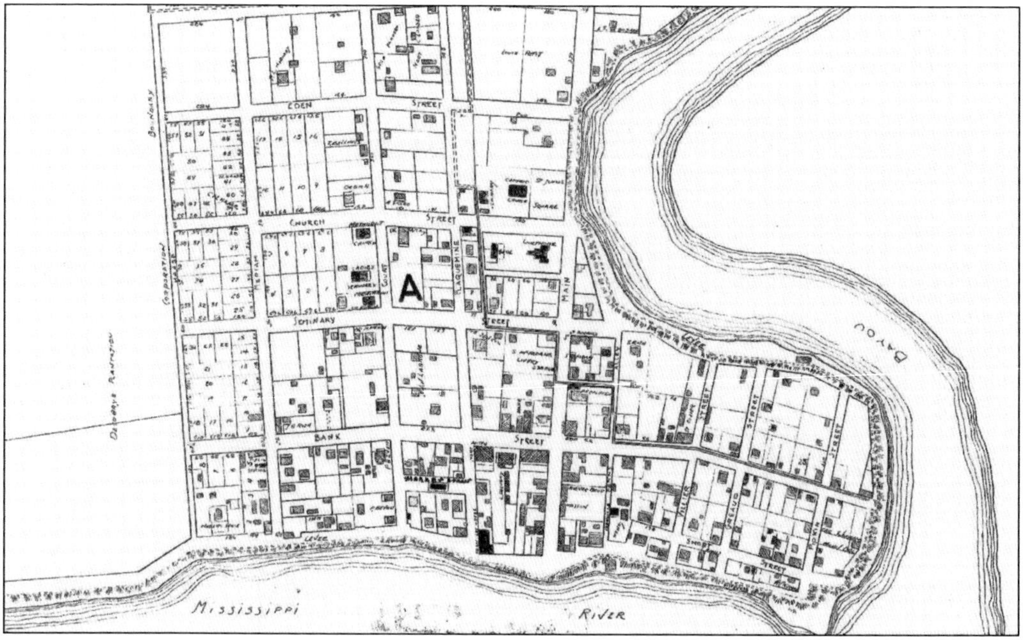

Between 1854 and 1930, the Mississippi River devoured over two blocks of Plaquemine. At the center of those blocks was Bank Street, which ran from north to south starting near Bayou Plaquemine. Bank Street was the street of commerce for the young town. It brimmed with merchants, grocers, barbers, printers, blacksmiths, coopers, carpenters, lawyers, apothecaries, and an abundance of coffee houses, saloons, and inns. As cave-ins along the river increased in frequency and size, locals fought to preserve as much of Bank Street as possible, refusing to give up on the valuable property. The above map is a portion of a c. 1854 map of Plaquemine by Michael Gill. Below is the 1884 map by Charles Dickinson, showing caves and levee changes until 1893.

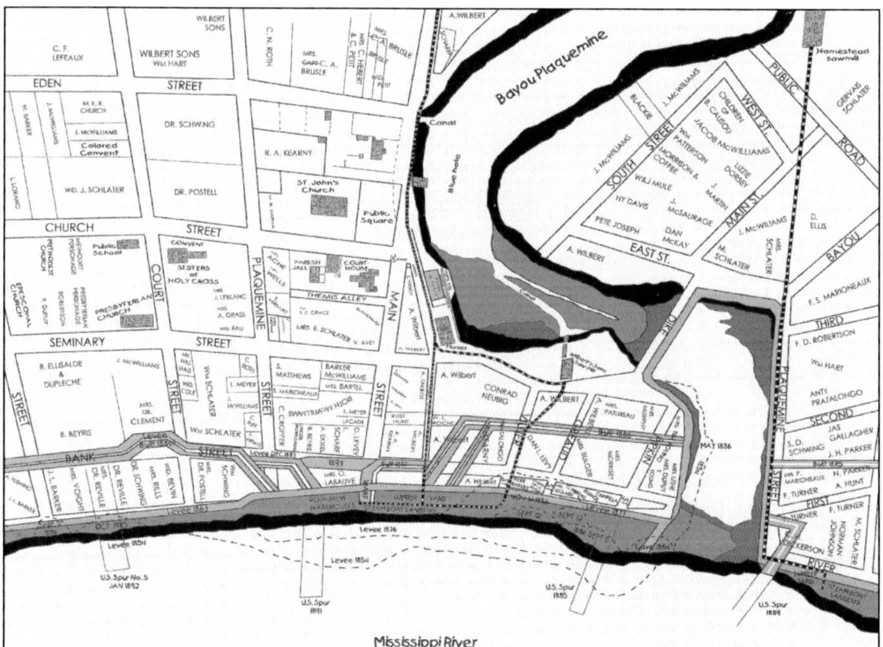

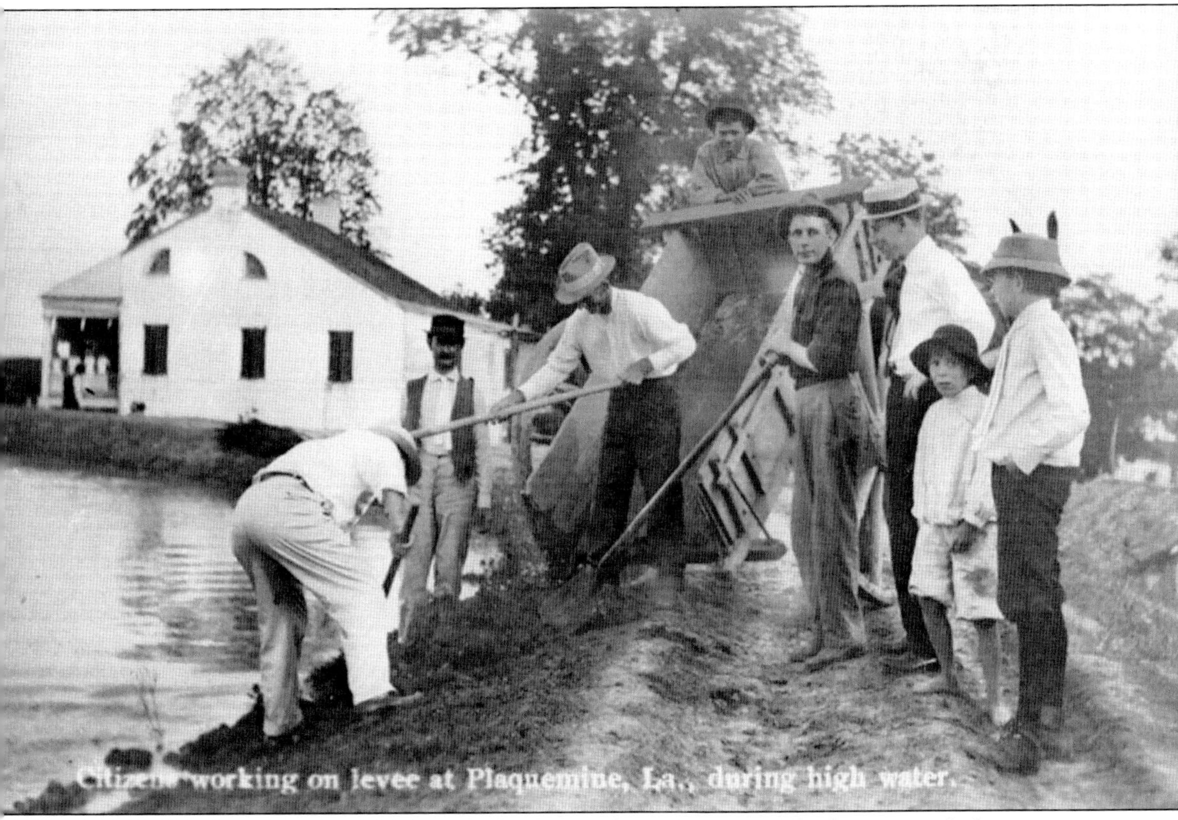

After a cave-in, the state engineers would come to Plaquemine to study the area and plan a new levee a safe distance from the river. In 1886, the new levee was drawn to line Seminary Street. However, local landowners petitioned the board to adjust the line to save a portion of Bank Street. They argued that this adjustment would make a safer and better levee because Bank Street was built up with oyster shells, bricks, and other hard debris. The board did not agree, but allowed locals to build the levee at their own cost. The citizen's levee caved in 1893, and residents still wished to build the new levee as close to the river as possible because they did not want to give up more property. The board agreed to a compromise but predicted another cave-in would follow. This c. 1912 photograph shows residents working on the remaining Bank Street levee in preparation for high water. (Courtesy of Tony Fama.)

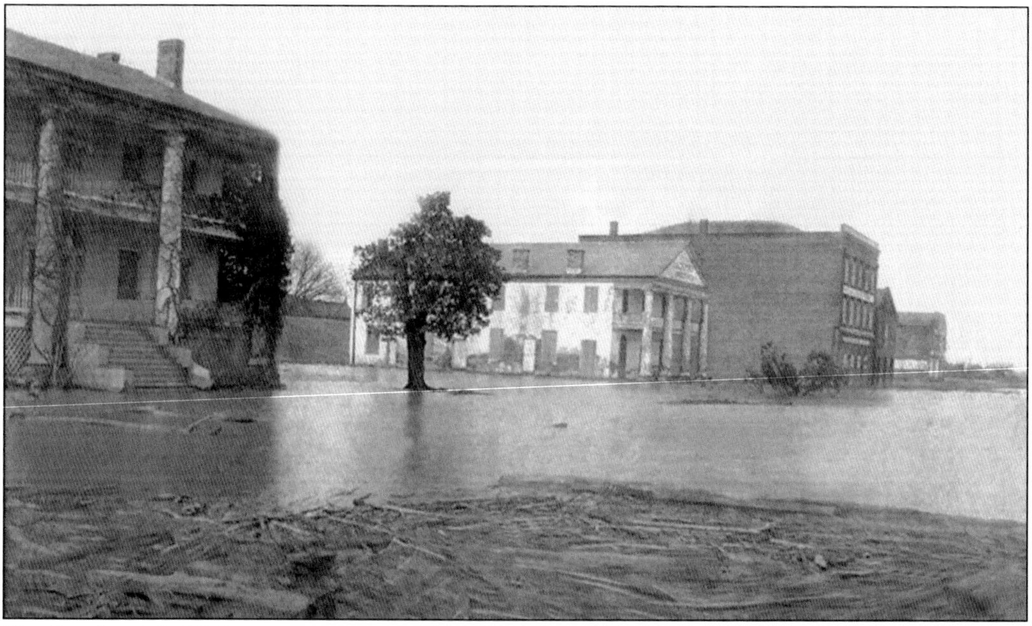

On October 28, 1897, a cave-in occurred in the levee that the *Iberville South* declared would be "the last of Bank Street." The levee was moved nearer to Seminary Street, abandoning several buildings, including those visible in this c. 1898 photograph. From left to right are William Schlater's residence, Plaquemine's first bank building, and the Roth and McWilliams store. (Courtesy of Tony Fama.)

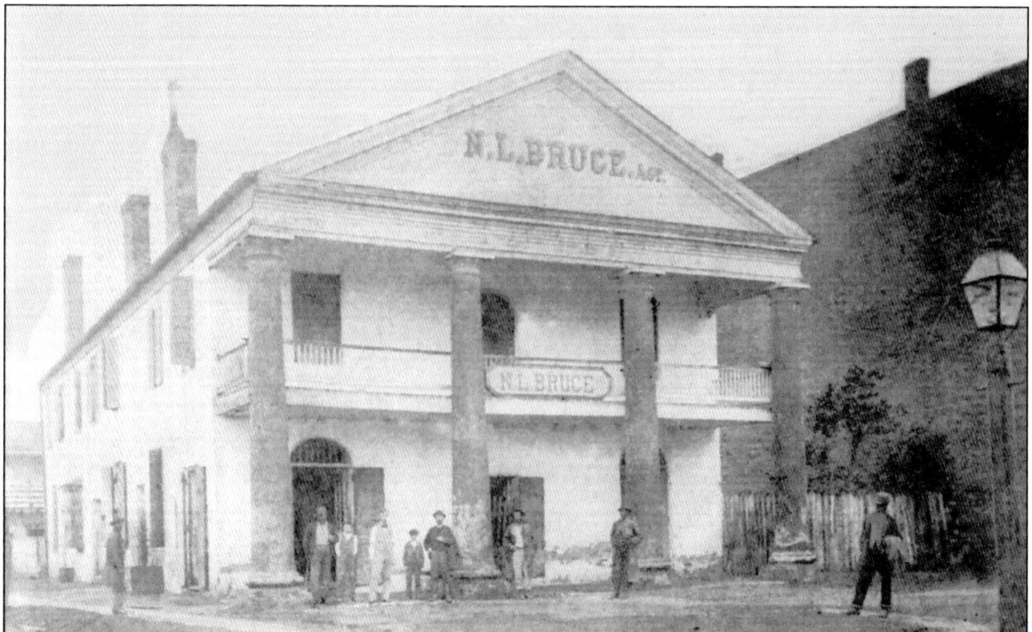

This c. 1874 photograph shows the first bank in Plaquemine, the Union Bank of Louisiana, built in 1837 on the corner of Bank and Plaquemine Streets. In 1856, it served as the Tuttle House Hotel. At the time of this photograph, Nathan L. Bruce used the building as a dry goods store, living on its second story with his family. It was torn down in August 1898.

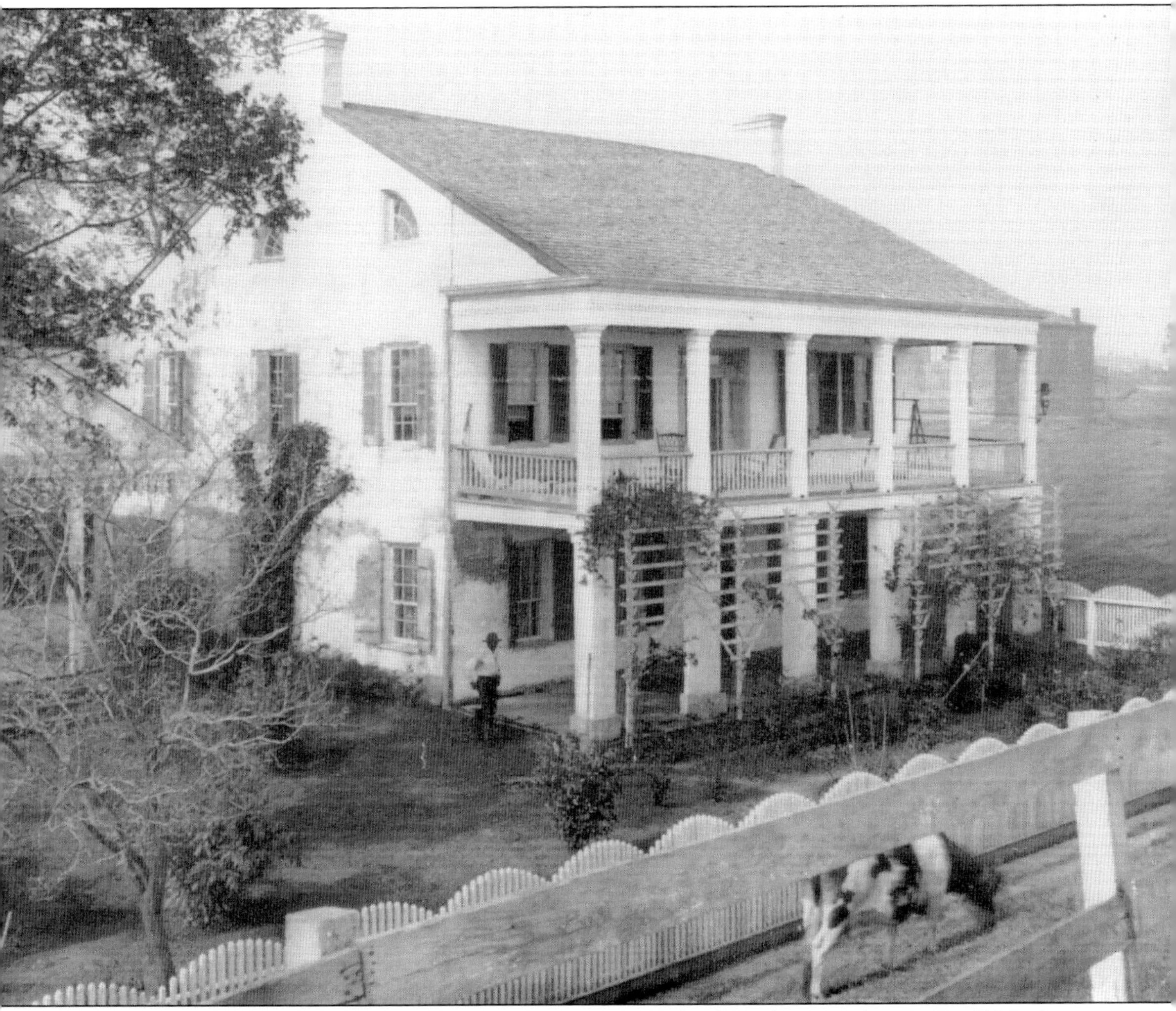

The only building to remain after the 1897 cave was Dr. Charles Clement's house. In 1886, the levee was placed around the home to preserve it and its history. It was one of the first two-story homes in Plaquemine, built in 1828 on the corner of what became Bank and Court Streets. Clement was from Poughkeepsie, New York. After graduating from medical school, he followed his two brothers to Louisiana. He became one of Plaquemine's first settlers and in 1826 married Henrietta Desobry. After the 1897 cave-in, the state engineers determined the home was a safe distance from the cave and connected the new levee line with the house's levee. However, despite the town's efforts to persevere the beautiful home, between 1912 and 1916, the river claimed it.

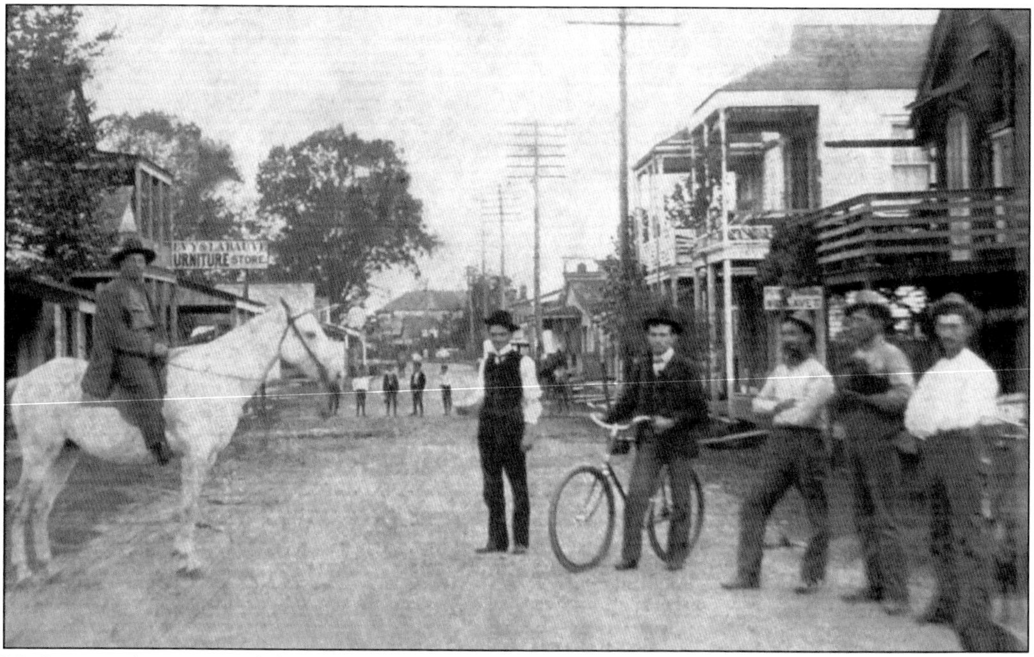

Unfortunately, cave-ins did not cease after 1897 but instead followed residents into the 20th century. Above is a c. 1900 photograph of Seminary Street with businesses along its east side. After the loss of Bank Street, several companies picked up and moved to places throughout Plaquemine. Some, such as the Roth and McWilliams store, moved up the block to Seminary Street. The east side of Seminary Street was not lost to the levee until 1930, when the US Army Corps of Engineers built the levee as it stands today. The photograph below was taken on January 1, 1942, on top of the levee looking down Main Street. (Below, courtesy of IPL.)

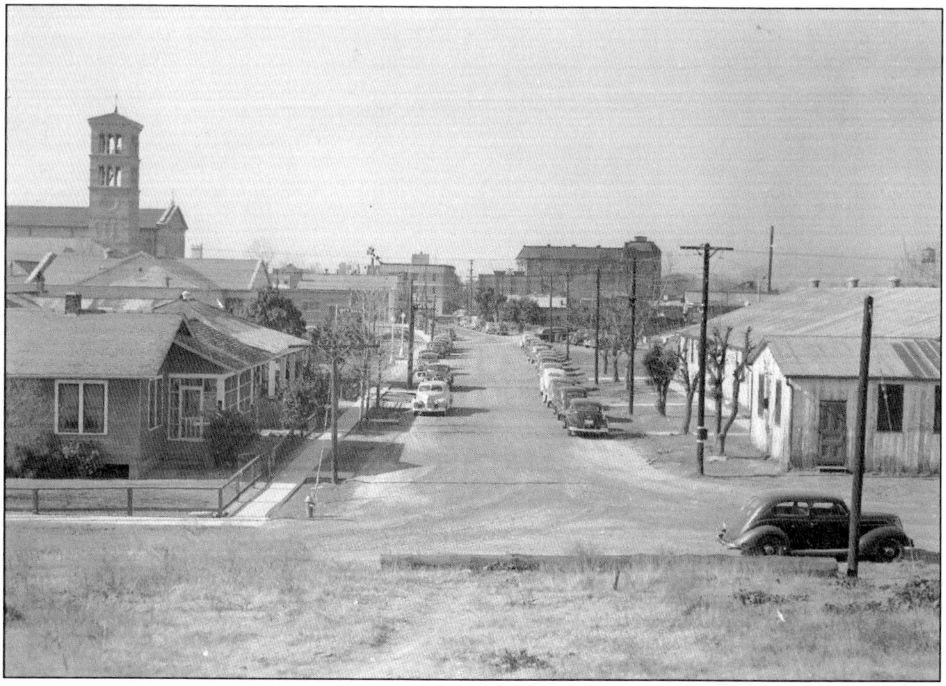

Three

SUGAR COUNTRY

The sugar industry became an essential part of Iberville's economy early in the 19th century. Sugar and cotton were the main crops produced in antebellum Louisiana, but sugar soon became south Louisiana's primary export. The "sugar bowl" was made up of Ascension, West Feliciana, Iberville, and Plaquemines Parishes. Plaquemine, being the parish seat of Iberville, was described as the heart of sugar country.

Sugar planters relied on large crews of enslaved people to quickly harvest and mill the cane so that it could meet the market's demands. Even with the technological advances that the sugar industry saw throughout the early 1800s, it remained grueling and exhausting work. The industry peaked in the 1850s and suffered an immediate decline following the Civil War. In Plaquemine and throughout the state, planters had to develop a new system of farming. Some opted to hire gangs of laborers who were given housing on the plantation and a small weekly or monthly wage, while others moved to a tenant system that required landowners to provide their tenants with a house, land, and seed cane, while the tenants offered their labor. Once the cane was grown, the tenant delivered it to the sugar mill and was paid various prices. Before the war, each plantation had its own sugarhouse to process the cane into syrup. However, as the industry changed into a tenant system, fewer and fewer landowners kept their sugarhouses open. By 1998, only one, Cora Texas Sugar Manufacturing, remained.

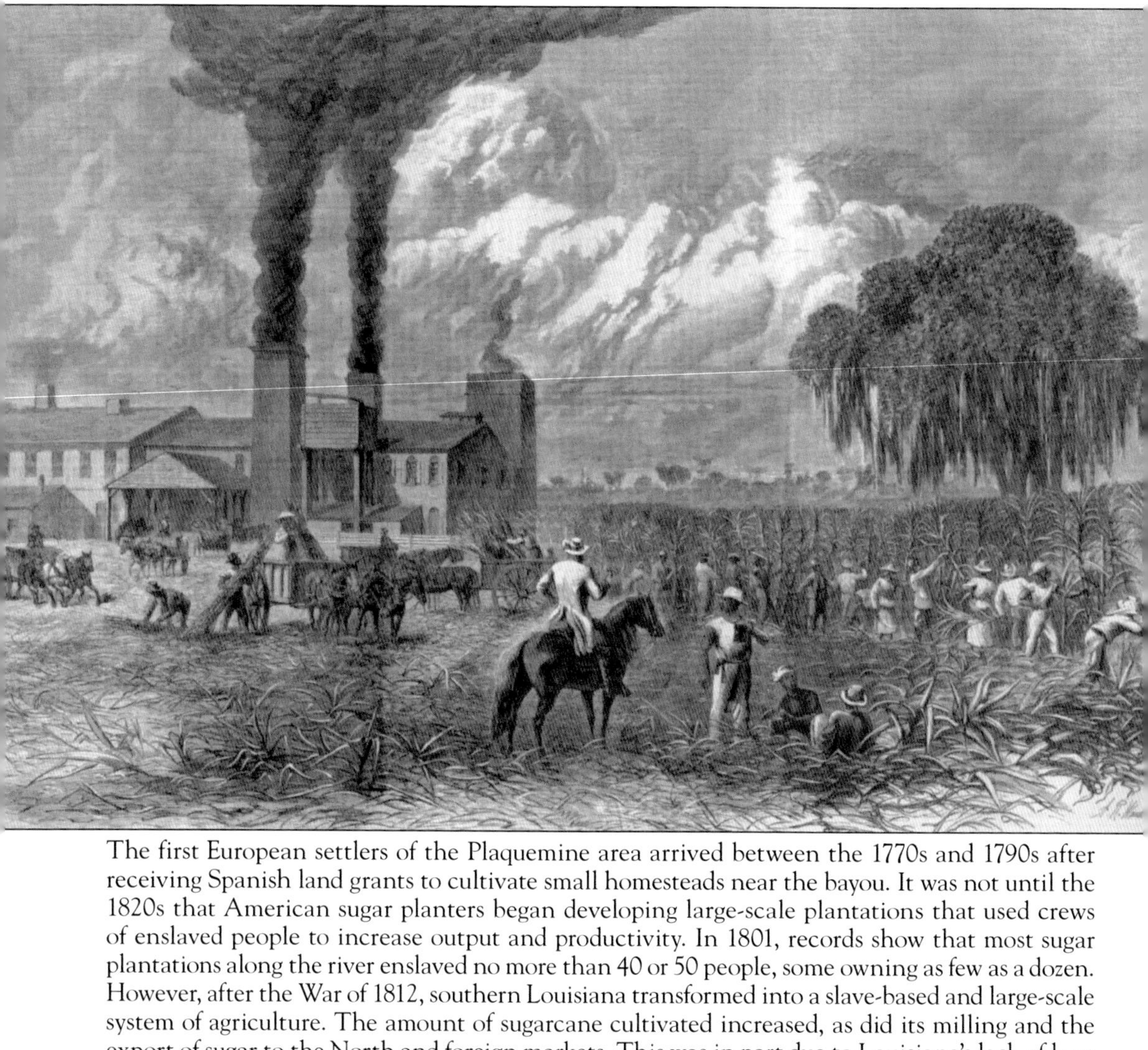

The first European settlers of the Plaquemine area arrived between the 1770s and 1790s after receiving Spanish land grants to cultivate small homesteads near the bayou. It was not until the 1820s that American sugar planters began developing large-scale plantations that used crews of enslaved people to increase output and productivity. In 1801, records show that most sugar plantations along the river enslaved no more than 40 or 50 people, some owning as few as a dozen. However, after the War of 1812, southern Louisiana transformed into a slave-based and large-scale system of agriculture. The amount of sugarcane cultivated increased, as did its milling and the export of sugar to the North and foreign markets. This was in part due to Louisiana's lack of laws on interstate slave trafficking, allowing the population of enslaved Africans to skyrocket. This illustration, *The Sugar Harvest in Louisiana*, was drawn by A.R. Waud and printed in *Harper's Weekly* magazine on October 30, 1875.

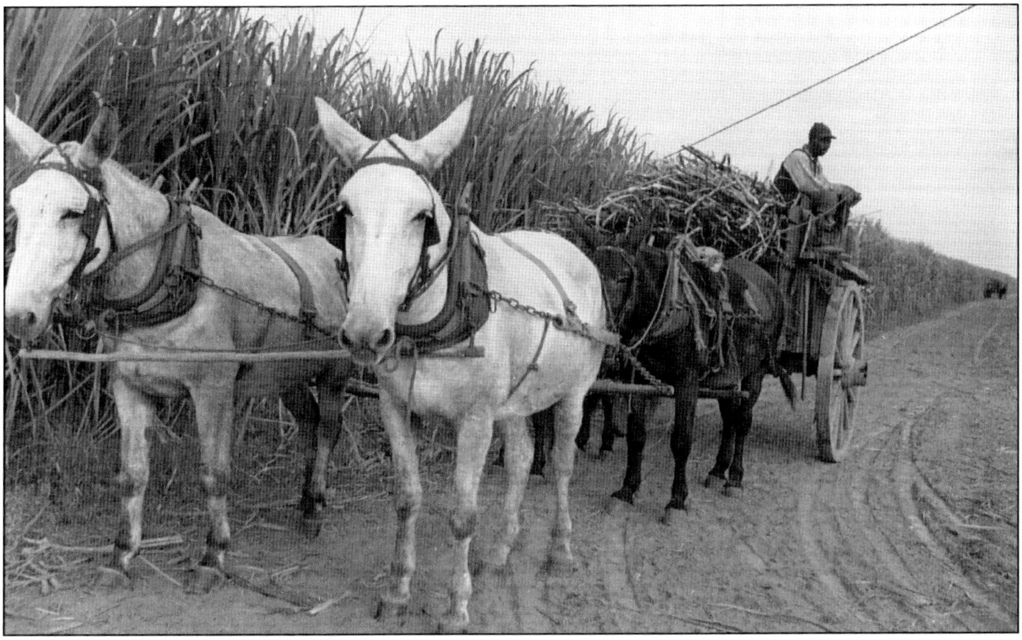

Joseph Erwin became a significant player in increasing the cultivation of sugarcane after the War of 1812. In 1807, Joseph and Lavinia Erwin migrated to Louisiana from Tennessee, building Home Plantation below the village of Plaquemine. After the international slave trade ended in 1808, Erwin became an interstate slave trader, acquiring enslaved black people from states like Maryland and Virginia and selling them to planters in Louisiana. This photograph is from around the 1920s. (Courtesy of IPL.)

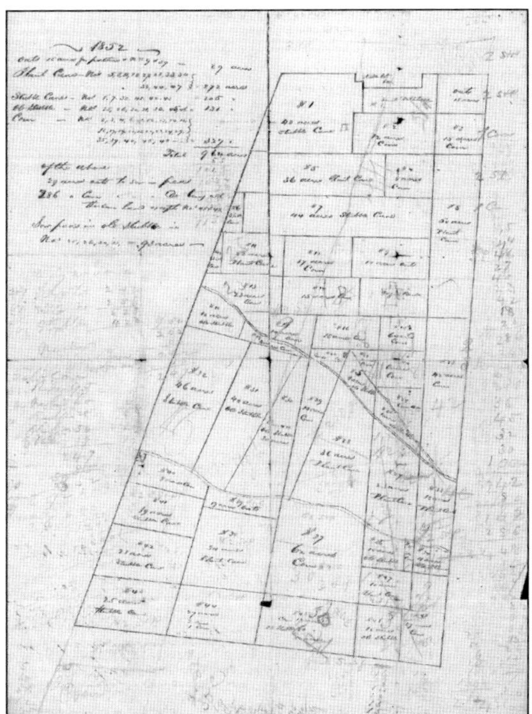

Joseph Erwin died in 1828, and his son-in-law Andrew Hynes took control of the property. When Hynes died in 1849, his son-in-law Edward J. Gay took over the estate, which was valued at $86,000 and enslaved 223 people. This c. 1852 agricultural map of the Hynes-Gay property shows how the fields were planned for planting different crops, such as sugarcane, corn, sweet potatoes, and oats, as well as cow grazing. (Courtesy of Louisiana State University.)

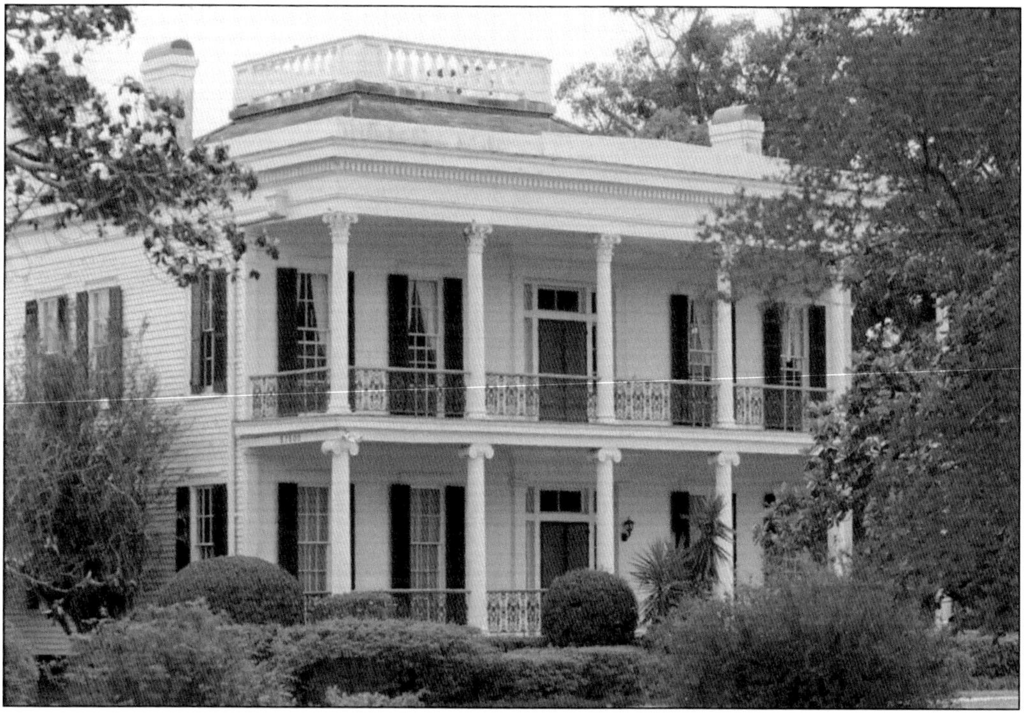

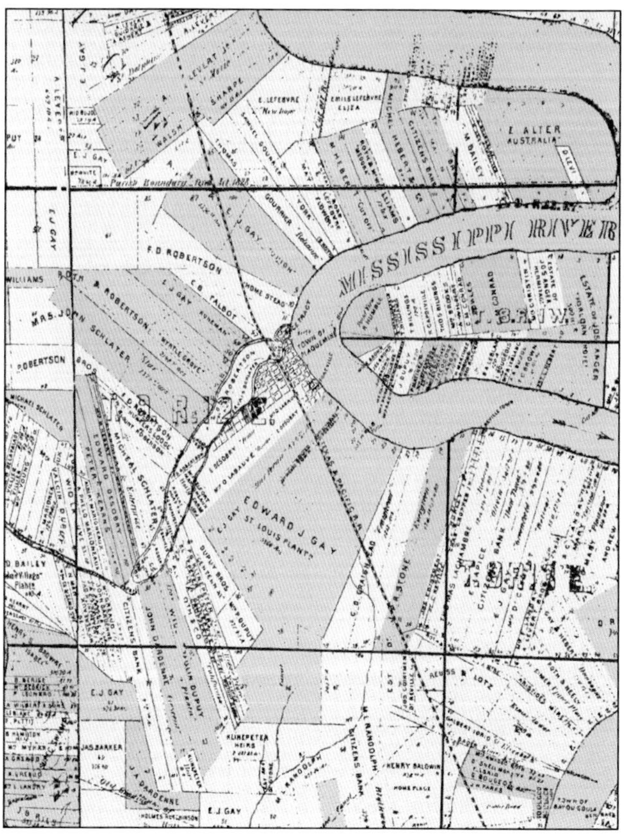

Edward J. Gay was a native of St. Louis, Missouri, and came to Louisiana after marrying Lavinia Hynes in 1840. In 1856, after inheriting Home Plantation a few years prior, he built a new house on the property and renamed the plantation St. Louis. (Courtesy of Tony Fama.)

After the Civil War, Gay expanded his financial interests by purchasing surrounding plantations through foreclosures and sales. This portion of the 1883 Charles Dickinson map is centered on Plaquemine and shows the surrounding landowners, including the Gay family's expansions.

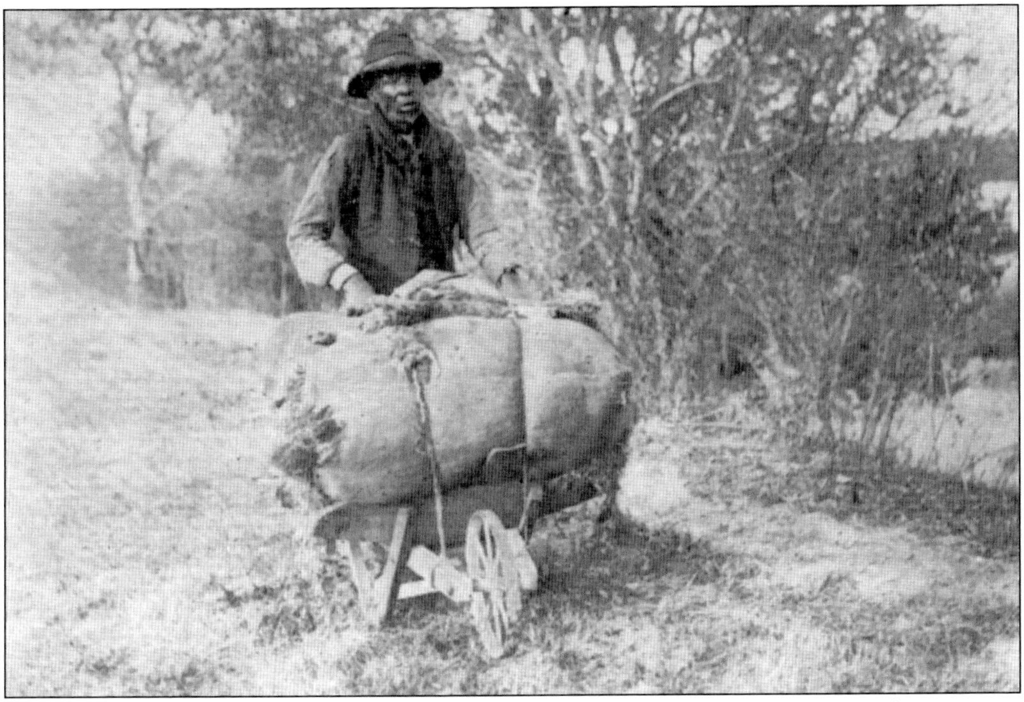

On St. Louis Plantation, some enslaved men and women turned to Spanish moss picking to earn a few dollars a year in the moss trade. Gay controlled their market activities, as he was responsible for selling the moss to Missouri furniture companies. Between 1849 and 1861, Gay sold over 1,000 bales of moss, but the enslaved moss pickers paid all the shipping and marketing costs. In the c. 1925 photograph above, a man holds a bale of Spanish moss. Those enslaved people who participated in the moss trade used their earnings to acquire items that slightly improved the bleakness of life in the sugar country, such as fabric to make their own clothing. The image below shows women cutting sugarcane near Plaquemine. (Above, courtesy of McNeese State University.)

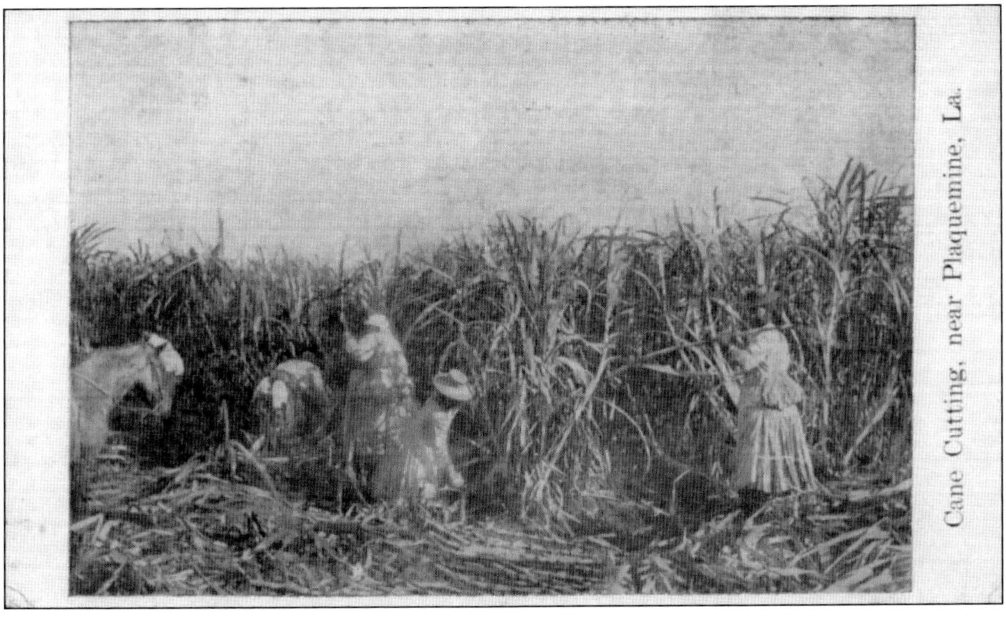

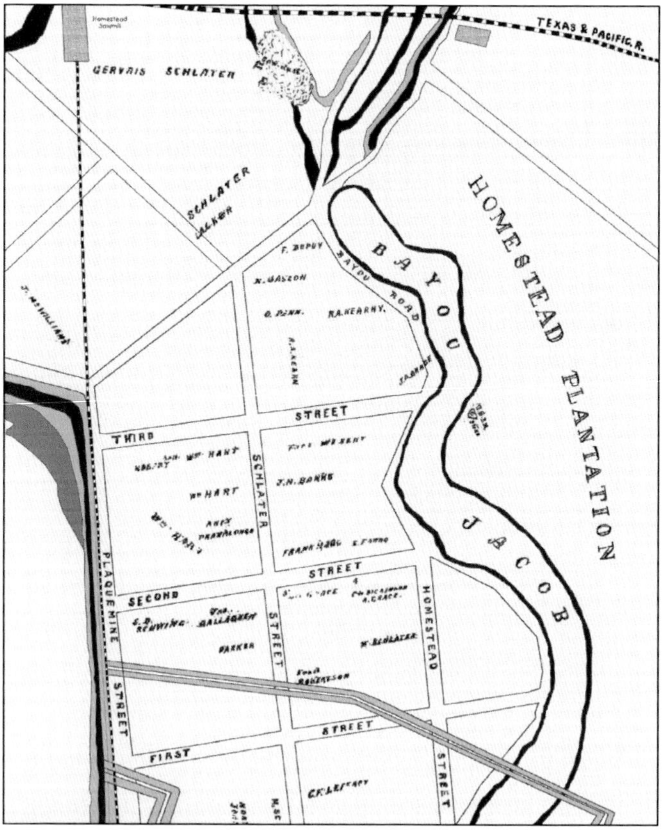

In 1774, Jacob Schlater, a native of Luxemburg, Germany, came to Iberville on a Spanish land grant and established the Homestead Plantation on Bayou Jacob. He married Barbara Kleinpeter, daughter of Johann Georg Kleinpeter, another European immigrant taking advantage of the land grants, in 1779. This portion of the 1884 map by Charles Dickinson shows Homestead's location on the bayou. His son Michael Schlater became one of the first notable sugar planters on Bayou Jacob, taking over some of his father's land and founding Enterprise Plantation further up the bayou, closer to Grand River. He built a 1,800-foot-long, 40-foot-wide sugar mill in 1847 to manufacture sugarcane and constructed his home in 1861. Below is a c. 1912 photograph of his home on Bayou Jacob. It burned down in 1942.

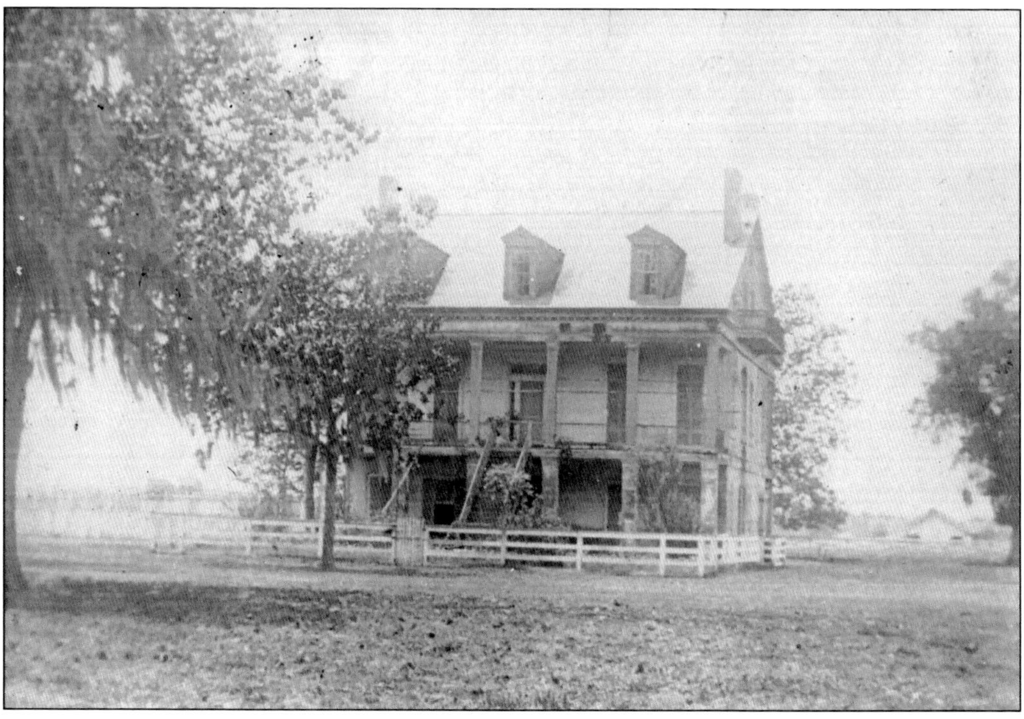

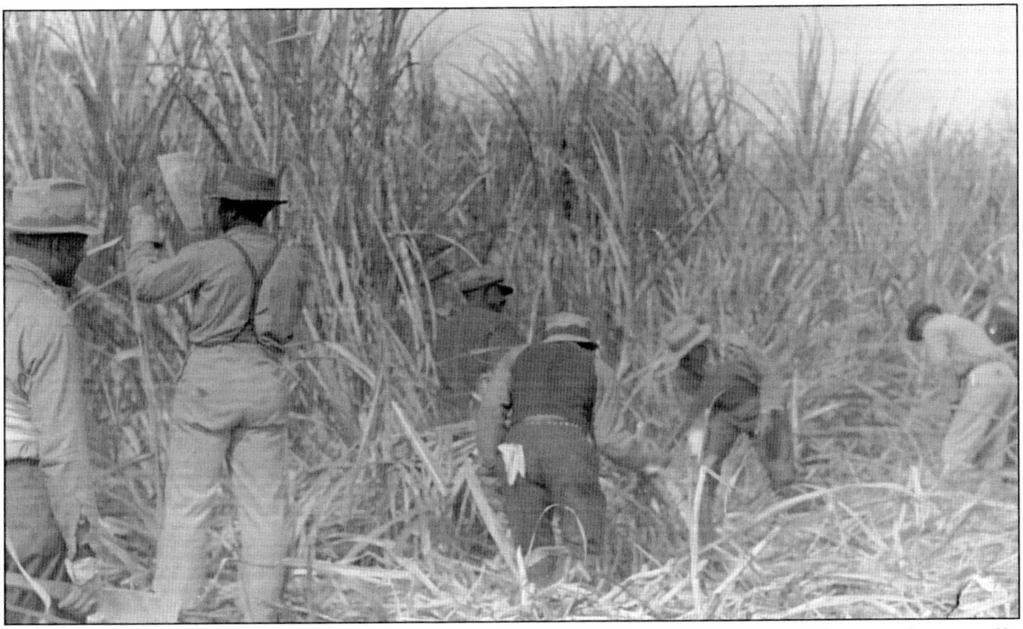

By 1850, the sugar industry was an essential part of Plaquemine's economy. The parish typically sent some 20,000 hogsheads of sugar to market annually. Sugarcane was planted in January and February and harvested from mid-October to December. However, due to Louisiana's temperamental climate, planters like Edward J. Gay were determined to harvest the crop quickly before the first frosts arrived. To do so, Gay classified his enslaved workers according to chore and assignment, subdividing his laborers into a set of teams that could meet the speed that "grinding season" demanded. He also preserved a small, all-male crew of kettle hands and engineers who aided Jacob Lennox, his enslaved sugar maker. Above is a c. 1920s photograph of workers cutting cane at Milly Plantation on Bayou Plaquemine. Below is a c. 1900 image of George M. Murrell Planting and Manufacturing Company's sugar mill. (Below, courtesy of IPL.)

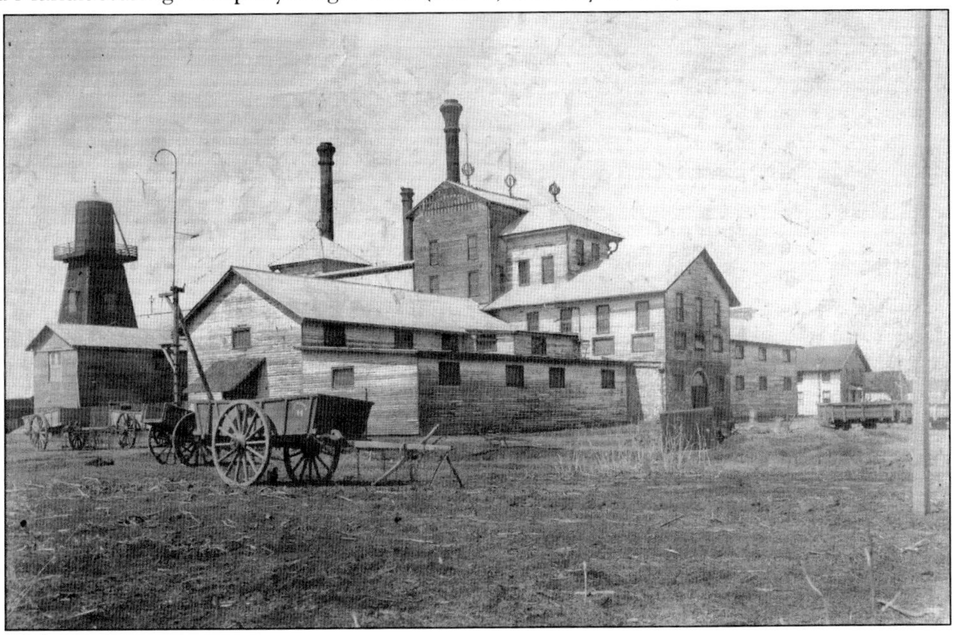

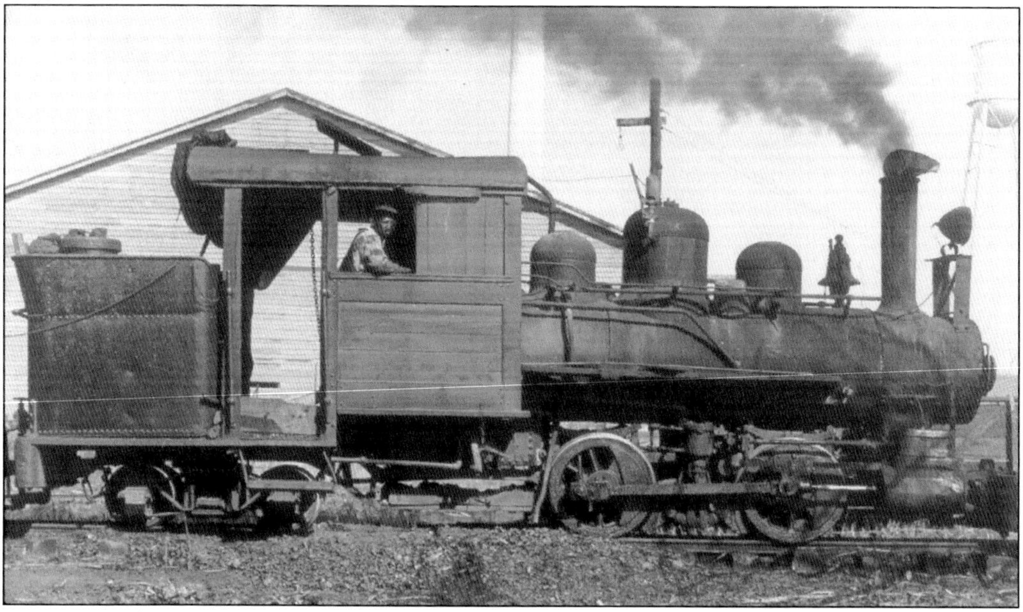

During grinding season, operations continued around the clock. The introduction of field trains that carried the stalk from the fields to the mills expanded the assembly line structure of the sugar mill and quickened the pace of fieldwork, resulting in greater urgency, stress, and risk on the mill floor. Inside the mill, laborers began the long, complex process of converting cane into brown crystalline sugar. In 1857, the local newspaper toured Dr. Henry G. Doyle's sugarhouse on Eureka Plantation near Bayou Goula. Doyle had modified his mill to have a platform overlooking the mill floor, from which he could monitor his enslaved workers throughout the night. Once the process was complete, the sugar was packed into hogsheads that held between 1,000 and 1,200 pounds. The c. 1975 label below is from J. Supples Sons Planting Company's last batch of Catherine's First Molasses. (Above, courtesy of Tony Fama.)

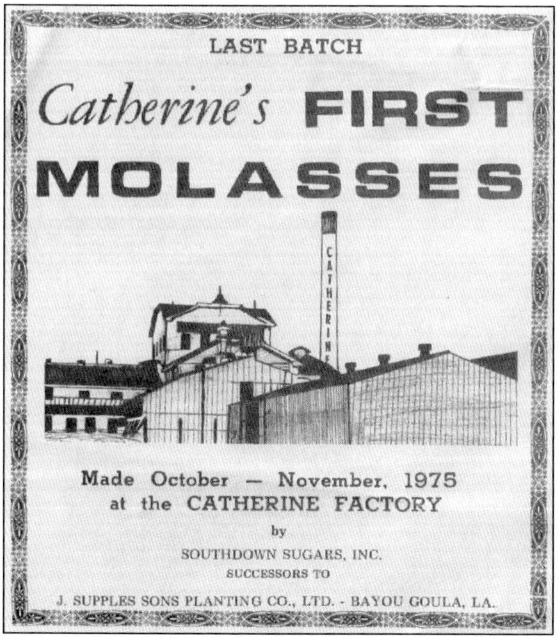

The introduction of the steam engine as a tool for sugar planters in the mid-1800s forever changed the flow of production for the sugar industry. By the late 1800s, most large-scale farms had built complete rail systems to carry their product across their plantations. In this c. 1930s photograph, a locomotive is seen next to a sugarcane hoist device in Iberville Parish. (Courtesy of Louisiana State Library.)

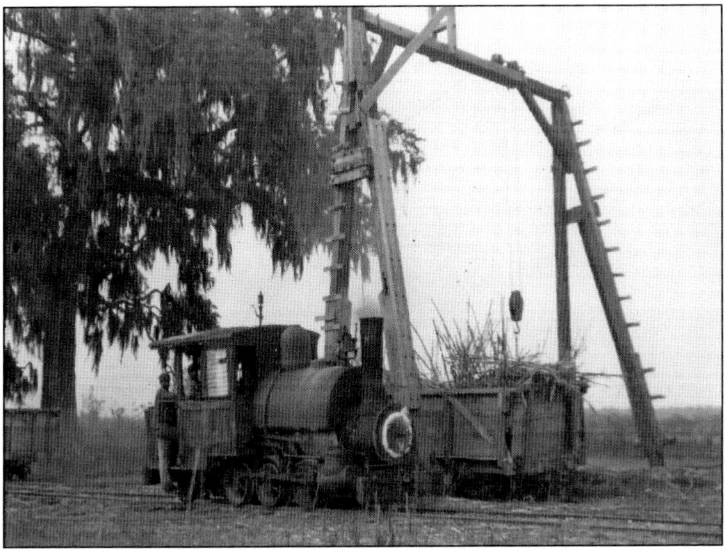

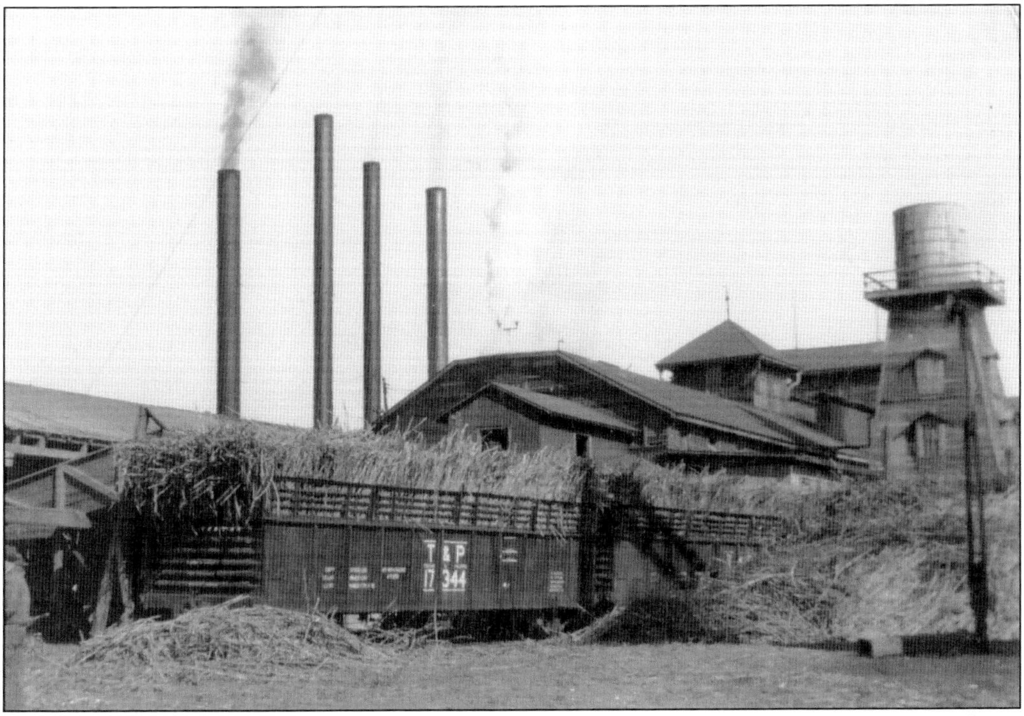

In 1892, Andrew H. Gay, son of Edward J. Gay, built a railway across the Mississippi River levee in front of Union Plantation, north of Plaquemine. The railway system connected to the other nearby plantations and carried the cane to Union Sugar Refinery. The railroad included about 159 railcars and two small switch engines. This photograph shows packed railcars at Tally Ho Sugarcane Refinery. (Courtesy of Louisiana State Library.)

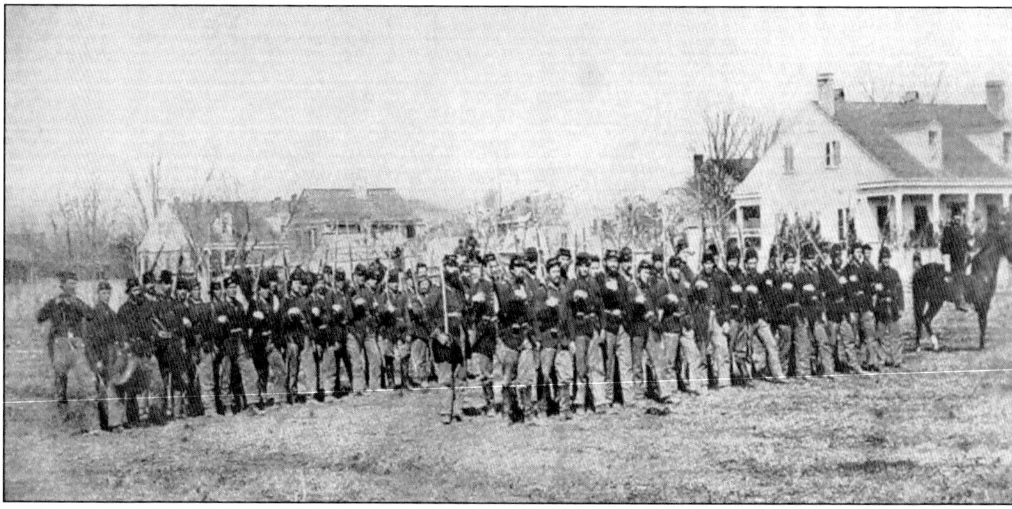

By 1860, Plaquemine was the largest town in the parish. Citizens began preparing for the state's secession from the Union by organizing their first military company, named the Home Sentinels, which joined Southern forces at the start of the war. After the capture of Baton Rouge in the summer of 1862, a small Federal garrison was sent to Plaquemine to occupy the town and use it as a supply line between New Orleans and Baton Rouge. As a result, Plaquemine saw many hit-and-run raids by Confederate guerrillas who sought to disrupt Union supply efforts. In 1864, the Union built a fort southeast of town at the head of what became Fort Street. Fortunately, the fort never saw combat. The above c. 1863 photograph shows the 42nd Ohio drilling in Plaquemine. Below is currency printed in Plaquemine during the war, dated March 1, 1862. (Above, courtesy of United States Army Military History Institute.)

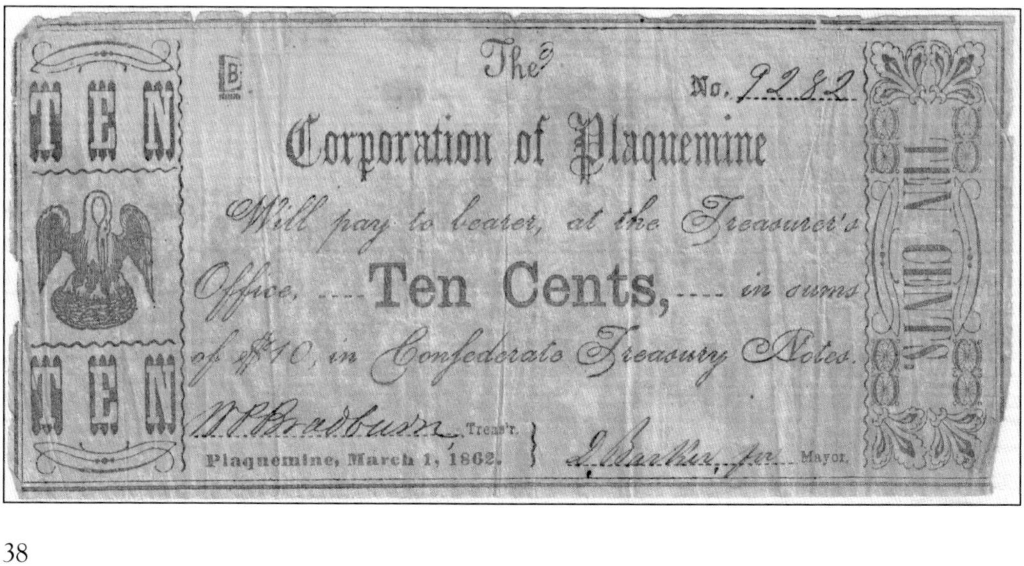

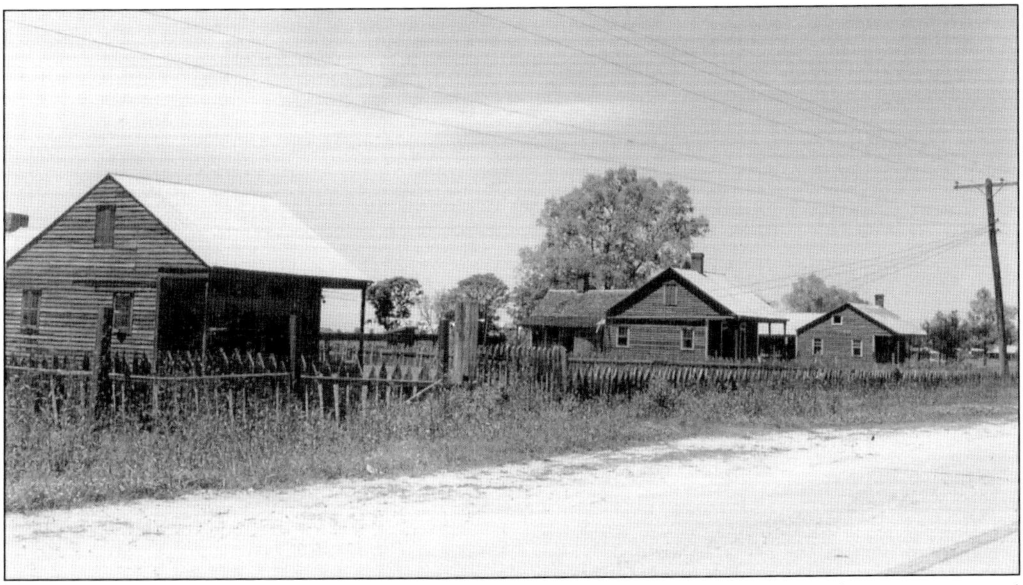

After the war, the sugar country was faced with significant difficulties as the international markets drove the price of sugar down at alarming rates. Additionally, there was a labor problem as Reconstruction-era planters were exceedingly dissatisfied with black labor. The *Iberville South* argued that a tenant system was the way to bring back Iberville's old sugar-producing ways, stating, "Mr. Gay at St. Louis and Mr. Ware at Belle Grove as well as Urquhart, Tuttle, and Nicol recommend this system." Pictured above are c. 1947 sharecroppers' homes on a sugar plantation near Plaquemine. In the 1870s, the Gay family attempted to bring Swedish and German immigrants to farm their plantations. However, both attempts failed, as the Europeans did not grow accustomed to the industry's harsh labor conditions. But by 1900, more than 10,000 Italian immigrants worked in the sugarcane fields across south Louisiana, including plantations around Plaquemine. Still, African Americans made up the majority of cane workers. (Above, photograph by Todd Webb, courtesy of Louisiana State Library; below, courtesy of IPL.)

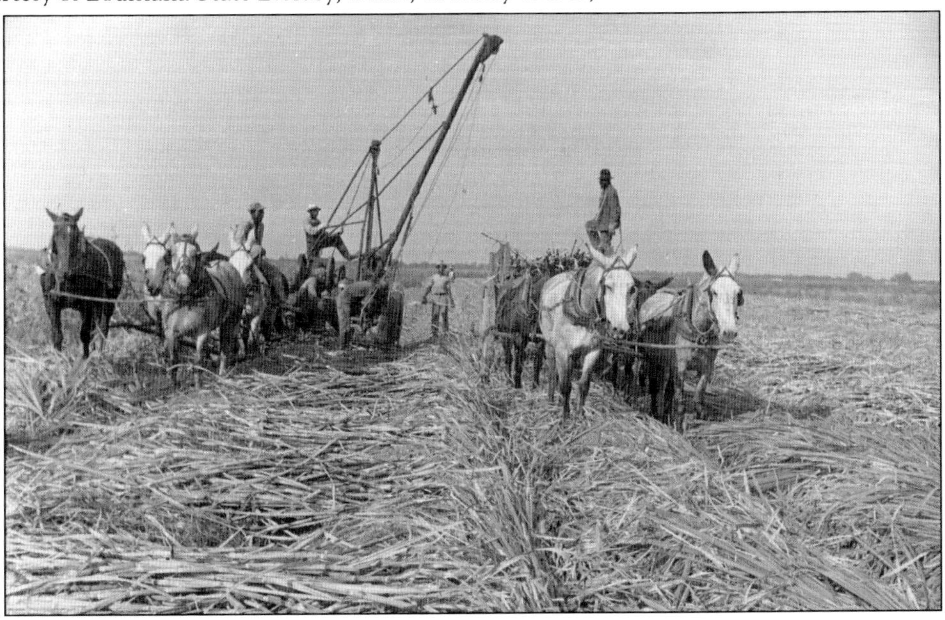

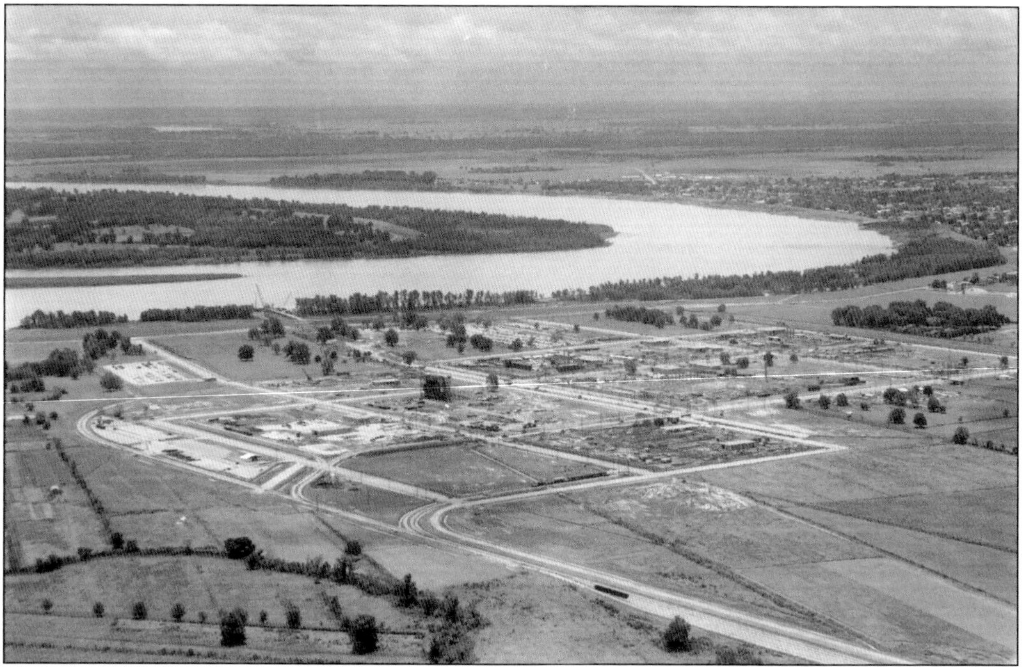

By the mid-1950s, what had been rural and green sugarcane country for nearly 150 years developed into a new industry. In 1958, the Dow Chemical Company began production on the west bank near Plaquemine. It purchased 1,700 acres of land, including the acreage of Union and Mayflower Plantation, in 1956 and started constructing facilities to manufacture chloroethene solvents and ethanolamines. Other industries followed to the west bank in the following decades. These two aerial photographs show the Dow Chemical Company's early beginnings on the Mississippi River. The above picture is from the 1950s; below is from the 1960s. (Both, courtesy of Dow.)

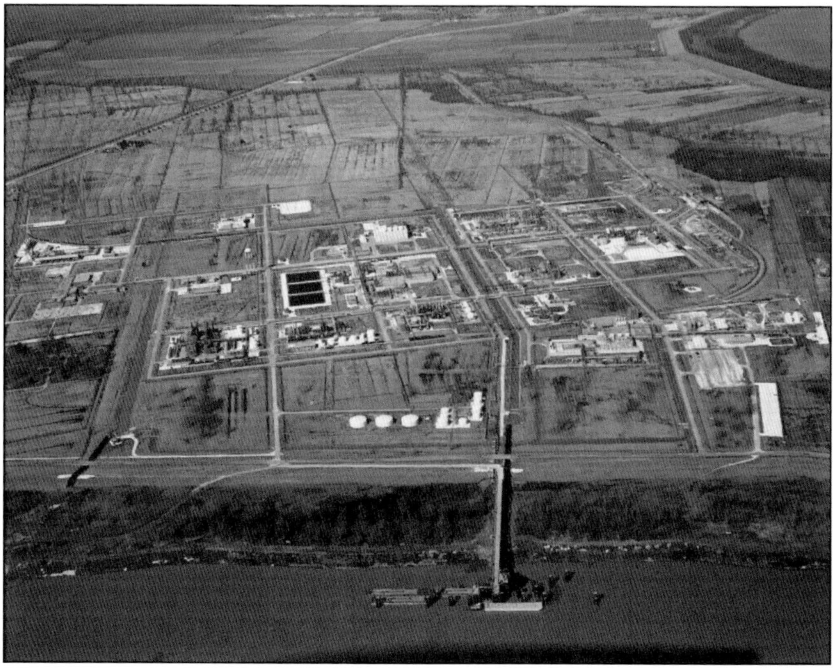

Four

Cypress City

Between 1890 and 1910, Plaquemine was known as the Cypress Capital of the World. The city was home to several lumber companies that cut a record number of cypress timber daily. The cypress lumber industry in Louisiana experienced a massive boom in the 1880s as seasonal flooding in the Atchafalaya Basin increased. Loggers readily adapted to the excess water, using the dry season to "ring" the great cypress trees in the swamp and the spring floods to cut the trees and float them to the sawmill.

In Plaquemine, many townsfolk invested in "swamping." Merchants, doctors, lawyers, city officials, and more purchased thousands of acres of swampland and employed loggers to gather the cypress to sell to the sawmills lining Bayou Plaquemine. The *Weekly Iberville South* in December 1886 reported, "At present, Bayou Plaquemine, from the Mississippi to about six miles up, where deep water is reached, is a shallow stream almost covered by the cypress logs floated in from the swamp to the sawmills."

Unfortunately, the boom of the cypress lumber industry was short-lived. By 1927, the great red cypress forests were depleted. While other species continued to be logged on a smaller scale, Plaquemine's lumber industry was gone with the trees.

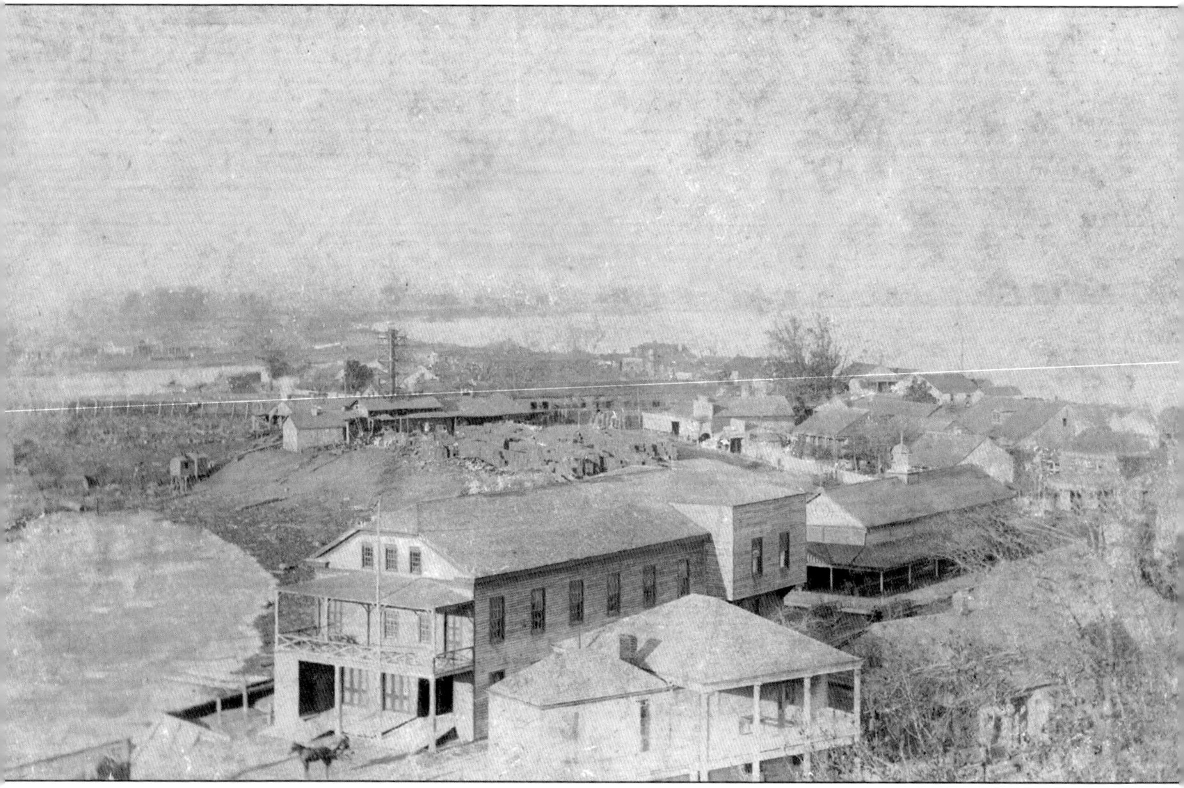

Although there were sawmills in Plaquemine and Iberville Parish since the early 1800s, the town's lumber industry did not fully develop until 1868, when Anton Wilbert opened the Little Jim sawmill on Bayou Plaquemine. Wilbert was a native of Koblenz, Germany, and moved to Plaquemine around 1848, where he began working as a cabinet maker. After the Civil War, he bought a cotton gin near the Plaquemine dike and converted it into a sawmill, discovering that cypress lumber and shingles were in high demand. Wilbert and his six sons became Iberville's lumber industry pioneers, owning one of the most successful lumber companies in the state. This c. 1880 photograph shows the Little Jim sawmill and lumber yard on Bayou Plaquemine. When it first opened, it cut around 8,000 feet of lumber a day, and the *Iberville South* stated that "day in and day out, the hum of the Little Jim [is] heard on Bayou Plaquemine." The mill closed in 1888 when planning for the lock began.

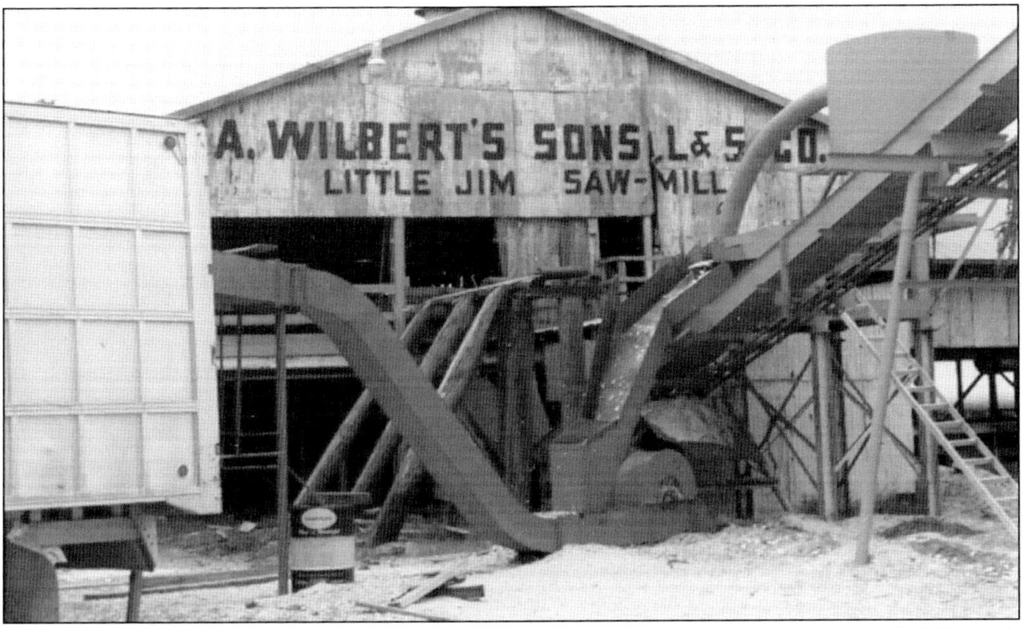

In 1887, following their father's death, the Wilbert sons were incorporated under A. Wilbert's Sons Lumber and Shingle Company. They then built two more mills that opened around 1888: the Anton sawmill and the Big Jim sawmill. In 1892, the company employed 50 skilled mechanics and 500 laborers. (Courtesy of Tony Fama.)

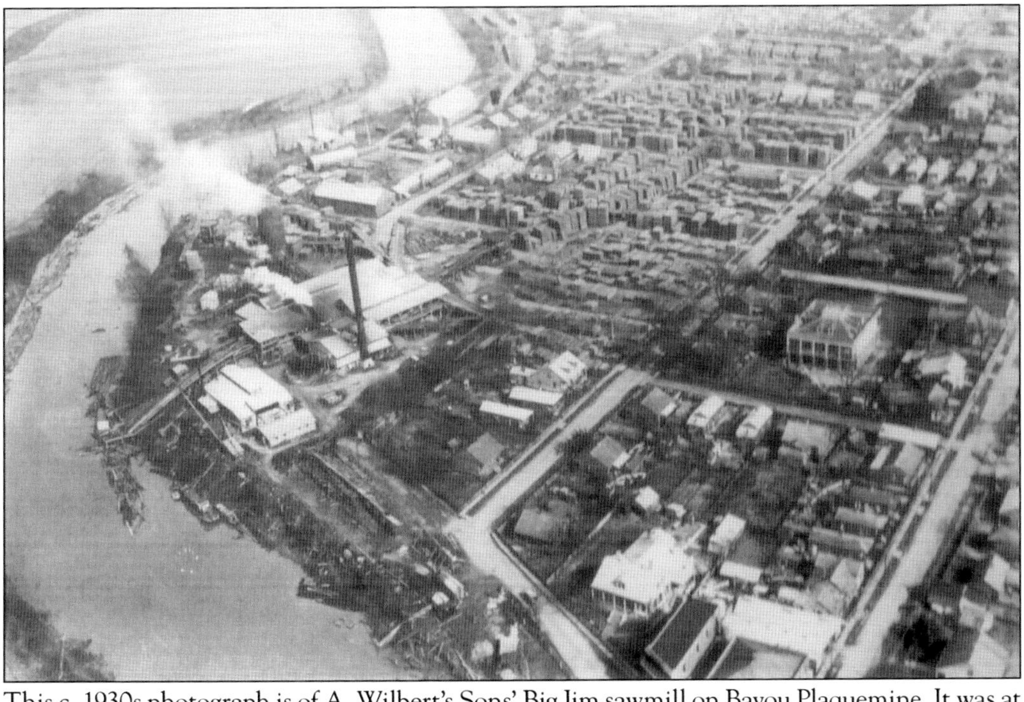

This c. 1930s photograph is of A. Wilbert's Sons' Big Jim sawmill on Bayou Plaquemine. It was at the end of Plaquemine Street, along Bayou Road. When first built, it could turn out some 30,000 feet of cypress lumber a day, and the mill workers' salaries ranged from $1 to $10 per day. After over 50 years of service, it was destroyed in a fire on March 18, 1940.

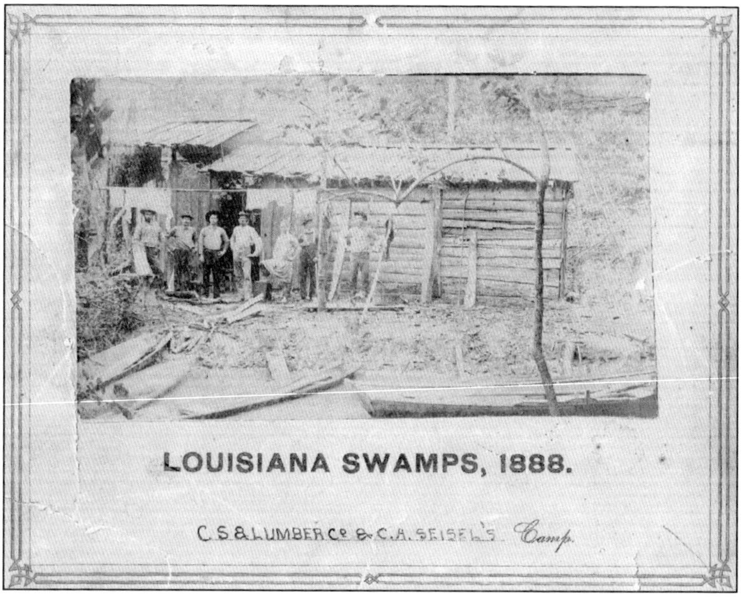

The Cypress Shingle and Lumber Company is considered the second-oldest lumber company in Plaquemine. In 1883, it erected a large shingle and lumber mill on Bayou Plaquemine about two miles from town. The company was run by Dr. S.D. Carpenter and Edward Shields, with Edward B. Schwing as the secretary. This c. 1888 photograph is of the company's lumber camp in the cypress swamps. (Courtesy of IPL.)

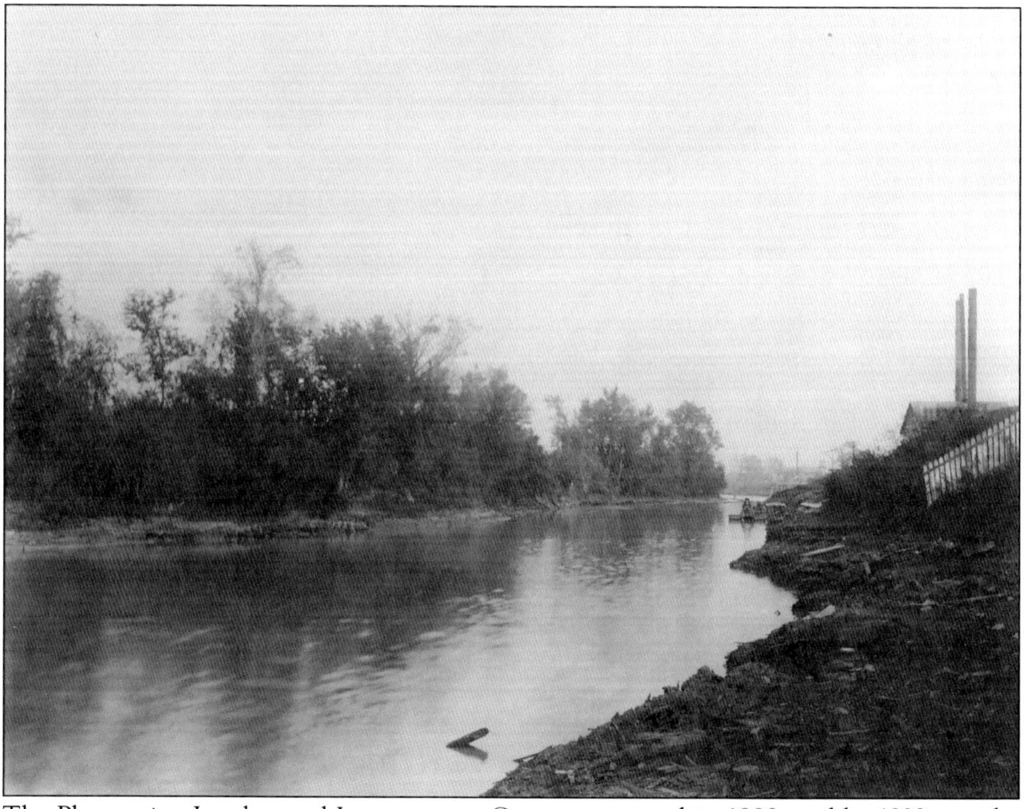

The Plaquemine Lumber and Improvement Company opened in 1888, and by 1892 was the largest lumber company in town. Pearl Wright, A. Baldwin, and Samuel G. Knowlton were in charge of operations. They had six mills at one point, but only four remained in operation due to fires. These were the Morning Glory Shingle Mill, the Homestead Mill, and two mills at Indian Village. In 1901, A. Wilbert's Sons bought all their shares. (Courtesy of IPL.)

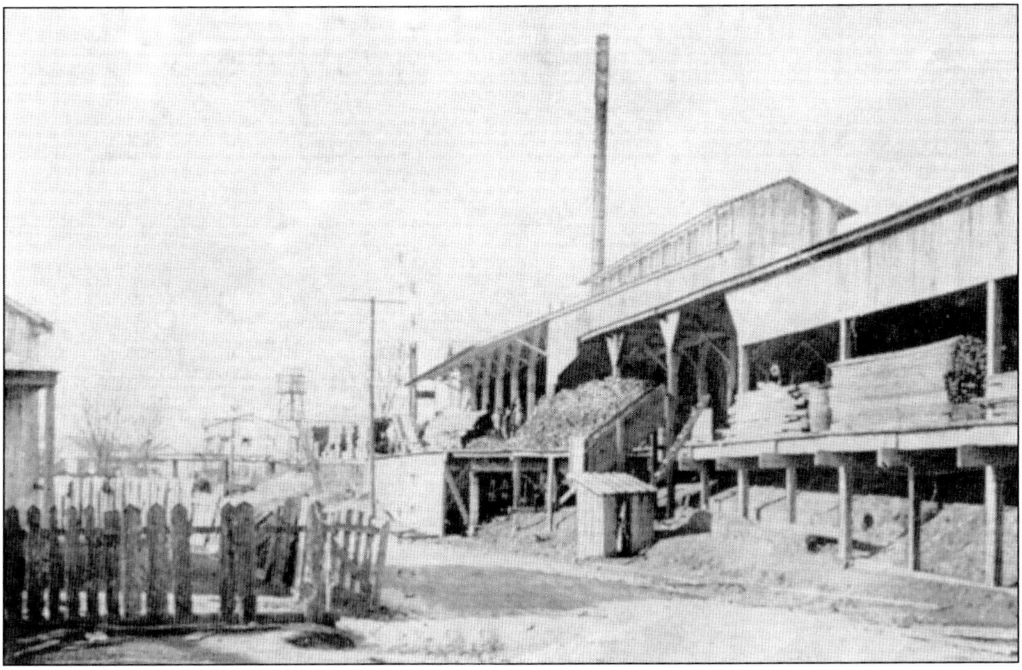

The Levert Lumber and Shingle Company was owned by John Baptiste Levert of New Orleans. He opened a Plaquemine firm in 1901 that was run by Levert's son-in-law Dr. Francis J. Kearny and John Deblieux. This c. 1906 photograph shows the planing mill built in 1902 on Bayou Plaquemine at Crescent, Louisiana, about five miles from town. (Courtesy of Tony Fama.)

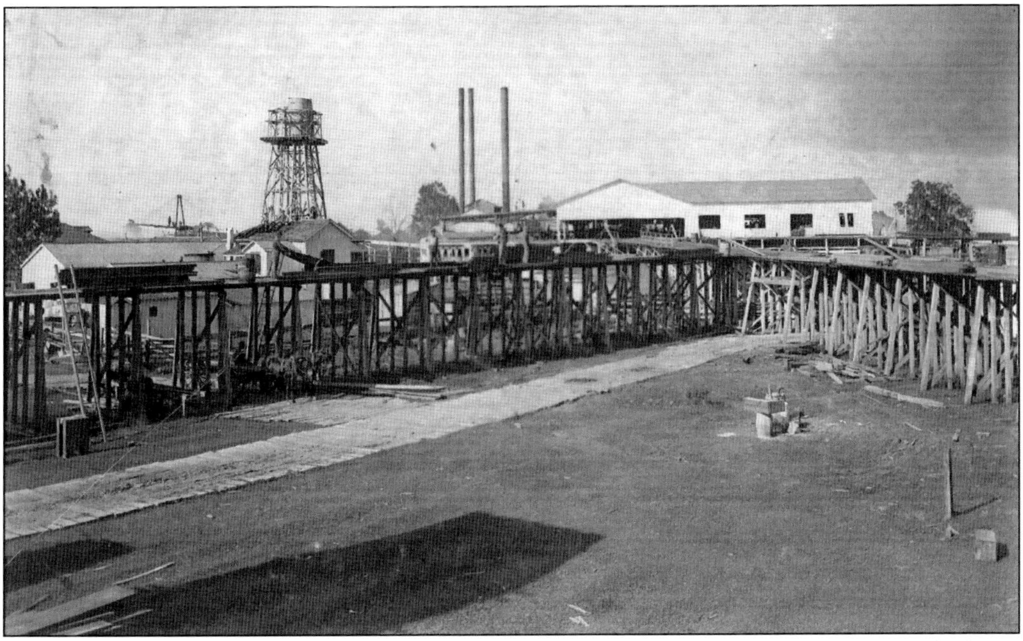

This is the Cockle Bur sawmill owned by August Levert and Company, a firm composed of Sen. August Levert, Francis J. Kearny, John Deblieux, and Samuel P. Schwing. It was about five miles from town on Bayou Plaquemine. During the small depression in 1894, this was one of the two sawmills to remain open in Plaquemine, the other being A. Wilbert's Sons' Anton mill.

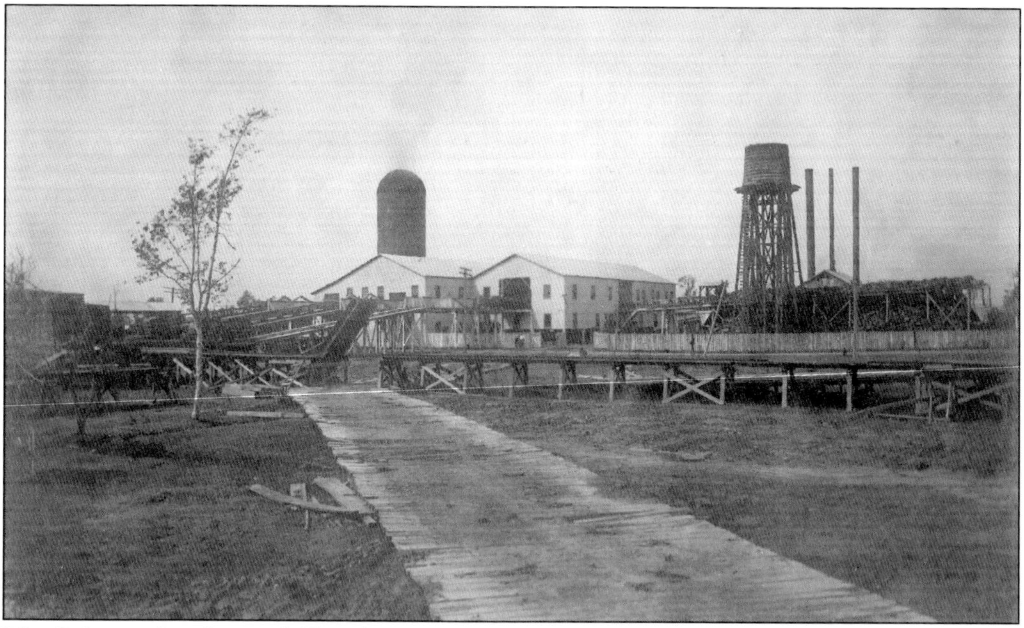

The Schwing Lumber and Shingle Company opened in 1901 under the direction of brothers Edward B. Schwing and Samuel P. Schwing, after both had been in the lumber industry for several decades. This c. 1906 photograph is of their sawmill about a mile from town. The mill was rebuilt in 1908 after a fire.

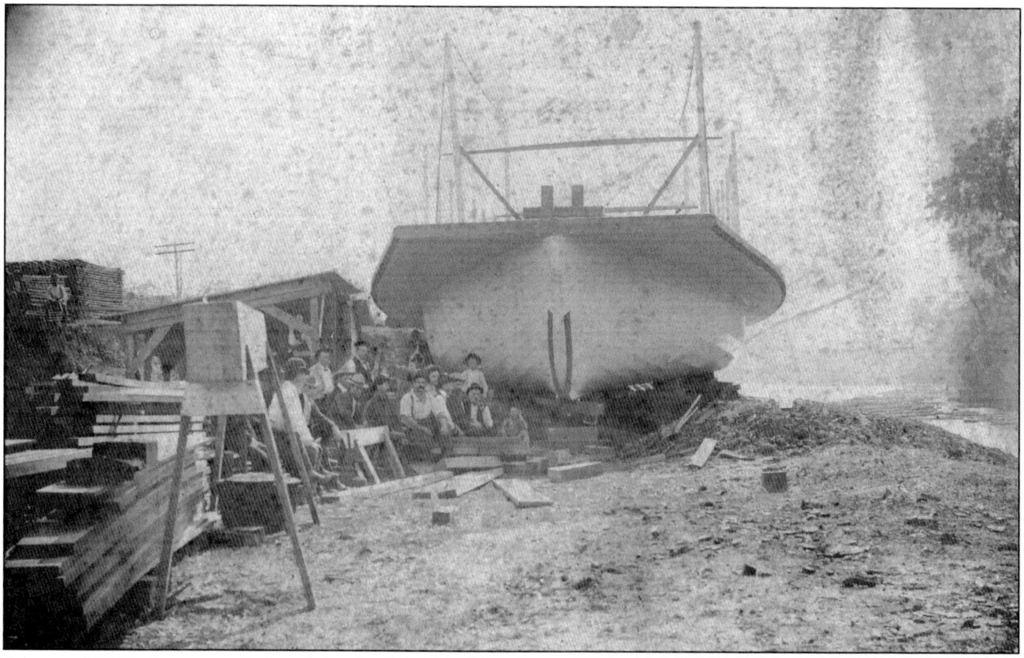

This c. 1903 photograph is of the building of the steamboat *Carrie B. Schwing*. The *Carrie B.* was built to be used in Bayou Plaquemine to conduct the Schwing Lumber and Shingle Company's affairs, including towing timber. The boat first set sail on March 26, 1904. After being rebuilt once due to fire, the steamer was finally put out of commission in 1946 when it burned and sank in the Mississippi.

The lumber cut in the swamp was arranged into log booms that sometimes extended half a mile, as the lumbermen were paid for every thousand feet of timber cut. The booms were pulled out of the swamp by steamboats. Loggers followed in flatboats or putt-putt boats to prevent log jams, some even riding on top of the booms. In the c. 1930s photograph at right, the *Carrie B. Schwing* is pulling a log boom to the Schwing sawmill. The picture below shows a smaller boom being floated in Bayou Plaquemine. (Right, courtesy of Linda Bezet; below, courtesy of IPL.)

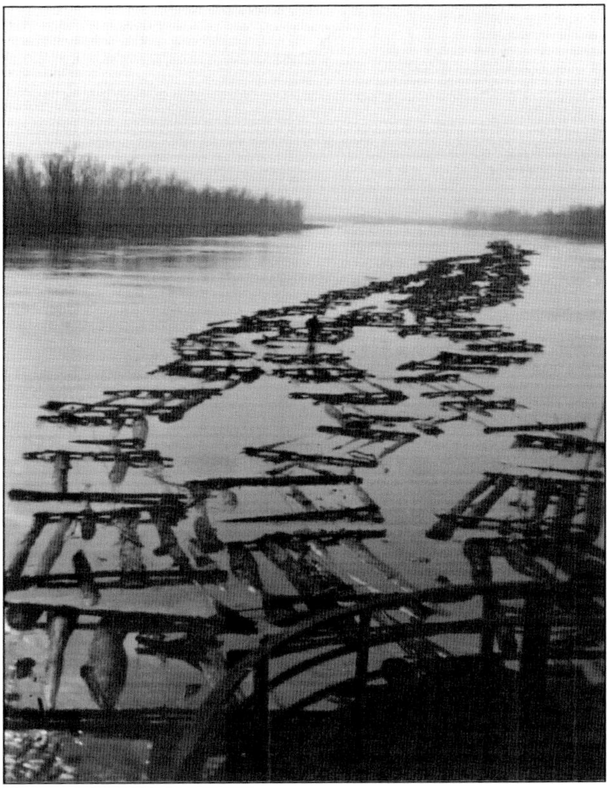

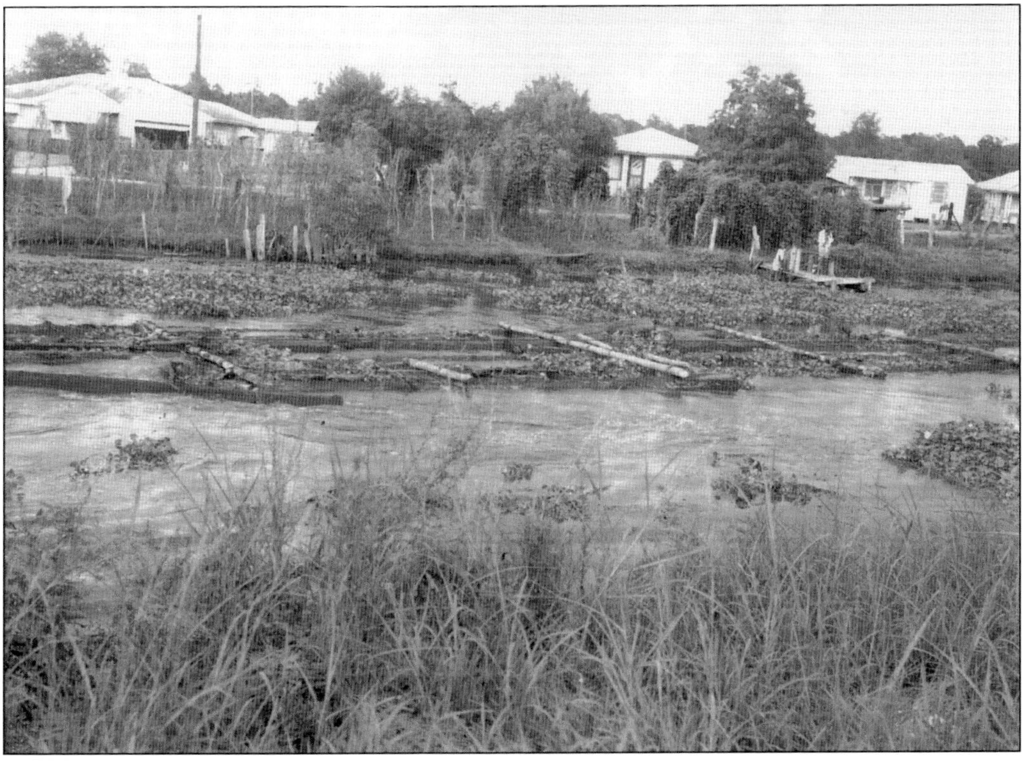

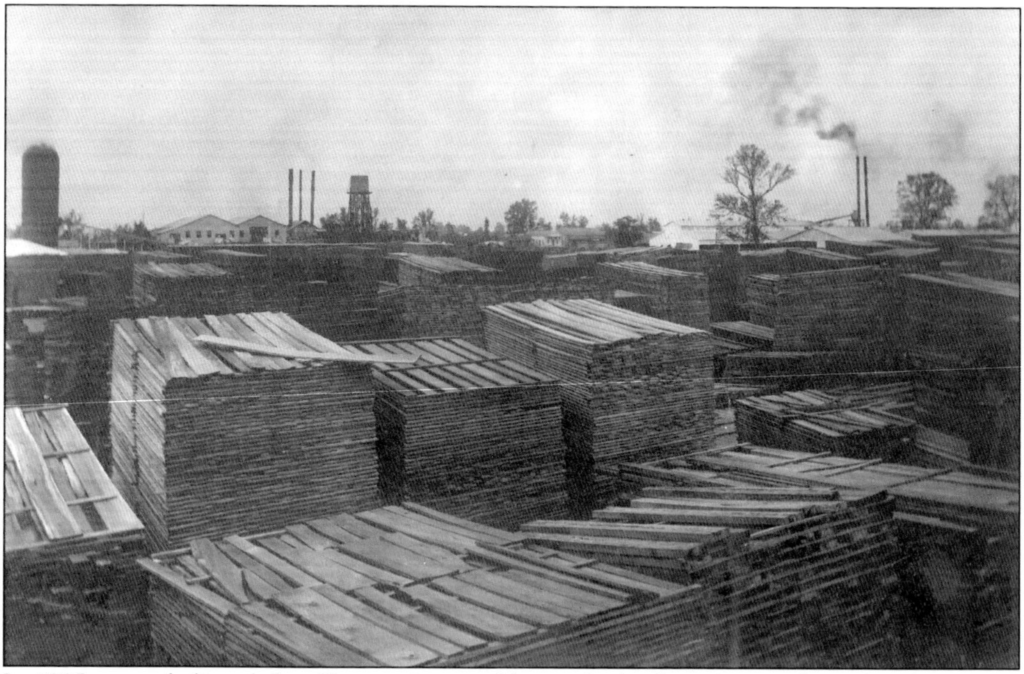

In 1885, many believed that Plaquemine would soon be leading the state's market for cypress lumber. Generally, the mills operated from six in the morning to six in the afternoon, so long as there was daylight. They were also prepared to furnish all kinds of sawed or split lumber, such as building material, sugar coolers, cisterns, hogshead and barrel staves, and shingles. By the 1890s, the Plaquemine mills' product was sought after by builders and lumber dealers throughout the United States. The above photograph is of the Schwing Lumber and Shingle lumber yard, and below is the planing mill, which opened in 1905.

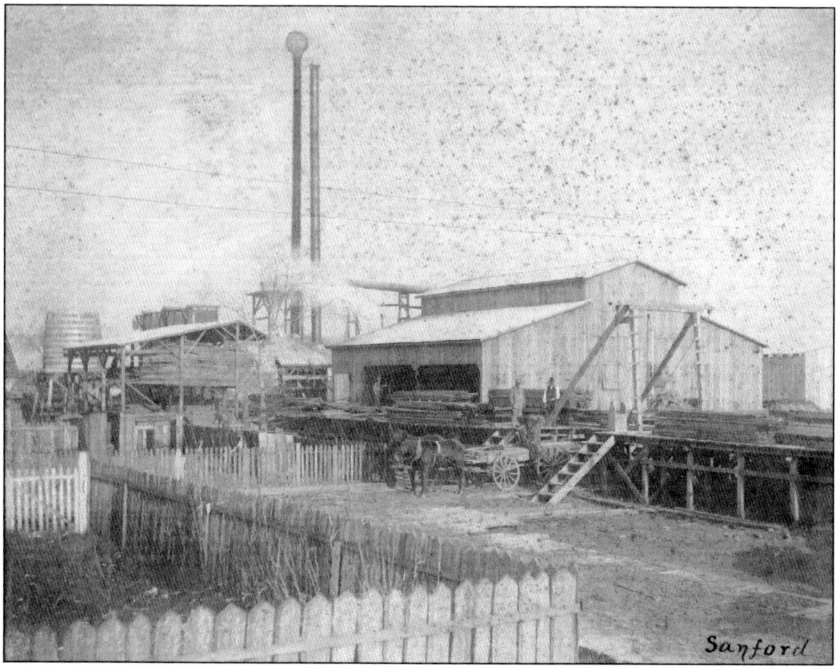

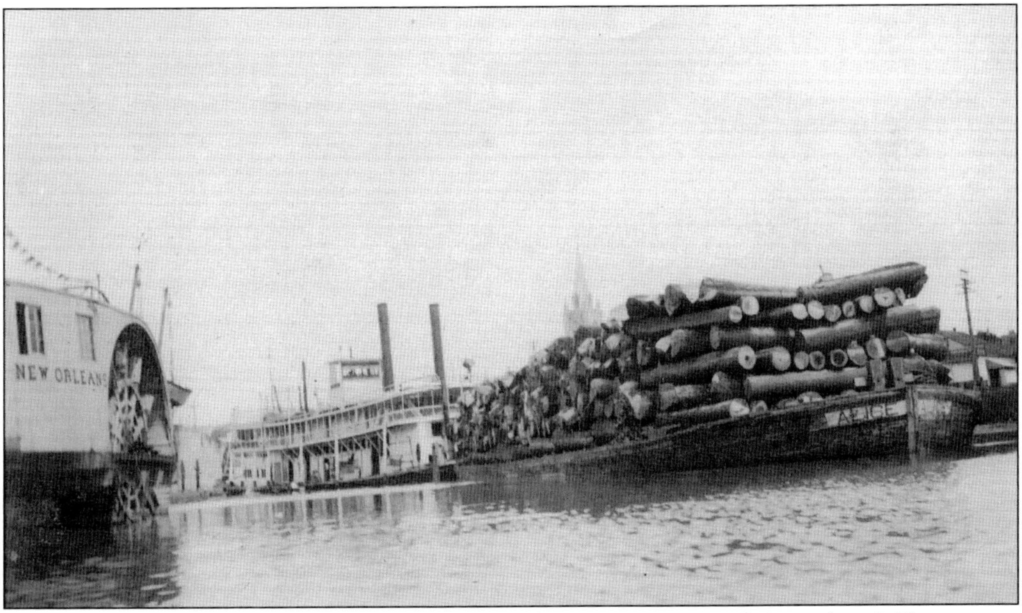

The lumber milled in Plaquemine was sent to market on steamers and the railroad. Plaquemine was only 85 miles from New Orleans by rail, and its location on the Mississippi connected it with a vast shipping network. Lumber shipped from the local mills supplied a market from Maine to Mexico, and according to the *Iberville South*, was used "to build many a cottage and mansion in the cities of the North and East." (Above, photograph by William Stadeker, courtesy of IPL.)

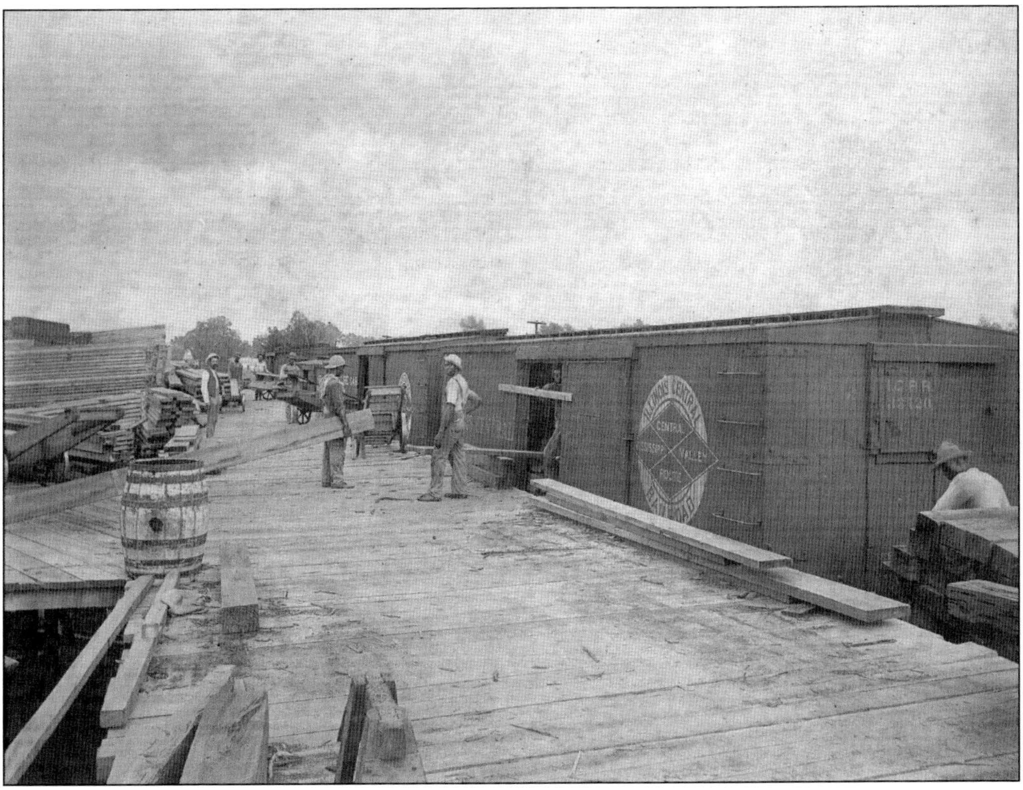

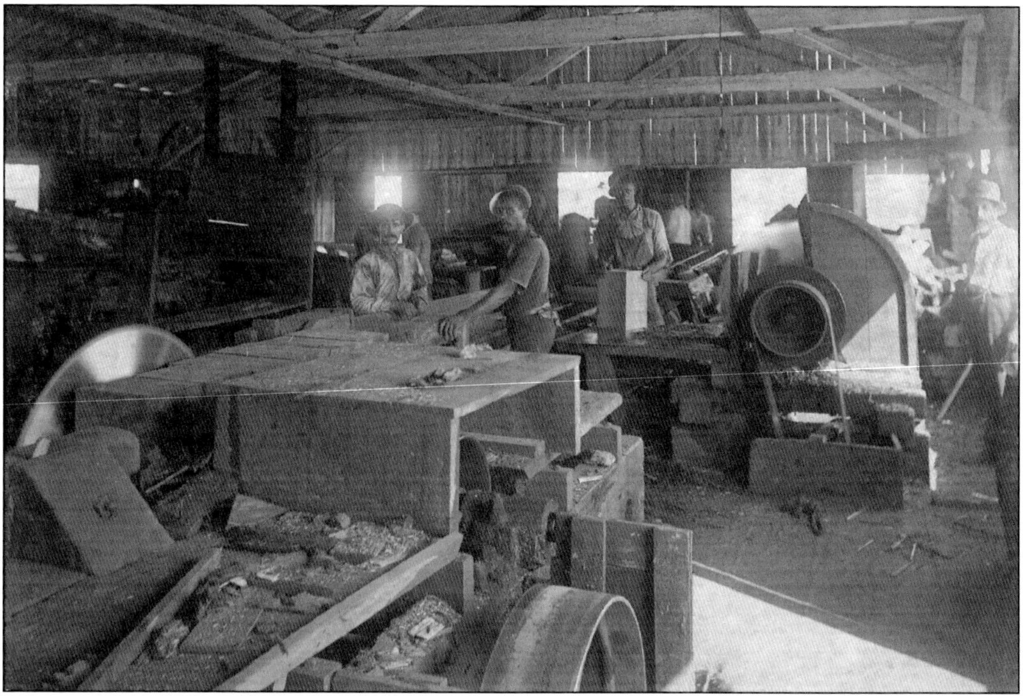

Trouble for the lumber industry began with the national panic of 1907. Before it, the price of lumber was abnormally high, as were the wages of mill workers and loggers. When the panic hit, the price of lumber dropped almost below the cost of production. Many sawmills across the state were forced to close, while others ran on short time and cut wages. In Plaquemine, mill owners worked to remain open because they knew if they closed, half of the community would be unemployed. By 1910, Plaquemine emerged from the depression, but the lumber industry remained in decline. Pictured above is the interior of the Baist Cooperage and Lumber Company's sawmill. Below is the Schwing Lumber and Shingle Company's lumber yard around 1905.

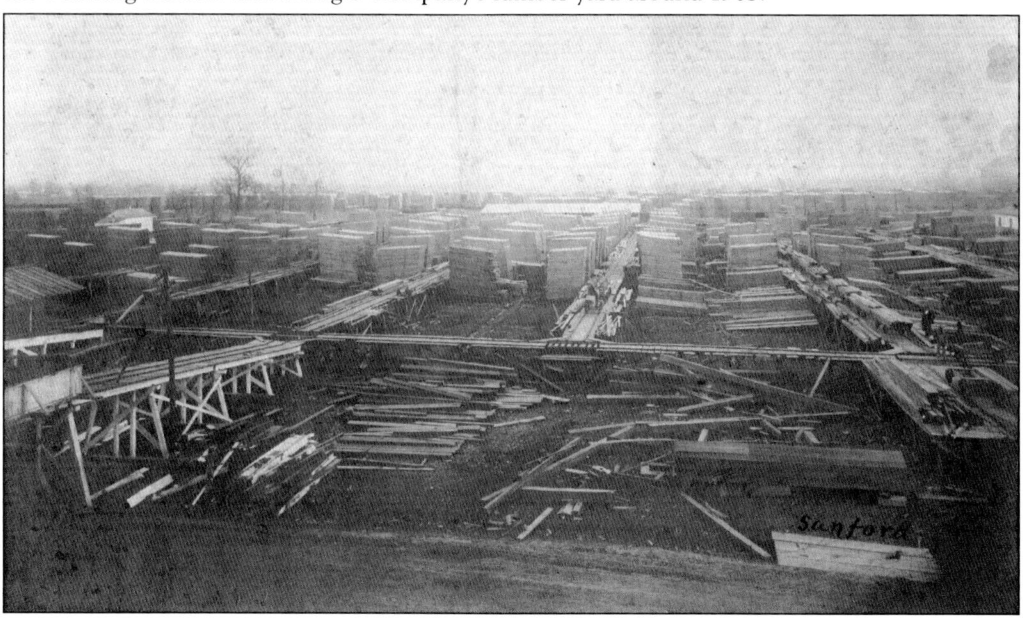

Five

Businesses, Buildings, and Landscapes

Early merchants and entrepreneurs embraced Plaquemine's role as a trade center, establishing hotels, taverns, and coffeehouses for travelers and opening many businesses that benefited the new industry the trade route supplied, such as Nadler Foundry and Machine Shop. As the town expanded outward, away from the river, new neighborhoods emerged that the city eventually annexed. Duttonville was along Main Street past Railroad Avenue. It was named after John Dutton, an Iberville Parish judge. Jeffersonville, Trinityville, and Haaseville made up the rear of Plaquemine and included the blocks between old Haase Street and Plaquemine Street. Fortville was about half a mile from the corporation limits and was named after the Federal fort built in 1864. Most of its residents were of African descent. The Desobry addition is named after the Desobry family that owned Irion Plantation. After Henry Desobry died in 1883, the city of Plaquemine incorporated his land. The Labauve addition was also added toward the end of the 19th century. By 1924, Dupont and Dupont building company advertised new bungalows in the Labauve Annex. Other additions included Seymourville along Louisiana Highway 1 toward White Castle, Turnerville, and Dupont Annex.

In this chapter, many of Plaquemine's most historic buildings and businesses are highlighted. While some of these buildings are long gone, they played significant roles in establishing the culture of Plaquemine.

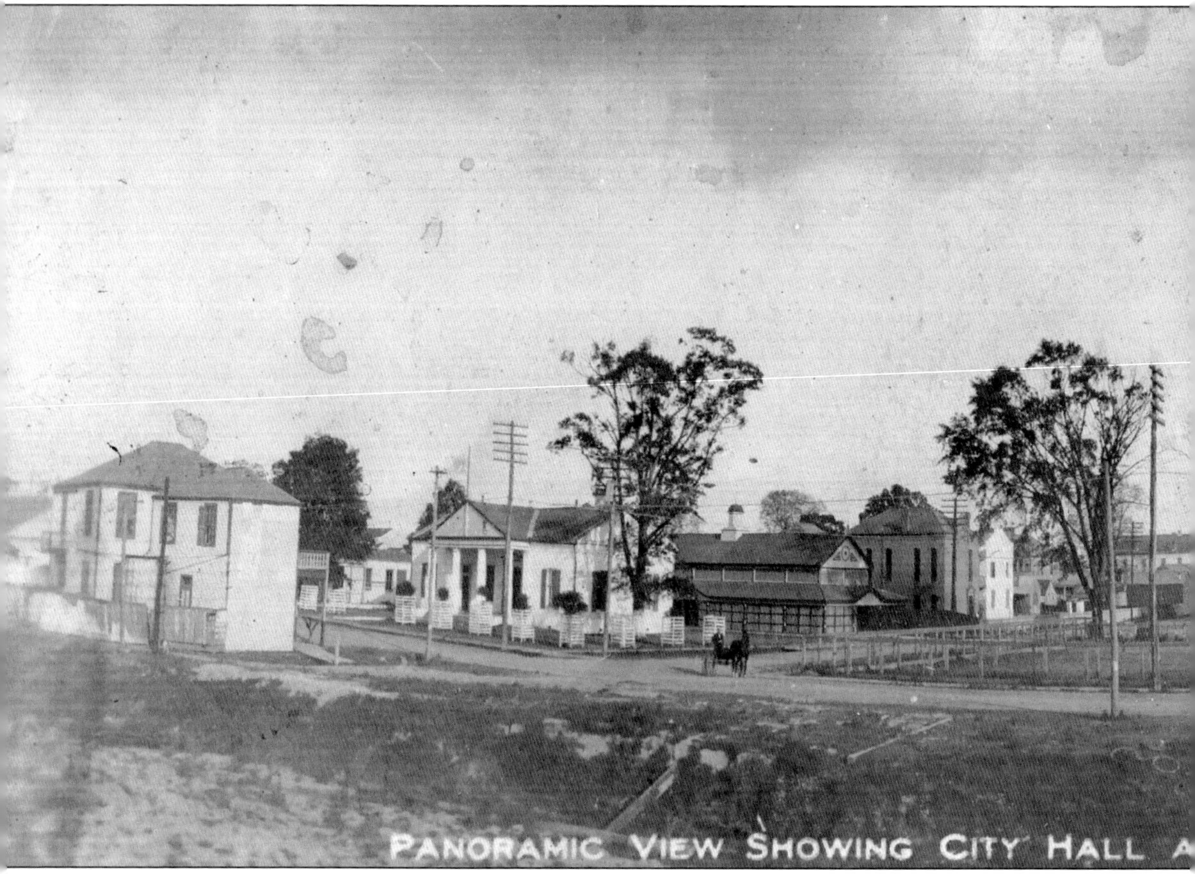

This c. 1908 panoramic photograph shows a section of Main Street. At far left is a commercial building that housed a barber, a saloon, and a tailor. Across the street is the Greek Revival–style building that was used as the city hall. Behind city hall are the Public Market and the parish jail. At center is St. John the Evangelist Church. Note the absence of the parochial school building

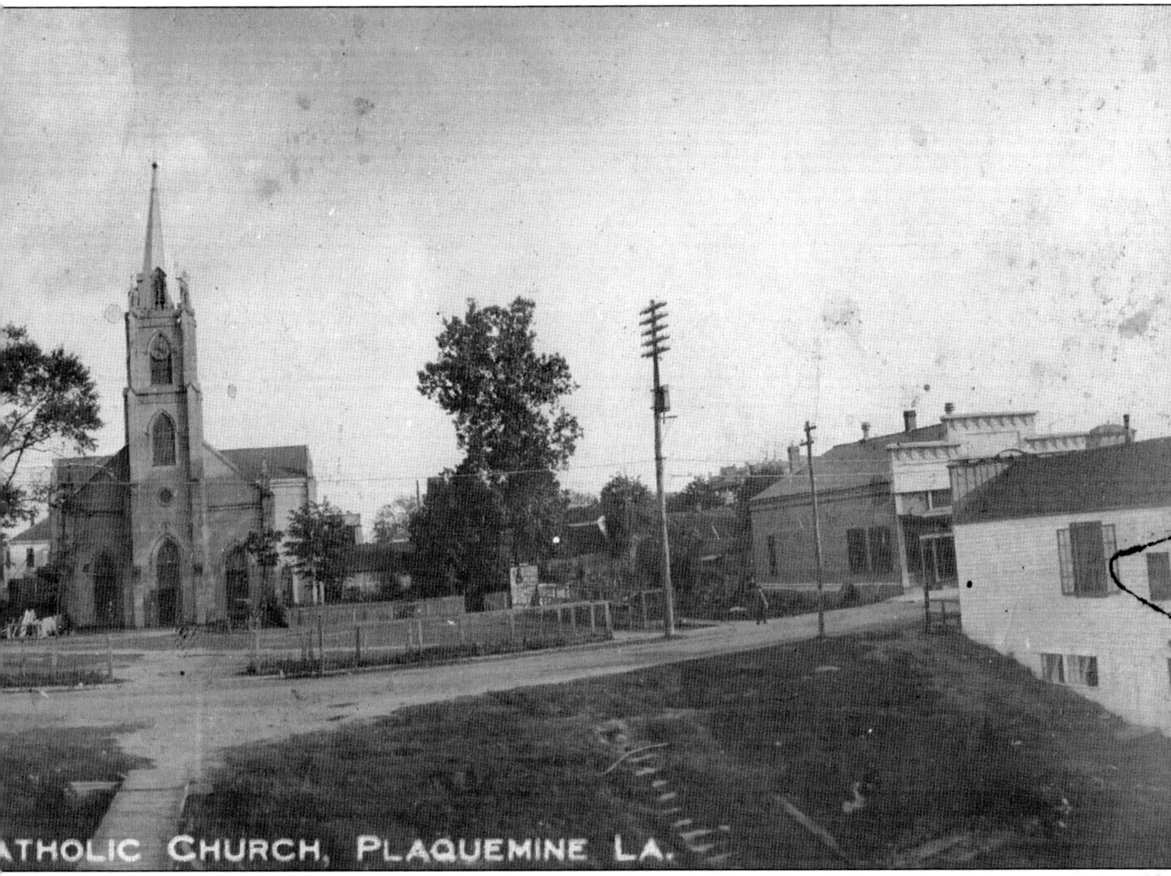

to the left of the church, as it burned down in 1907 and was not rebuilt until 1910. On the right of St. John is another commercial building, built in 1905, that was split between F.L. Trepagnier and Brothers Jewelers and Iberville Bank and Trust Company. Finally, across the street from the jewelers and bank was a tinsmith.

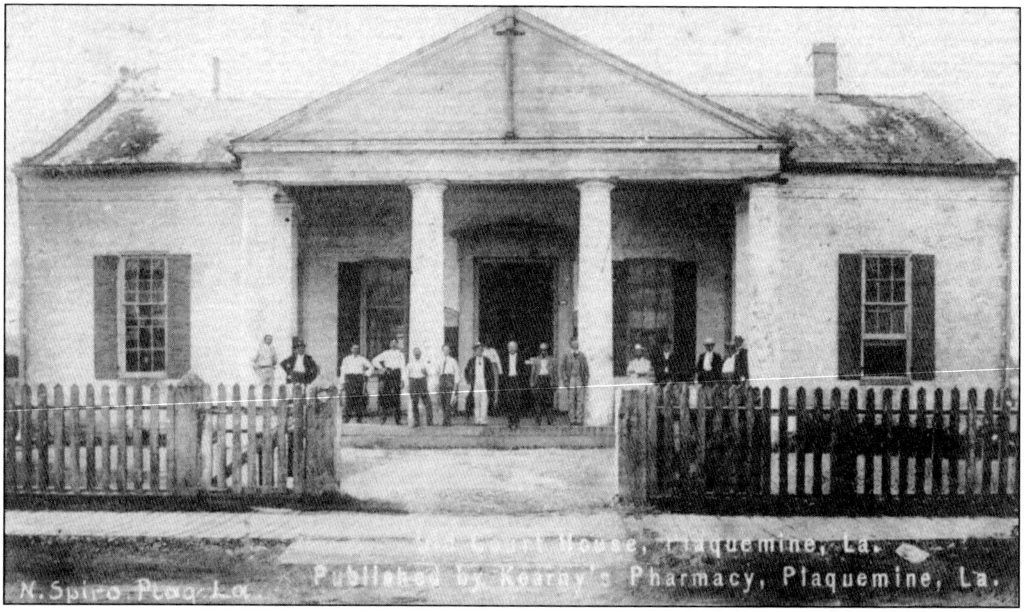

Fondly remembered as "the Old City Hall," this building first opened around 1850 as the Iberville Parish Courthouse. In 1848, the parish police jury contracted Thomas and George Weldon, two Irish immigrants out of Natchez, Mississippi, to construct a courthouse and jail in Plaquemine. By the 1880s, caves along the Mississippi River began to increase, resulting in growing concern over the courthouse's proximity to the river. The parish had also grown in size due to the lumber boom, and many residents wished to build a larger and grander courthouse a safe distance from the Mississippi. In 1906, the parish moved into its new courthouse on Railroad Avenue, selling this building to the City of Plaquemine to use at city hall, which it remained until 1985. In June 2000, the Iberville Museum opened in this historic structure.

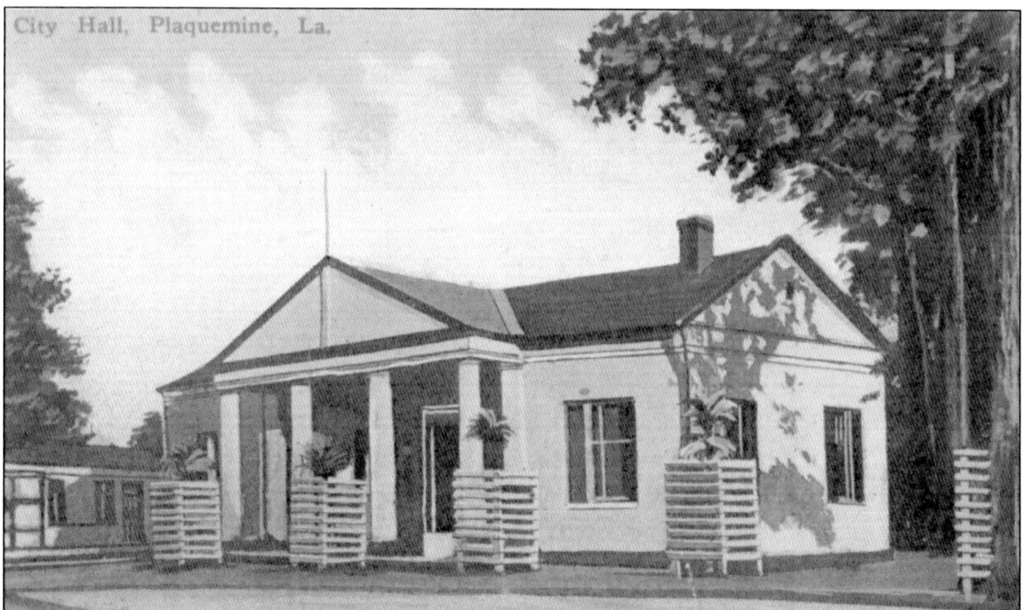

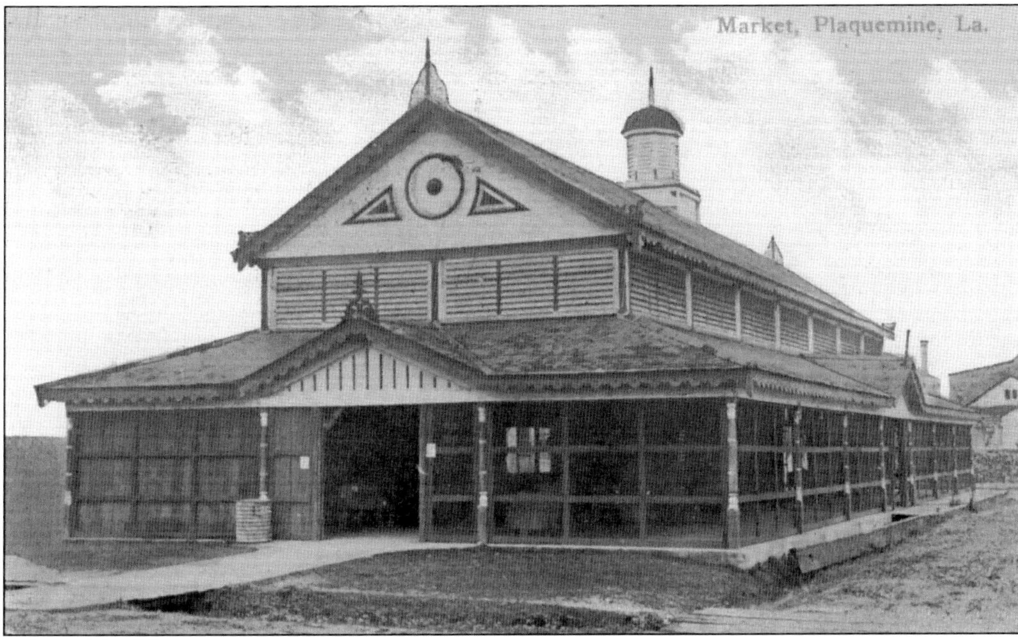

The Marionneaux Market was first located in Turnerville near the bayou, but by August 1882, the 100-foot-long, 40-foot-wide market was rebuilt on Fenn's Alley in Irishtown. It contained 12 stalls and boasted fresh eggs, vegetables, fruits, butter, fish, meat, and game. In 1883, the Marionneaux family sold the market to the city, renaming it the Public Market. After the 1896 cave-in, the building was moved to Main Street in front of the Catholic church. But when the city purchased the old courthouse to use as city hall in 1906, the market moved behind the building, where it remained until its closure in the 1920s. The image below is of the 1916 Plaquemine Fire Department and schoolchildren in front of city hall and the Public Market, taken by Duncan's Studio in Plaquemine.

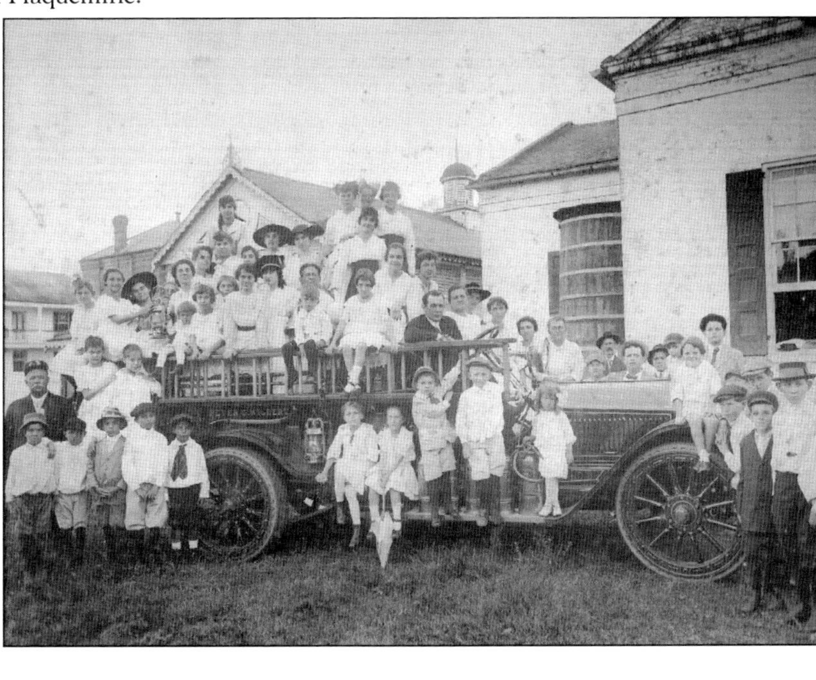

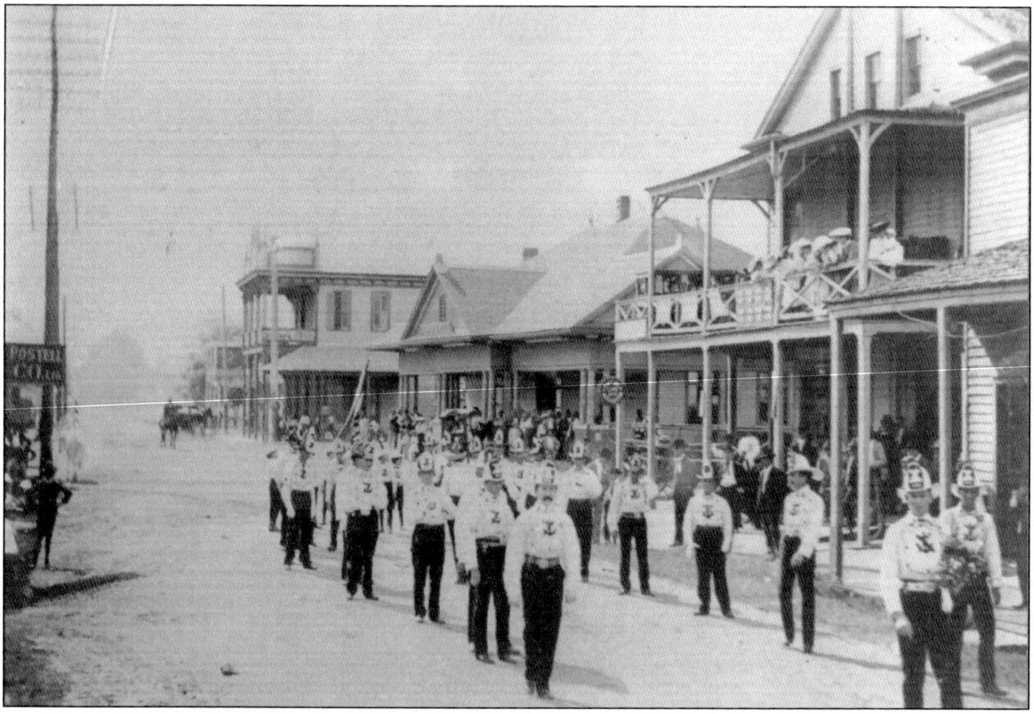

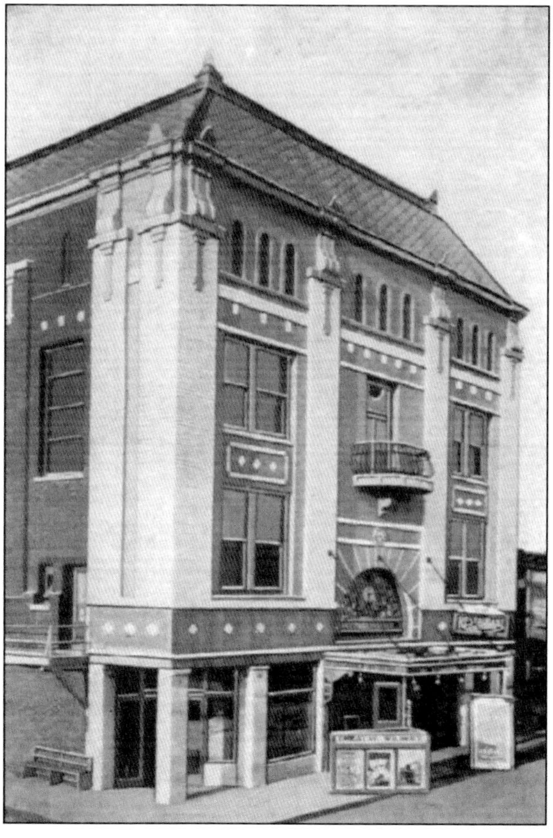

This view down Main Street was taken during a Firemen's Carnival parade in 1906. The two-story building with the balcony on the right was the Hope Opera House, which opened there in 1897. The city moved it from its original location on Fenn's Alley after the 1896 cave-in. The railroad depot sits to the left of the opera house, with the Cosmopolitan Hotel and Bar and the Marchal Bakery following.

Wilbert Theatre opened in 1918 after the Wilbert family purchased the Hope Opera House and replaced it with a larger and more modern structure. The new theater cost $80,000 and was four stories high. It seated 1,300 people and sported a 40-by-52-foot stage that hosted opera and ballet companies until the introduction of movies. The building was eventually torn down when Citizens Bank and Trust expanded.

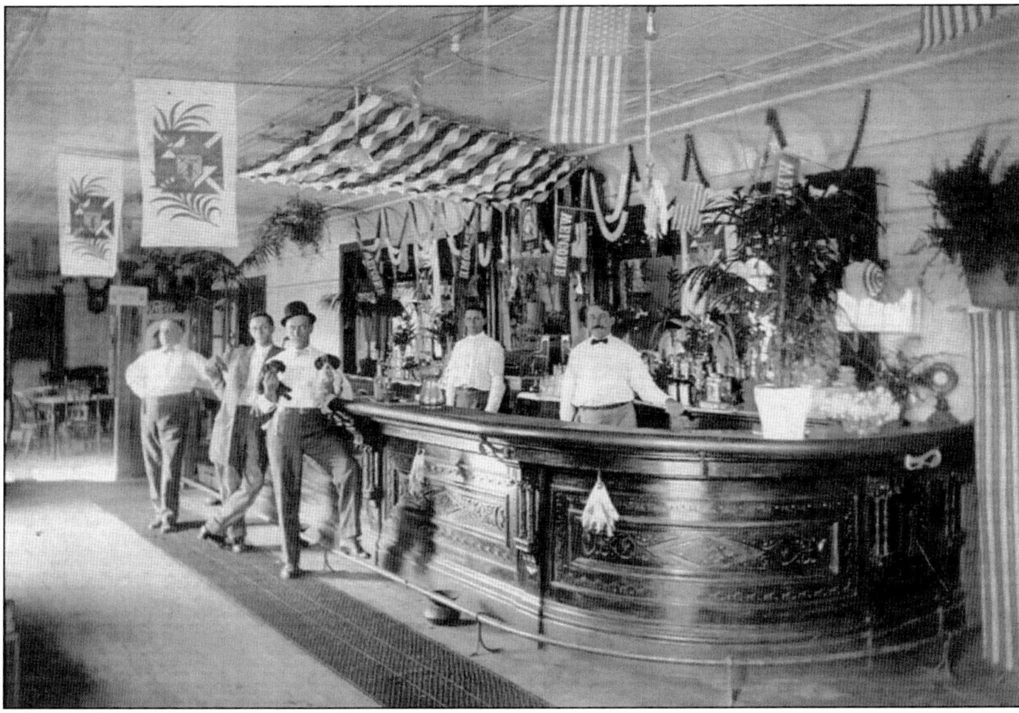

Lionel Delacroix was the manager of Wilbert Theatre until the late 1930s, when he built his own theater, Osage Theater, on Court Street. However, this c.1918 photograph shows the cocktail lounge inside the Wilbert Theatre. The building also included a barbershop with a street entrance. (Courtesy of Tony Fama.)

Pictured here is a crowd of locals waiting for the Knights of Columbus toy giveaway for Christmas 1946. From left to right are the Wilbert Theatre, the Knights of Columbus Hall, and Lee Miller's appliance store.

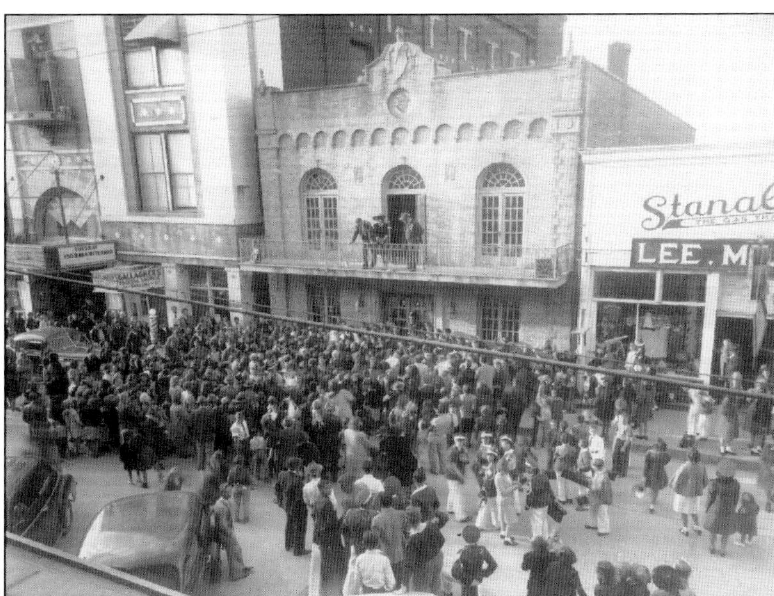

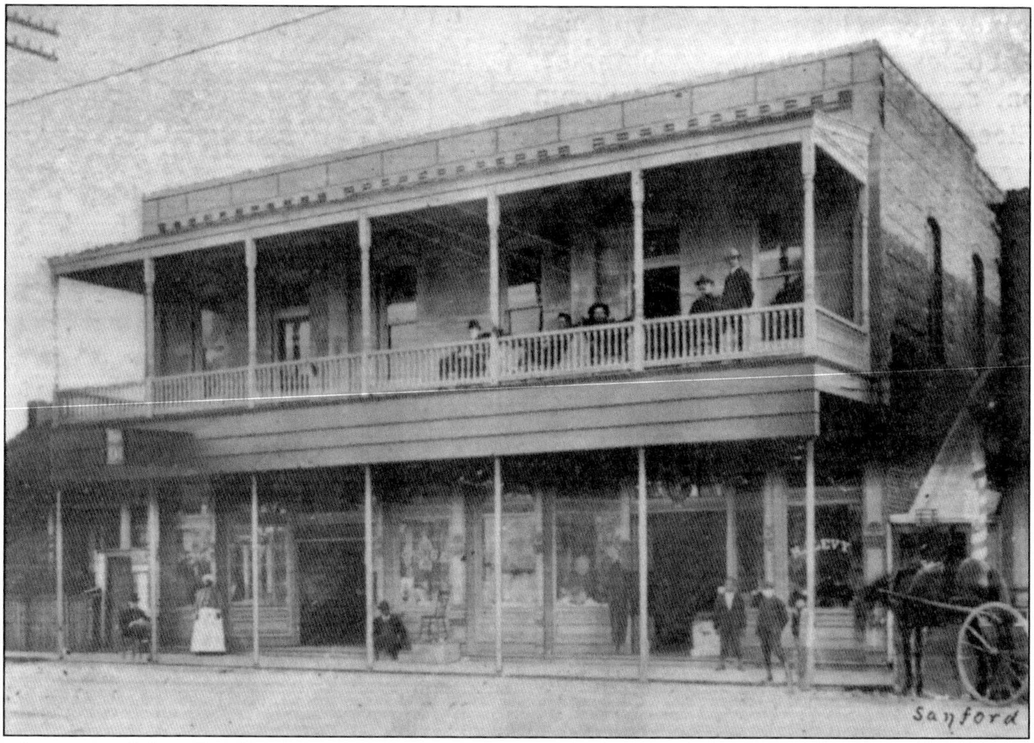

This is the Scharf building on Main Street, pictured around 1906. Leon Scharf built it in 1893. Initially, it was a one-story building that housed J. Levy and Company's men's clothing store and Holloway-Postell Drug Company. In 1905, the second story was added at the request of the Plaquemine Club. Pictured below is the Plaquemine Club reading room around 1905 on the second floor of the Scharf building. The Plaquemine Club was founded in 1900 and was first located above Barker's Pharmacy. The club also featured an assembly hall, parlors, and a billiards room. (Below, courtesy of Tony Fama.)

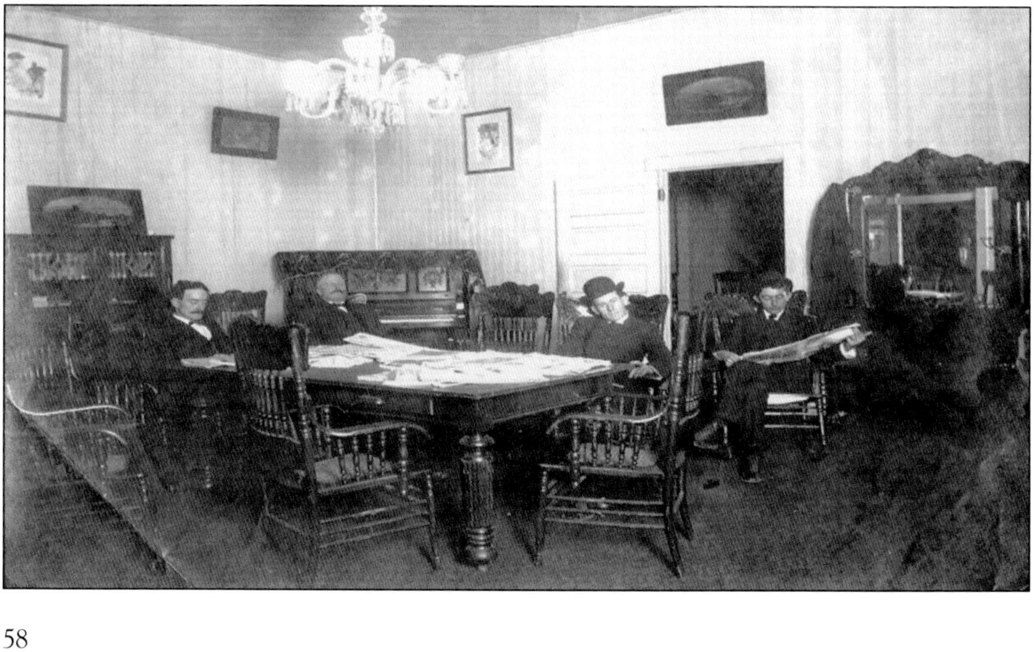

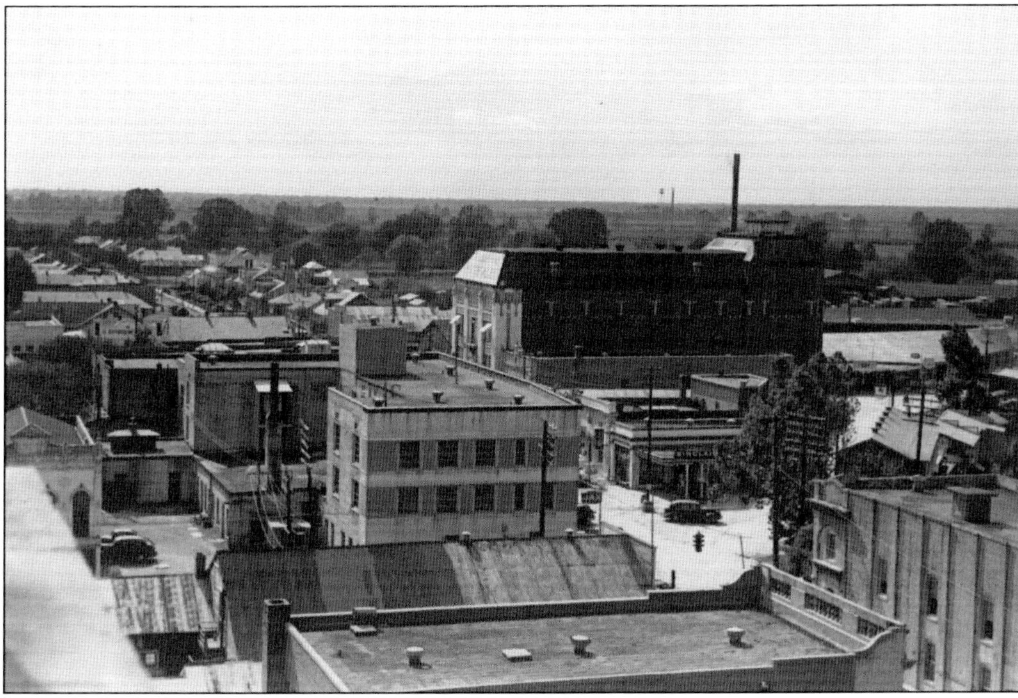

This photograph of Main Street was taken from the Catholic church in 1939 by Talbot Grant. The three-storied building on the corner of Main and Eden Streets is the Silber Hotel, originally known as the Central Hotel. The Silber brothers built it in 1914. In 1931, it was remodeled after a fire and renamed after the brothers. It later became Hotel Lamar and was torn down in 1976. (Courtesy of IPL.)

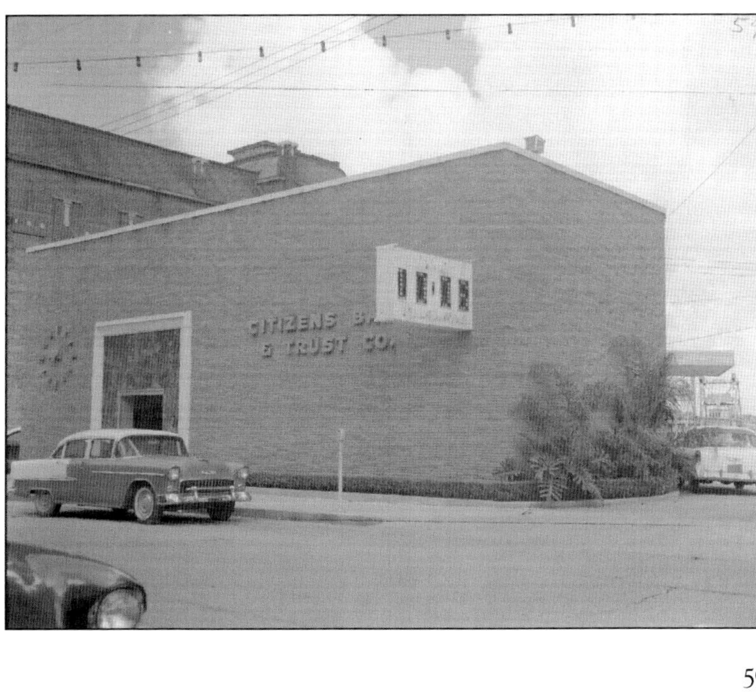

Citizens Bank and Trust Company opened in Plaquemine around 1918. In 1921, it opened at Main Street across from the Central Hotel. This photograph is by Joseph Ollis Dupont and was taken shortly after the bank was renovated in 1952, expanding into the Sinclair Gas Station. The bank was remodeled a second time in the 1970s. (Courtesy of IPL.)

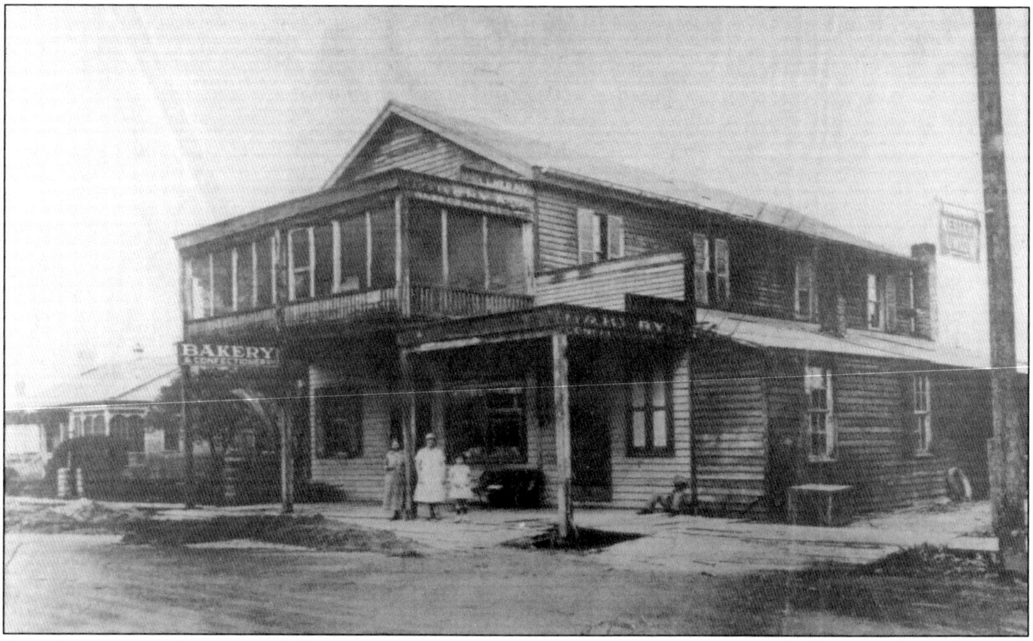

Charles N. Roth built this bakery in 1886 on Main Street. August Marchal purchased the building in 1917 and opened Central Bakery and Confectionery. In the 1930s, Marchal replaced the original bakery with a brick building. After he died in 1955, Joseph Varnel purchased the building and renamed it Bon Bakery. It closed in 1983.

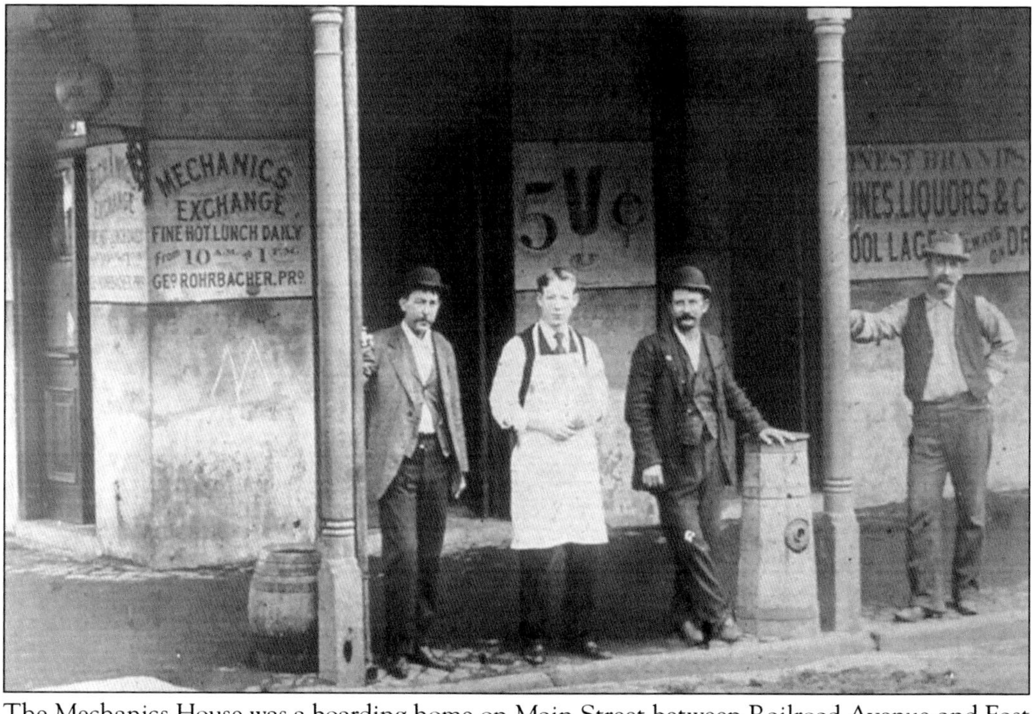

The Mechanics House was a boarding home on Main Street between Railroad Avenue and East Street. It was first managed by Ernest Putter and Henrietta D. Gross, German immigrants who moved to Plaquemine in the 1880s. This photograph was taken around 1890. (Courtesy of Tony Fama.)

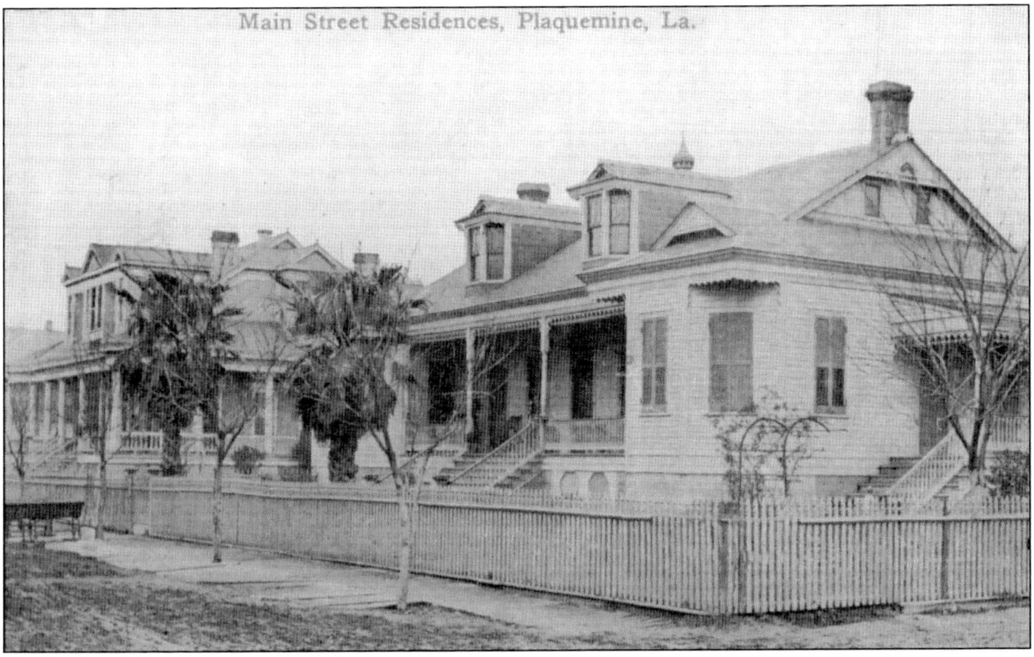

This c. 1914 postcard of Main Street residences features the Wilbert-Kirkland house (right), built by John Wilbert in 1900 in the Colonial Revival style, and the Wilbert-Bishop house (left), built around 1900 by Charles Wilbert as a Queen Anne–style cottage. (Courtesy of Louisiana State University.)

A. Wilbert's Sons Department Store opened in 1899 on Main Street between Railroad Avenue and East Street. In this c. 1909 photograph, standing in front of the store from left to right are Irwin Wilbert, Joe Trosclair, Omer Hebert, Clarence Briggs (with the broom), Louis Labauve, Grover Landry, Peter Wilbert, and Jules Durand (behind).

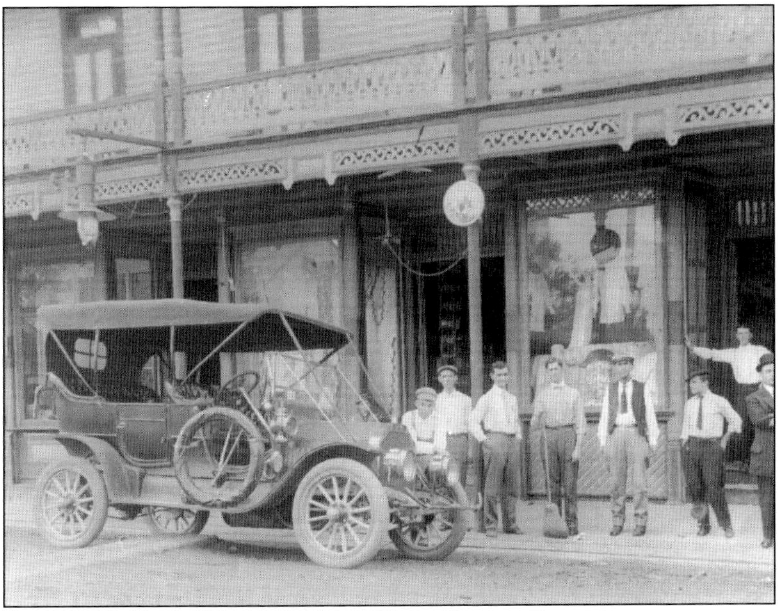

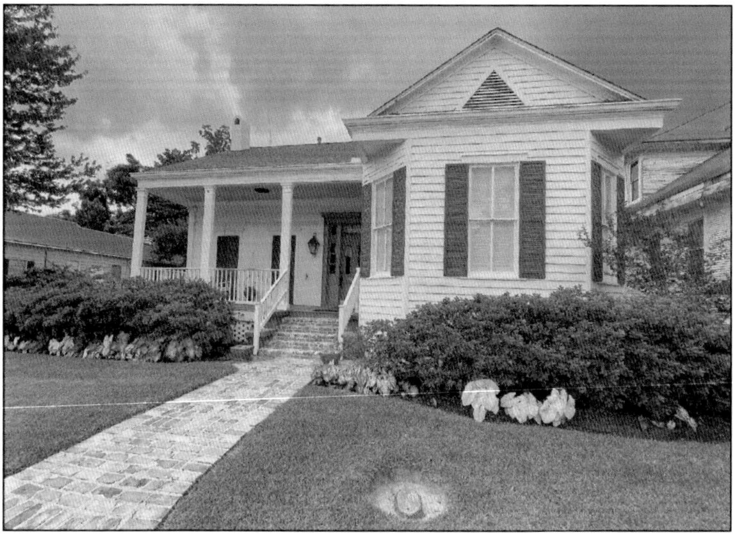

This Italianate cottage was built by Leonard F. Hooper in 1880 in Duttonville on Main Street, where it meets Federal Street. Hooper was a well-known carpenter in Plaquemine in the late 1800s, working as the contractor on many public buildings and residences in town. This later became the home of Charles Ernest and Elizabeth "Lizzie" Hebert. (Photograph by Meghan C. Sylvester.)

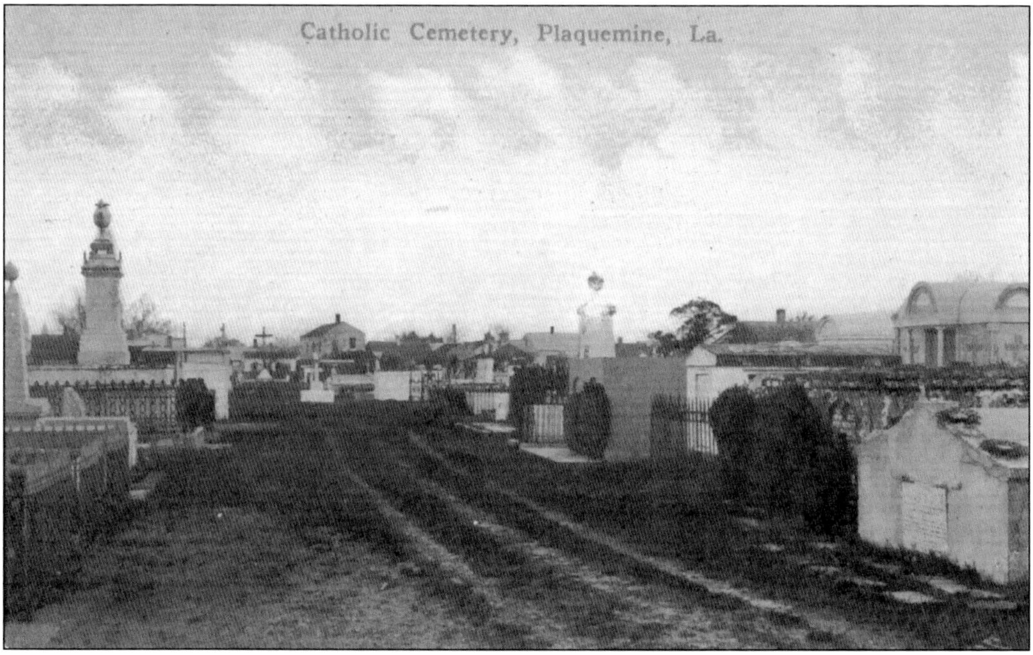

St. John's Catholic Cemetery is the oldest in Plaquemine. In 1840, Judge John Dutton donated the lot at Main and Hamilton Streets to the town. However, a few markers predate Dutton's donation. The adjoining lot at Main and Federal Streets was donated in 1852 for a Protestant cemetery. Finally, in 1856, the Hebrew Benevolent Society of Plaquemine established a Jewish cemetery at Federal and Division Streets.

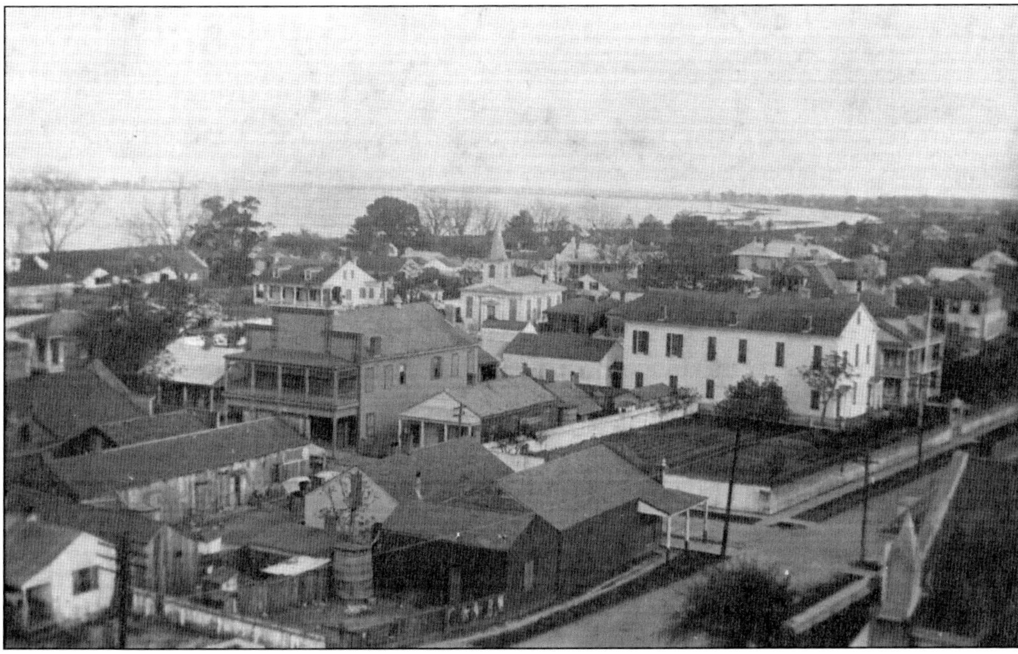

Pictured here is a bird's-eye view of Plaquemine in 1912. The photograph was taken from St. John Church and looks behind the church toward the Mississippi River. The two-story wooden building with a balcony at left was the old Neubig Dry Goods Store. The large Greek revival structure at right is St. Basil's Academy and Convent, and the small church with the steeple at rear center was the Presbyterian church.

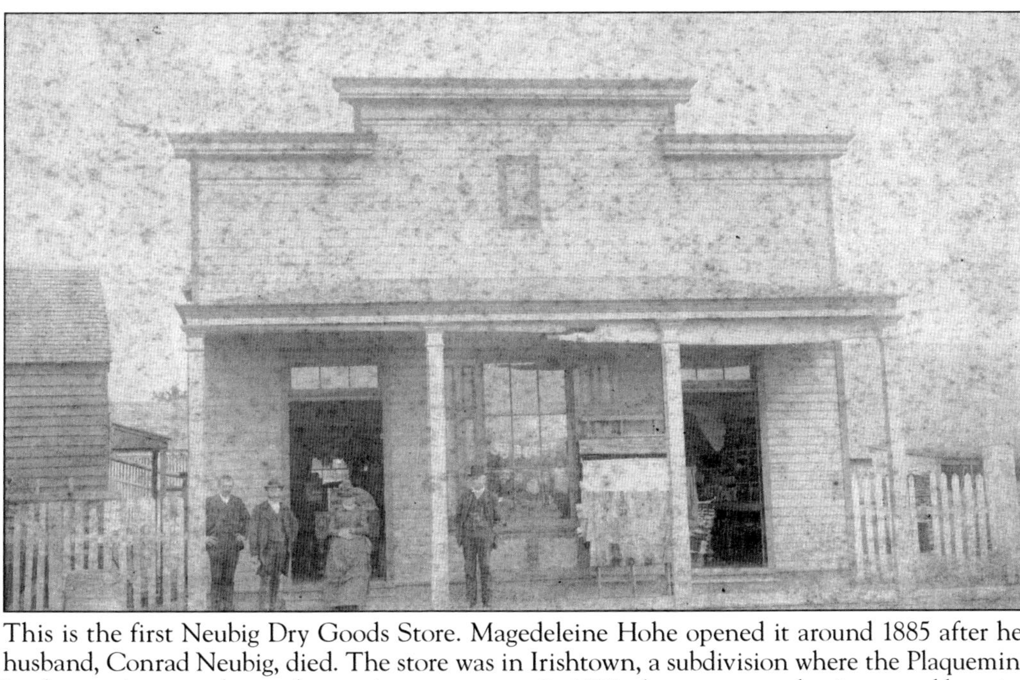

This is the first Neubig Dry Goods Store. Magedeleine Hohe opened it around 1885 after her husband, Conrad Neubig, died. The store was in Irishtown, a subdivision where the Plaquemine Lock now sits, next door to her son's grocery store. In 1893, the store moved to its second location on Plaquemine Street behind St. Basil's.

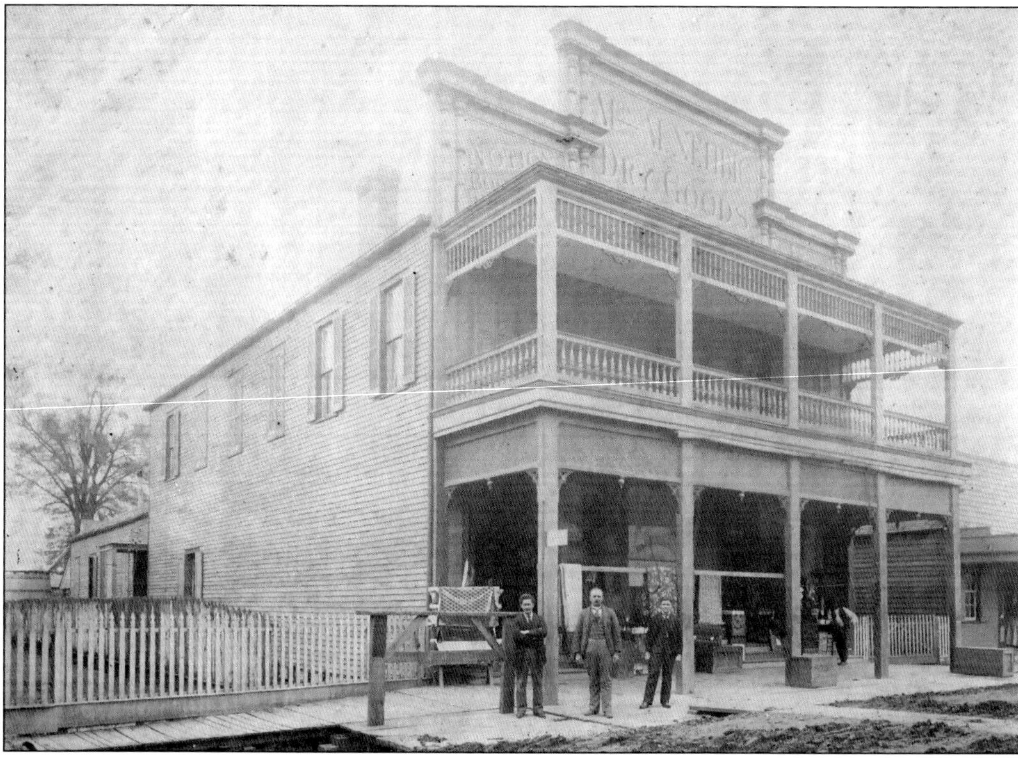

Magedeleine Hohe died in 1902 and passed the family business to her daughter Frances Neubig and son Christian Conrad Neubig. Pictured is the store's second location on Plaquemine Street. This location closed after the siblings built a new brick building at Eden and Plaquemine Streets. In the 1940s, the store was converted into apartments, but the building was eventually demolished. This photograph is by H.D. Hughes.

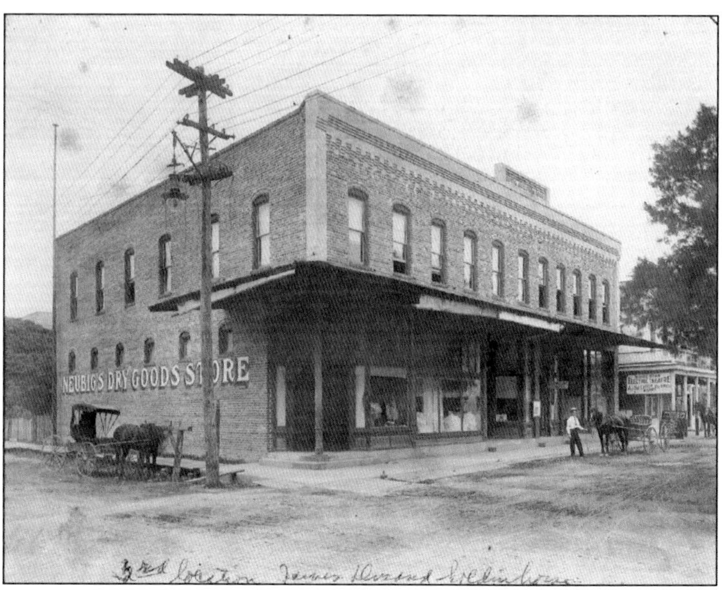

The final location of the Neubig Dry Goods Store opened in 1906 on the corner of Eden and Plaquemine Streets, where the St. John Church's parking lot now sits. The US government rented the right side of the building as a post office, and the top floor was used as a Masonic lodge. This photograph is from 1908. The store officially closed in 1934.

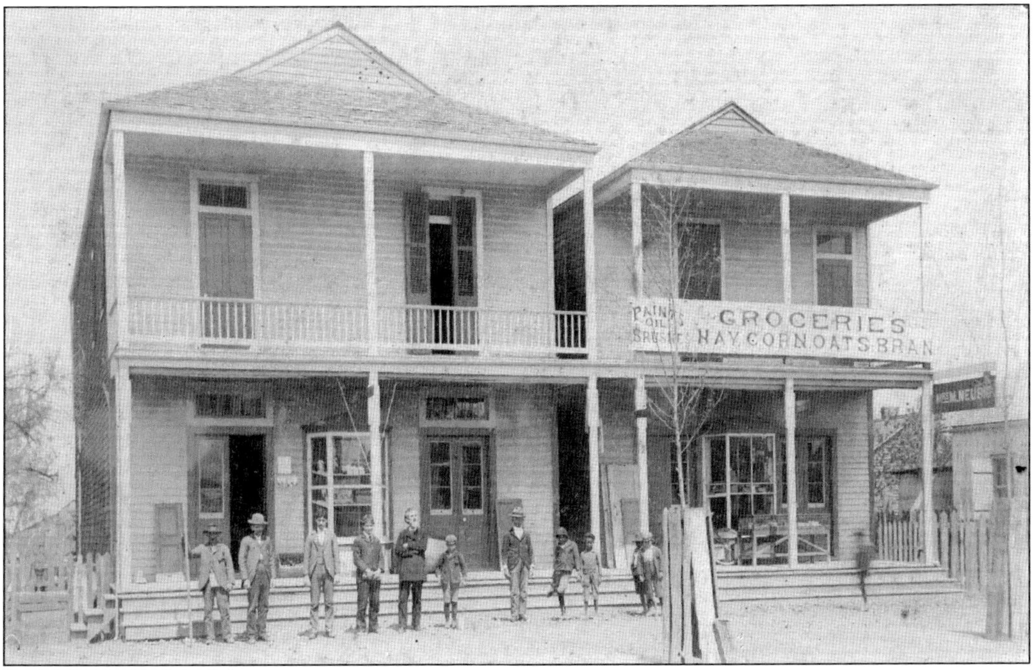

The Neubig Grocery store first opened in 1881 in Irishtown. Philipp Neubig, son of Conrad Neubig and Magdeleine Hohe, ran the store for his father. In 1893, he moved the shop to Nadler Street across from the Plaquemine dike in Turnerville. Pictured above is the grocery store's third building, which opened around 1899. It was at the corner of Laville and Turner Streets in Turnerville. Shown below is the interior of the store. A box of Kellogg's toasted corn flakes and minced meat sit on the counter. Standing in the aisle are Benjamin Tullier (left) and Philipp Neubig.

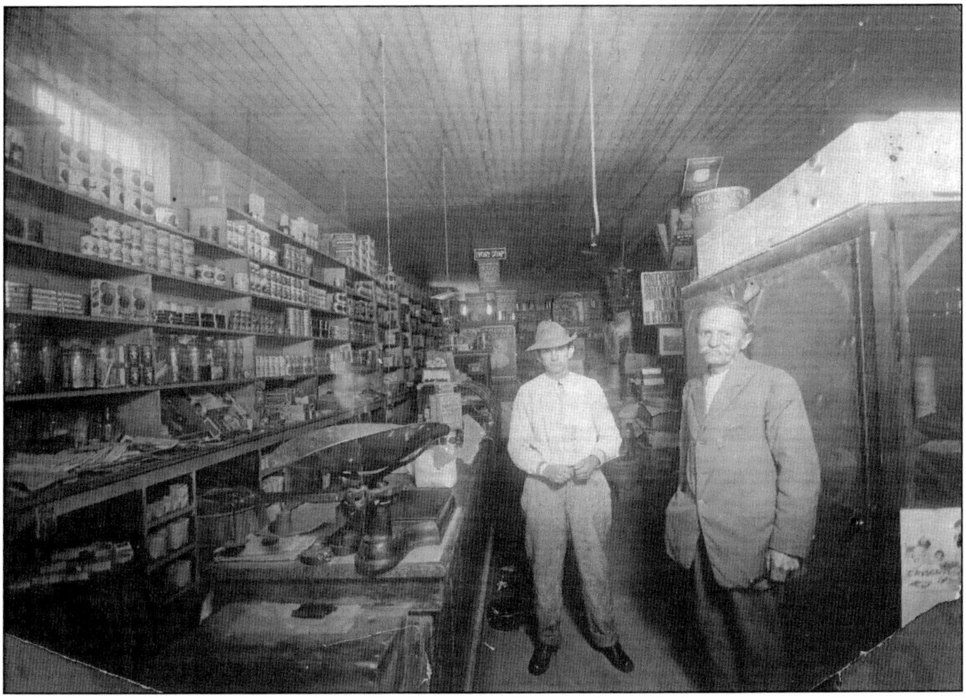

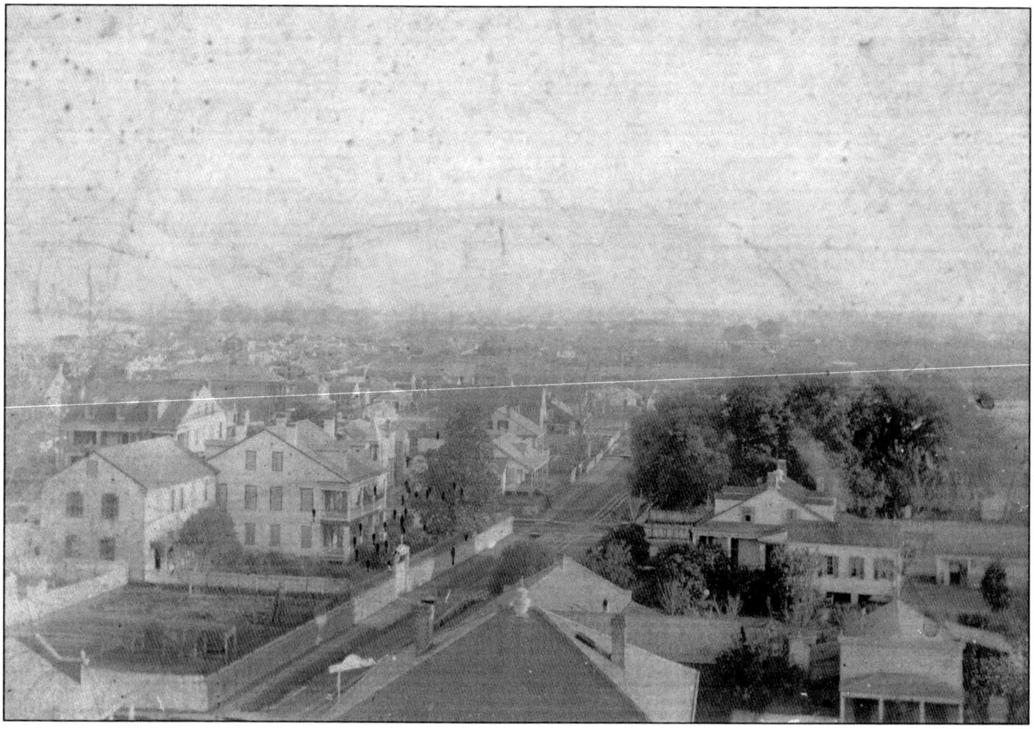

This c. 1880s view down Church Street again shows St. Basil's Academy and Convent (left). Next door to the convent on the corner of Court and Church Streets is a public school, and the two-story building to the left, behind the convent, is the Iberville Female Seminary. Across the street from the convent is a house commonly known as the Church Street House.

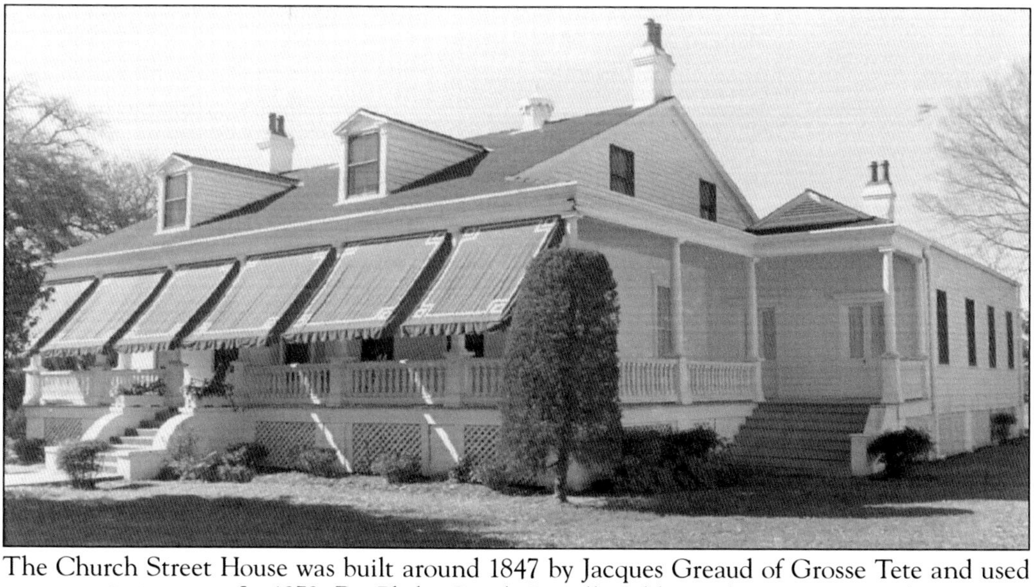

The Church Street House was built around 1847 by Jacques Greaud of Grosse Tete and used to entertain in town. In 1872, Dr. Philip Smith Postell and his wife, Margaret Pauline Logan, purchased the home after moving to Plaquemine from South Carolina in 1863. He practiced medicine in the little room with the porch entrance. In 2017, Walter and Melissa Cain purchased and restored the house. (Courtesy of Tony Fama.)

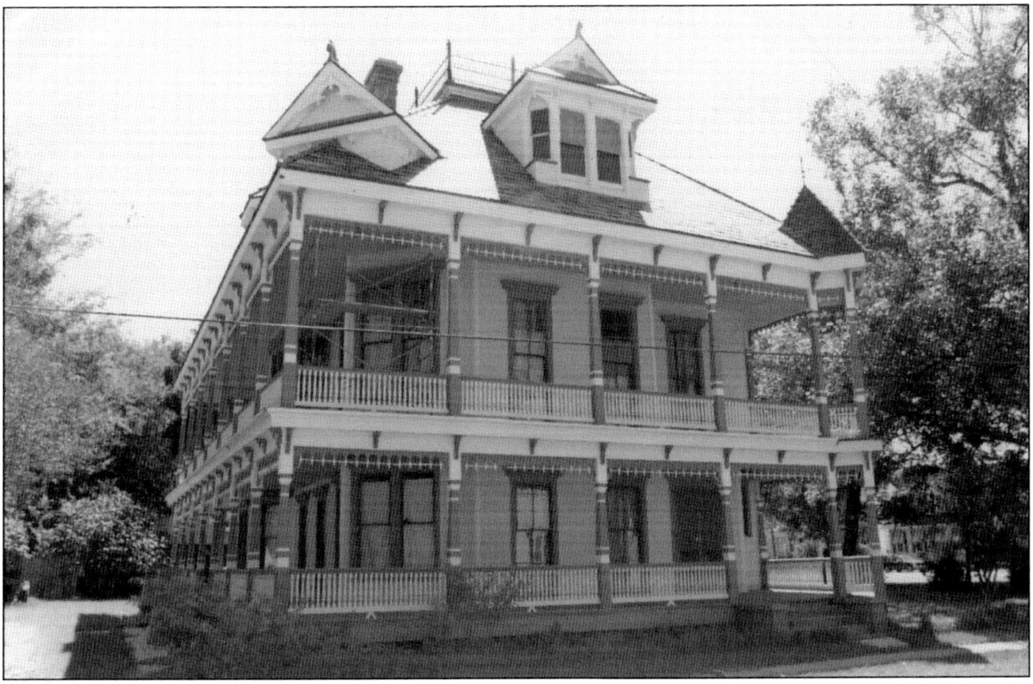

Sen. Frederic Wilbert built this three-story Queen Anne–style home in 1895. Wilbert served as the president of A. Wilbert's Sons Lumber and Shingle Company and constructed his home entirely of cypress wood. The house is on Court Street near the river. It was eventually purchased by Harry and Sue Hebert. This c. 1967 photograph was taken by Robert Mooney.

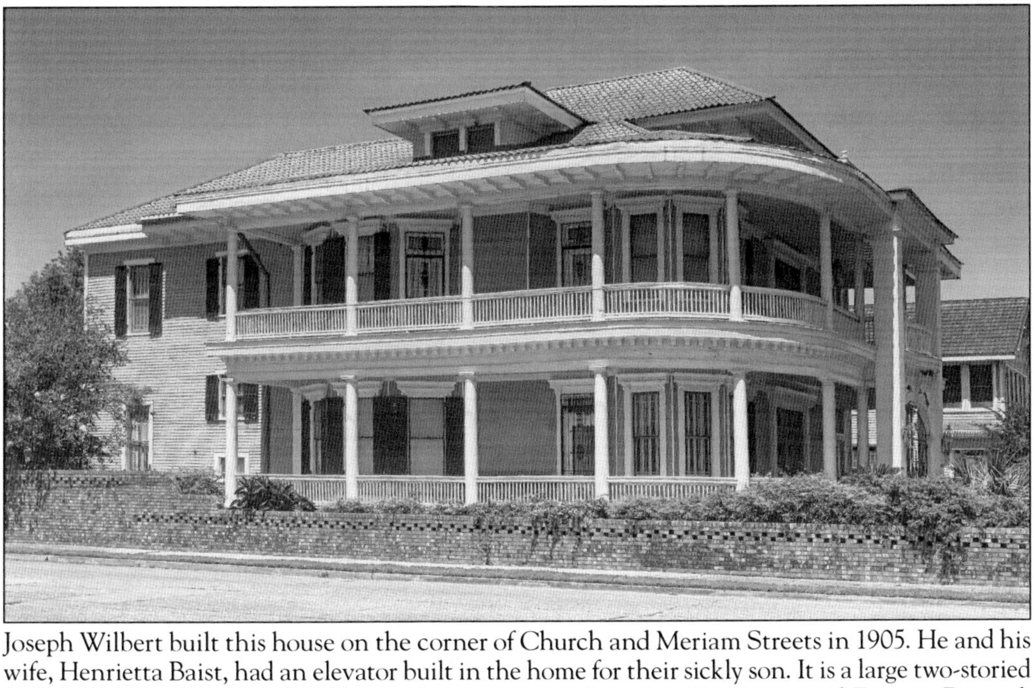

Joseph Wilbert built this house on the corner of Church and Meriam Streets in 1905. He and his wife, Henrietta Baist, had an elevator built in the home for their sickly son. It is a large two-storied Colonial Revival galleried residence. It later became home to Dr. James and Frances Durand. (Courtesy of Paul Bouy.)

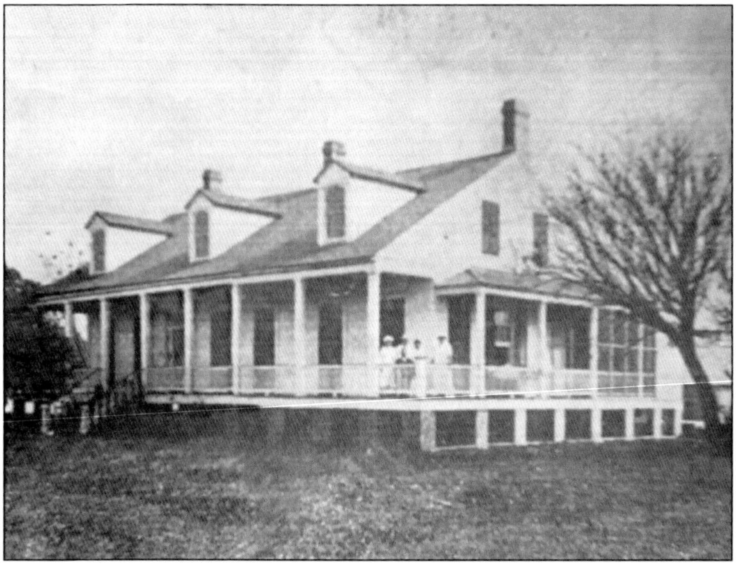

The Plaquemine Sanitarium was Plaquemine's first hospital. It opened on October 3, 1923, and was dedicated to the memory of the late Dr. Francis J. Kearny in June 1924. Pictured here is how it first appeared when opening on Church Street between Meriam and Haase Streets. The building was originally the Sebastian Hiriart residence, and was converted into a 15-bed hospital.

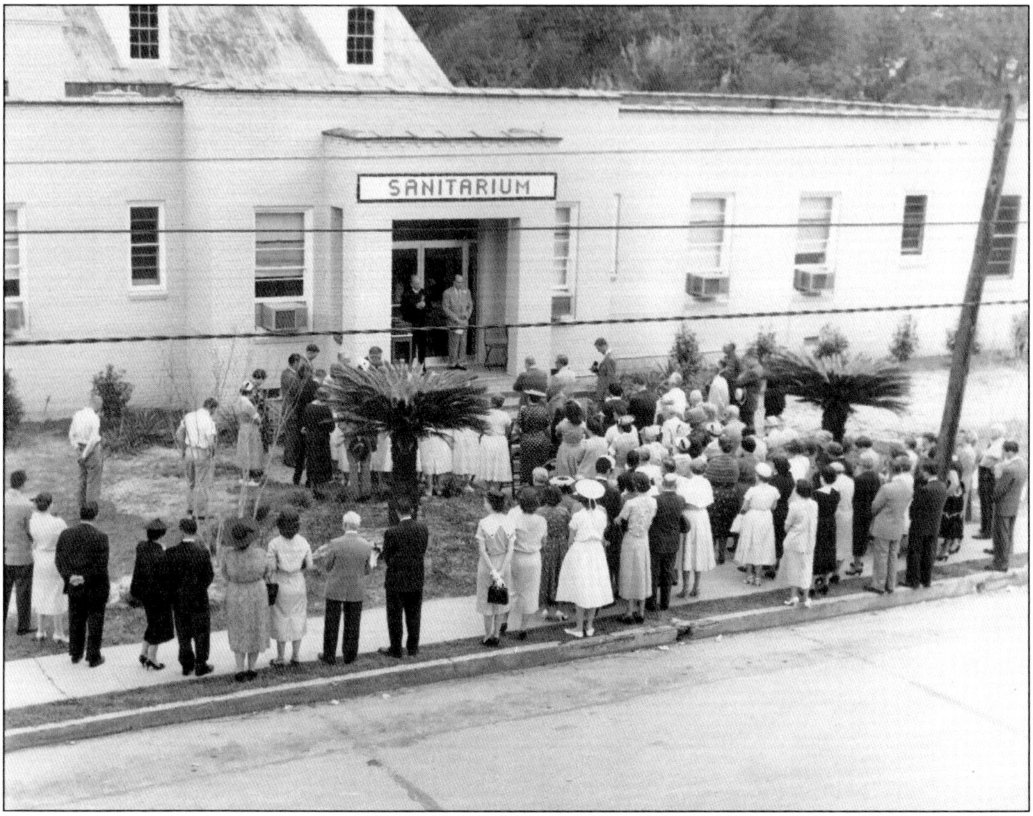

The sanitarium was later rebricked, and other buildings were added to its campus. Eventually, it was renamed Rhodes J. Spedale Hospital. This photograph by Bob Rogers was taken during a new hospital wing dedication ceremony. Dr. Rhodes J. Spedale and Fr. Leonard Robin stand at the front doors facing the crowd. In 1984, a new hospital was constructed on Tenant Road, and the Spedale Hospital was demolished around 2016. (Courtesy of IPL.)

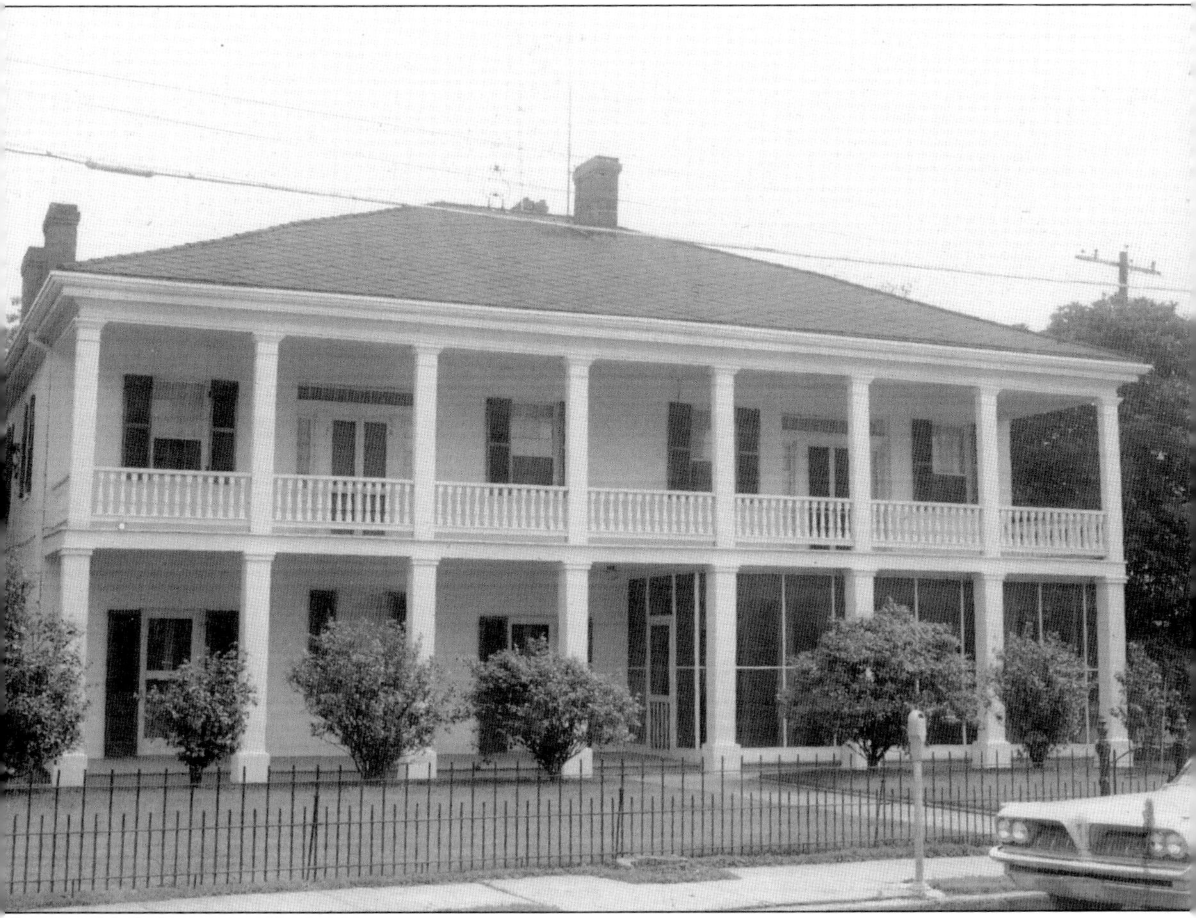

The Middleton house is one of the oldest standing houses in Plaquemine. It is believed to date to a 1779 Spanish land grant. In 1845, Joseph Schlater and Catherine Caulk purchased the home, and for the next 175 years, it remained in the same family. During the Civil War, a Federal gunboat in the Mississippi shot a cannonball through the home, leaving two of the brick walls demolished. Caulk later gifted the house to her granddaughter Marie Poynter after she married Dr. Sebastian Schwing of Rosedale, Louisiana. The couple raised nine children here, and the house was passed down to their youngest daughter, Maria Schwing. She married William Beverly Middleton of Mississippi in the 1910s, and it was then passed to their eldest son and then grandson. The home is of French Creole architecture and sits on the corner of Plaquemine and Eden Streets. (Courtesy of IPL)

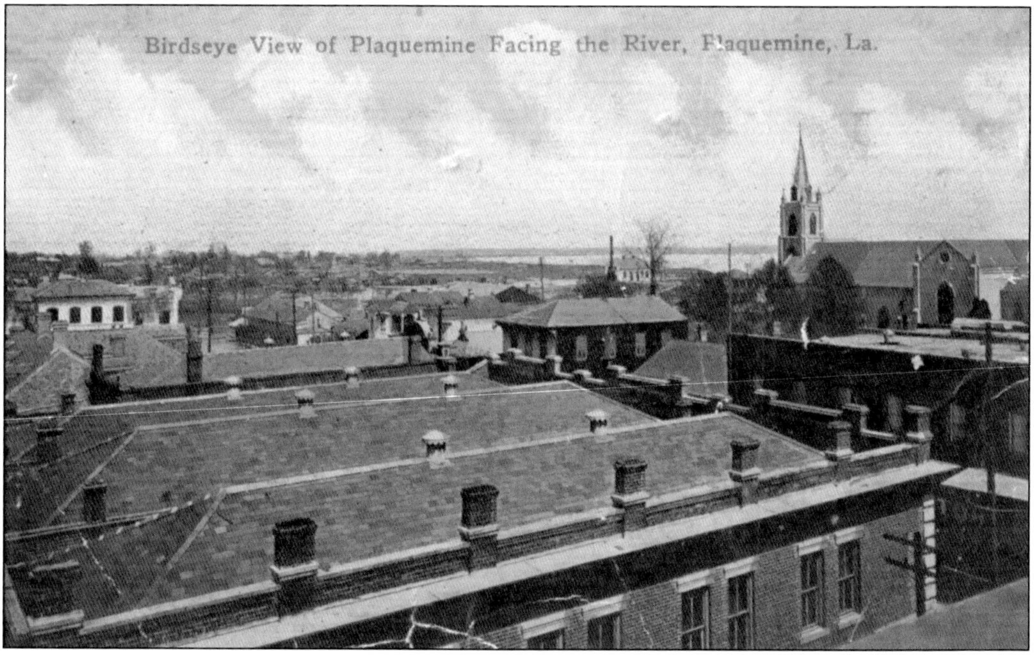

This c. 1910s postcard features a bird's-eye view of Eden Street. The building in the lower-left corner is the Roth Building, followed by the rooflines of People's Bank, the Brusle-Sherburne House, and the Brusle Building. Across the street from the Roth Building is the Neubig Dry Goods Store (lower right). St. John's Catholic Church is behind the Neubig building, and the Plaquemine Lock House is visible in the distance.

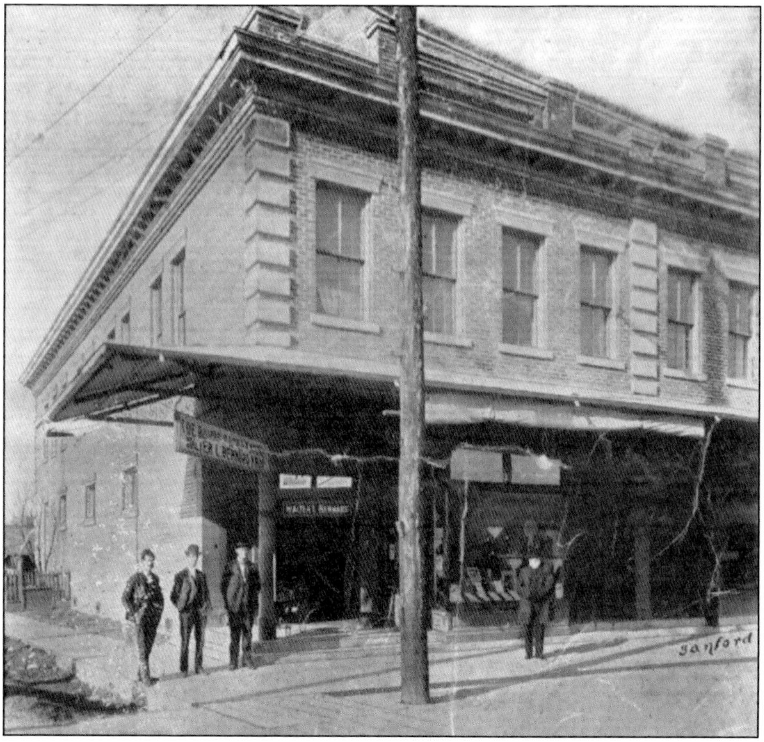

The Roth Building was completed in 1899 for Charles N. Roth. It was designed with three separate interiors. On the corner was Rouss Racket Store, in the middle was a furniture store, and on the right was Barker's Pharmacy. Later, the building housed a gentlemen's club, a men's clothing store, an art studio, and Son's House of Tools. Pictured here is the building in 1906 featuring Rouss Racket Store on the corner.

Barker's Pharmacy is one of the oldest continuously run pharmacies in Louisiana. The pharmacy first opened on Main Street near the courthouse in 1885. William Edward Barker, the pharmacy's founder, graduated from Tulane Medical School in 1865, opening a medical practice in Plaquemine. He first worked with Dr. Kearny's Pharmacy, and eventually opened his own pharmacy to gain quicker access to necessary drugs. The pharmacy moved to the Roth building in 1899, where it has sat since. This c. 1981 photograph is by Robert Mooney.

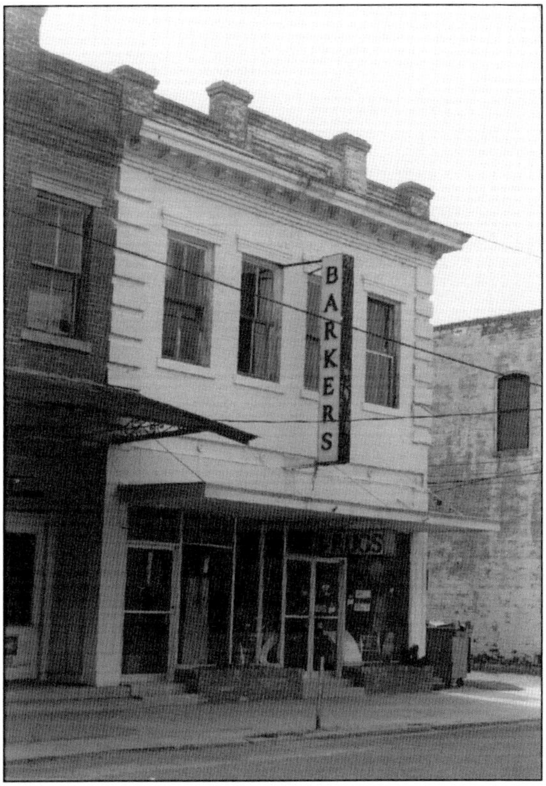

This old bank building was once known as the People's Bank, organized in 1899 under James E. Dunlap. It was later used as the dentist's office of Dr. L.P. Laville and his son Dr. James A. Laville. This photograph was taken by Robert Mooney in 1981, before the building's restoration through the Plaquemine Main Street program.

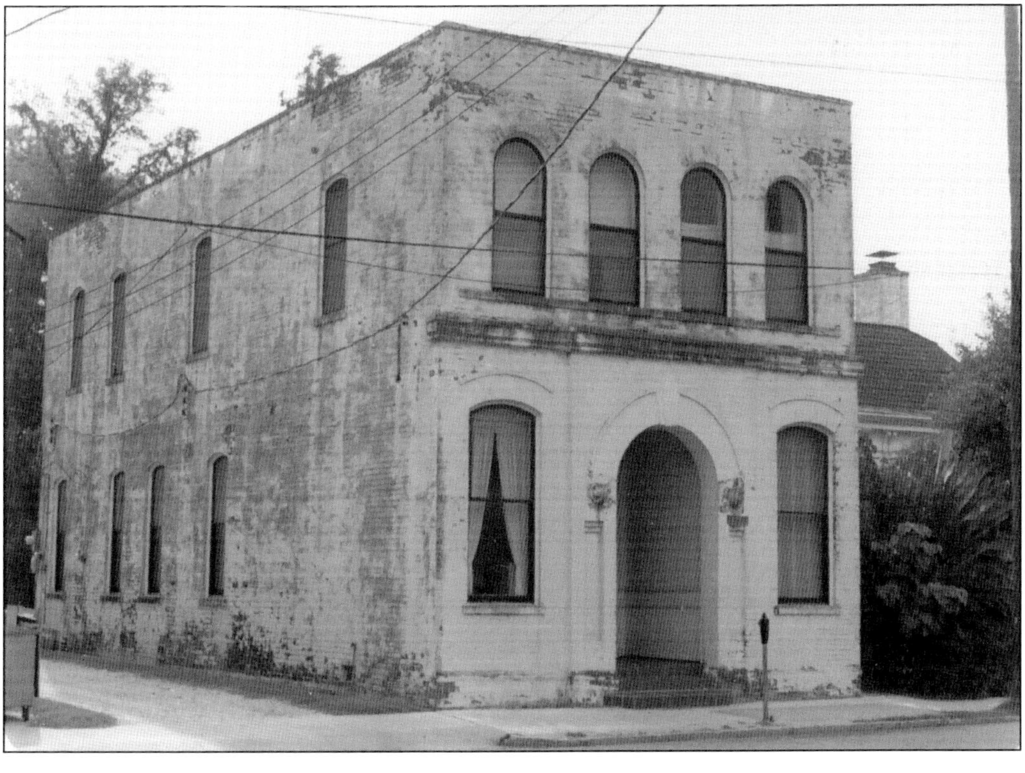

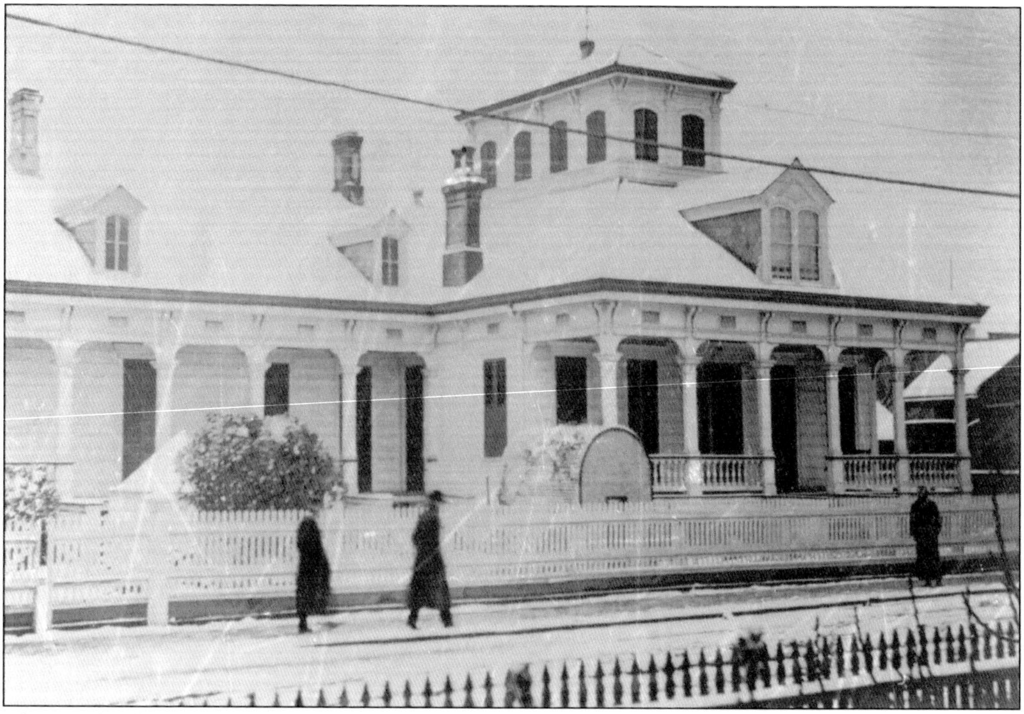

The Brusle-Sherburne House, later known as Plaquemine's "half house," was on Eden Street between Main and Plaquemine Streets. In 1883, Charles A. Brusle and Eugenie Dardenne built the home as a modern raised cottage, and it featured an observatory, library, and an interior bathroom. Above, the home is pictured c. 1899. In 1935, the house was cut roughly in half after the US government purchased the north side of the property to build a post office. Henry Sherburne, grandson-in-law of Brusle, continued living in the remaining portion of the house (pictured below), which was torn down in 2009. The photograph below was taken by Robert Mooney in 1981.

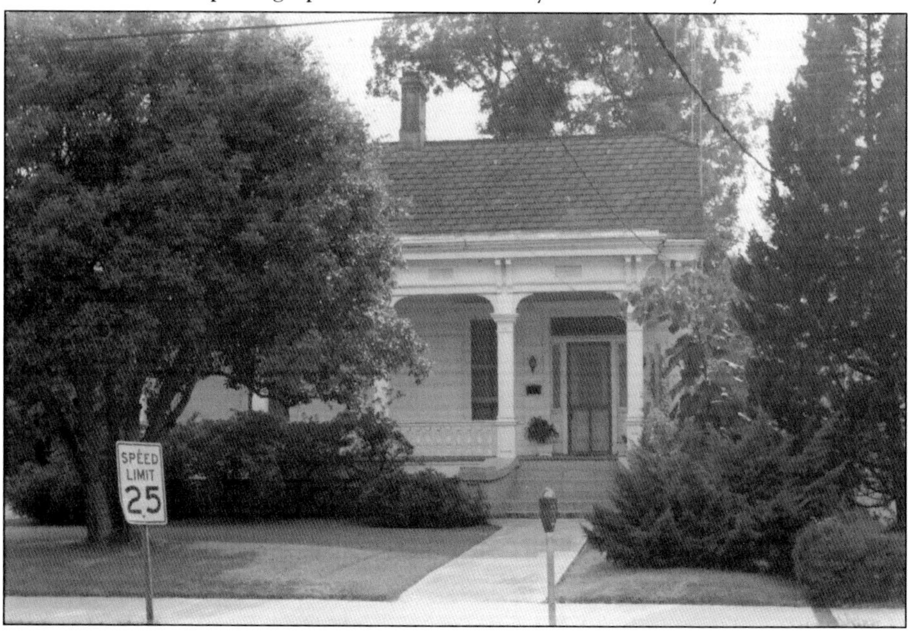

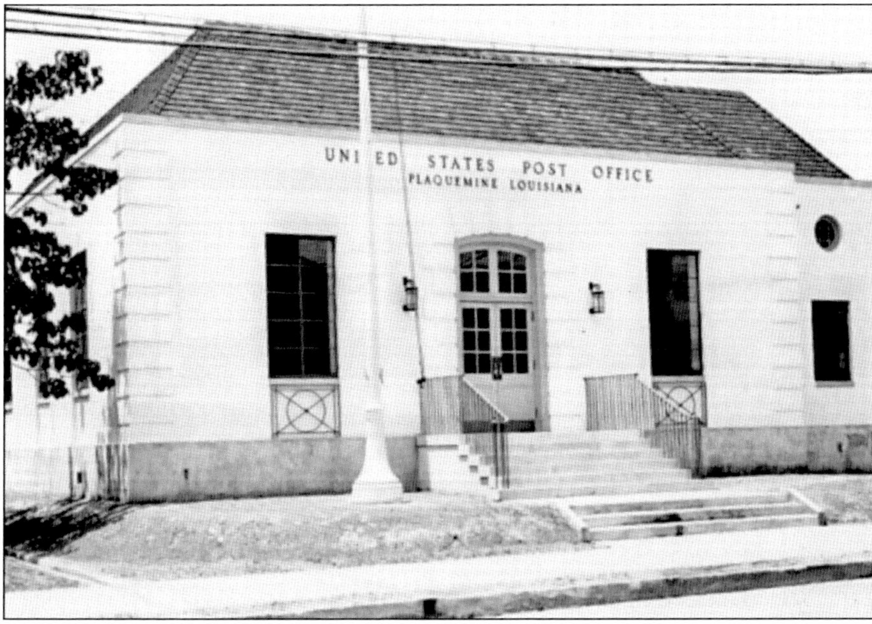

The first post office in Plaquemine dated to 1822 and was the second post office in the parish. It was called Bayou Plaquemine Post Office, with Louis Desobry as the postmaster, and was located at Bank and Main Streets. In 1866, the post office opened in William L. Roche's store on Plaquemine Street between Bank and Seminary Streets. However, as river caves increased around the 1890s, the post office moved into Sebastian Hiriart's drugstore on Plaquemine Street opposite the Neubig Dry Goods Store. In 1906, when the Neubig siblings built a brand new building at the corner of Eden and Plaquemine Streets, an up-to-date post office opened there too and remained until around the 1920s, when it moved to the Moise Levy building on Railroad Avenue. Pictured above is the post office around 1942 on Eden Street, which opened in 1936. Below is the building in 1981 in a photograph by Robert Mooney.

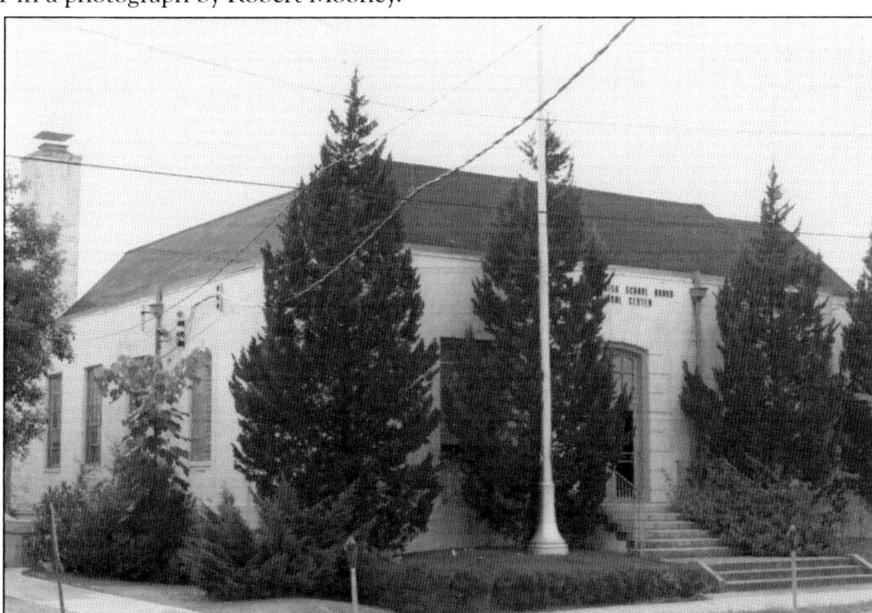

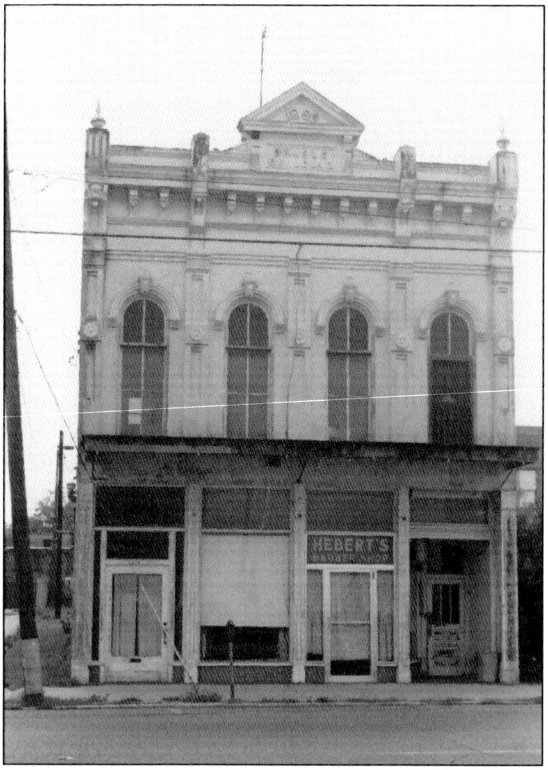

The Brusle Building first opened as the Bank of Plaquemine in 1889, and Jacob McWilliams served as the bank's president. In 1906, the Cumberland Telephone Company moved into its second floor, and the bank closed shortly thereafter. Over the next few decades, the building's main floor was used as a movie theater, drugstore, and Westinghouse Appliance Store. In 1972, Wayne Hebert opened a barbershop in the building. In 1993, Scott Stassi purchased the building and had it restored, turning the second floor into a residence. Pictured at left is the building in 1981 while it housed Hebert's Barbershop. The photograph was taken by Robert Mooney. (Below, courtesy of Paul Bouy.)

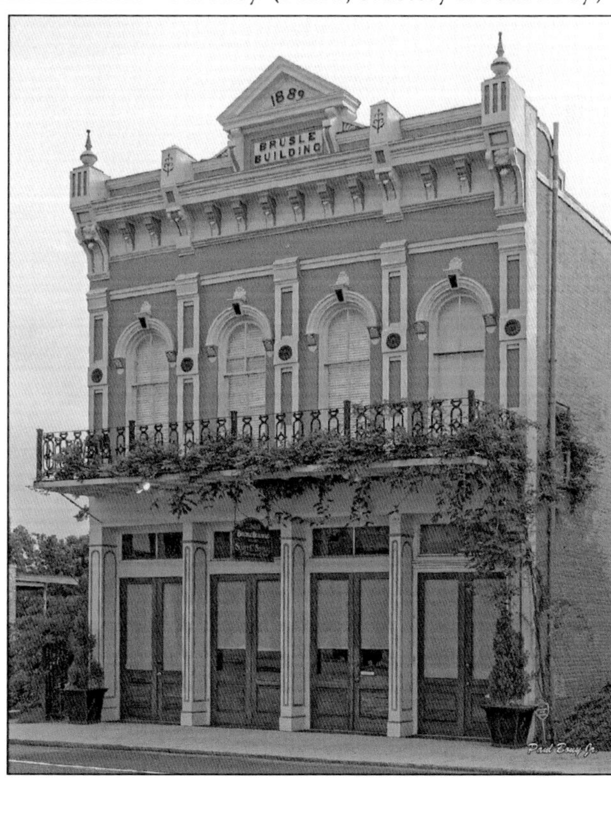

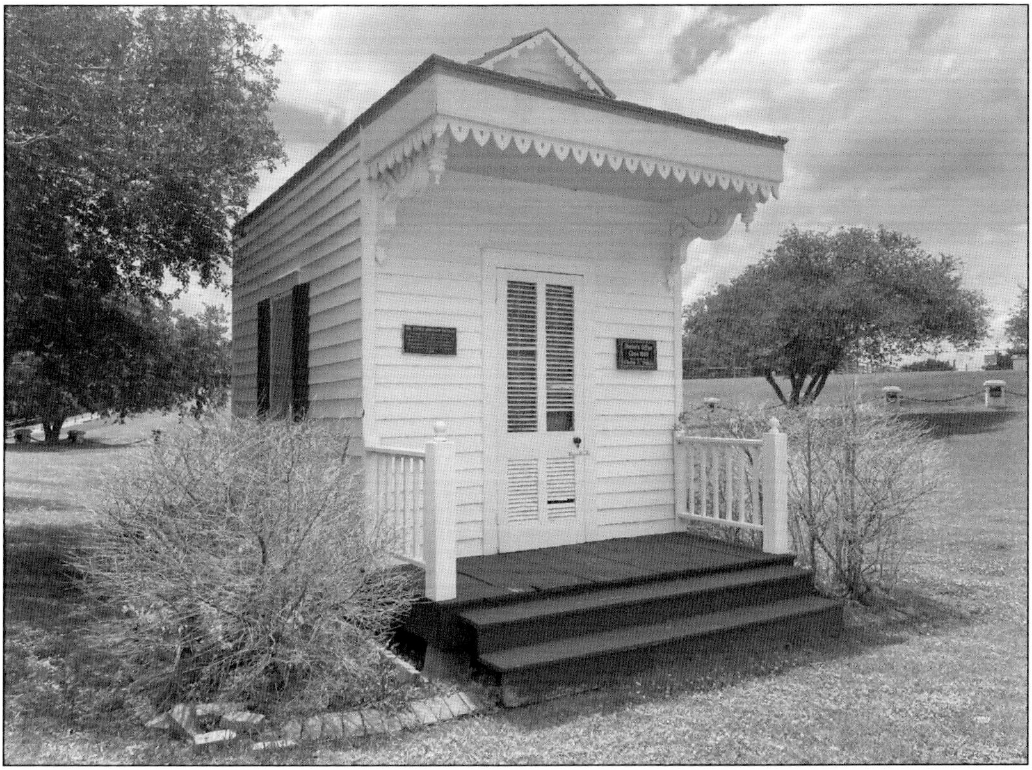

Dr. Emile Hiriart was born around 1858 to a family of doctors and druggists. He graduated from Tulane Medical School around 1880 and started his practice as a physician and surgeon in Plaquemine. He used the small one-room building above as his office until he died in 1895. It was located at his home on the southwest corner of Meriam and Eden Streets. The house was demolished in 1969, and the office was gifted to the Dekel family, who moved it to their home on Highway 75. In 1998, Clelie Dekle donated the building to the City of Plaquemine and it was relocated to the Plaquemine Lock Historic Site. At right is a store card for Dr. Hiriart's brother Sebastian Hiriart, who owned a drugstore on Plaquemine Street near Seminary Street. The two brothers worked closely together, providing residents with all their medical needs. (Above, photograph by Meghan C. Sylvester.)

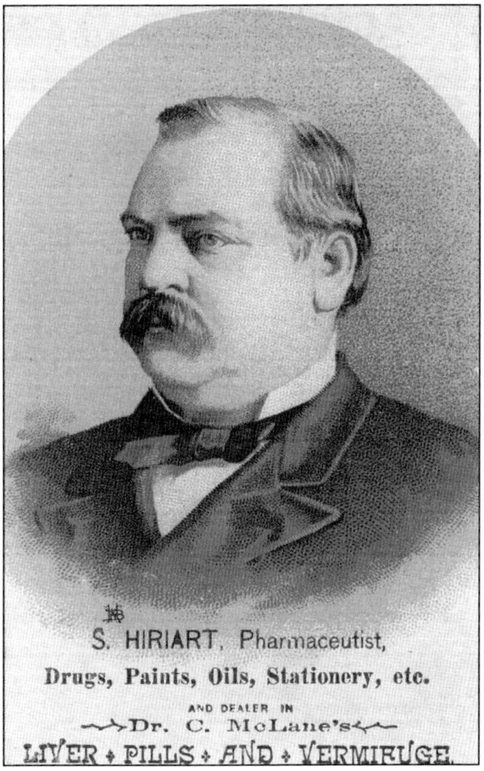

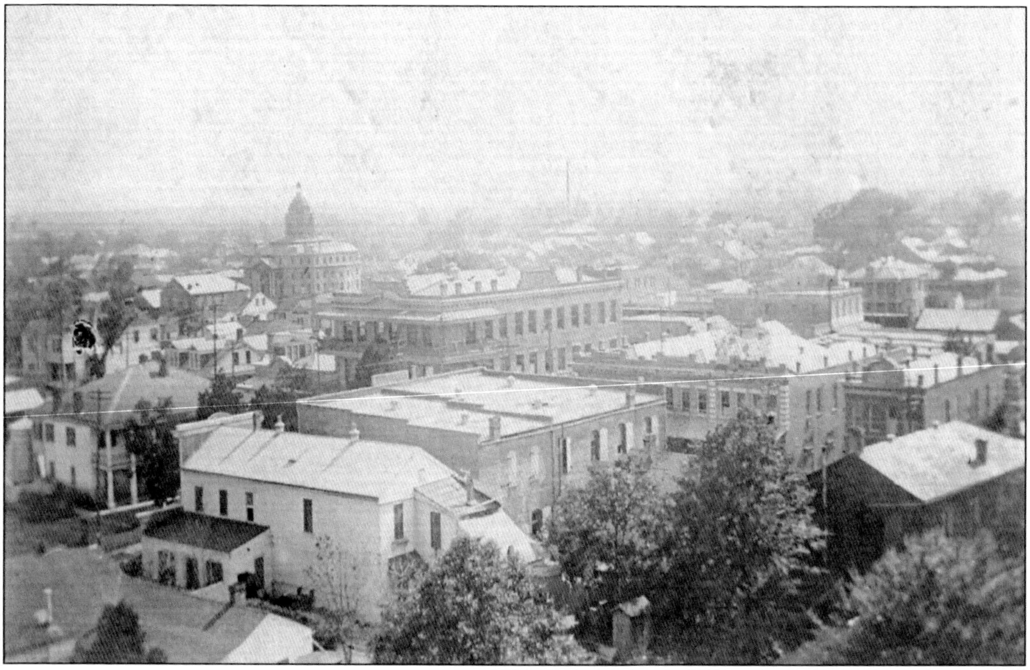

Pictured above is a c. 1912 view of west Plaquemine from St. John's Church. On the left is the Middleton House with the Neubig Dry Goods Store across the street. The Roth Building and the People's Bank are on the right, and the large three-story building at center is the Wilbert building. It opened on Eden Street in 1906, after the Grace Brothers' building on this lot burned down. The building housed several medical offices as well as the People's Drug Store. Additionally, the Bluestein's Clothing Store was on the first floor, and the third floor was used as a dance hall. Below, folks play tennis in an empty lot on Eden Street on the side of the Wilberts' undertaker parlor, built in 1907 next door to the Wilbert building.

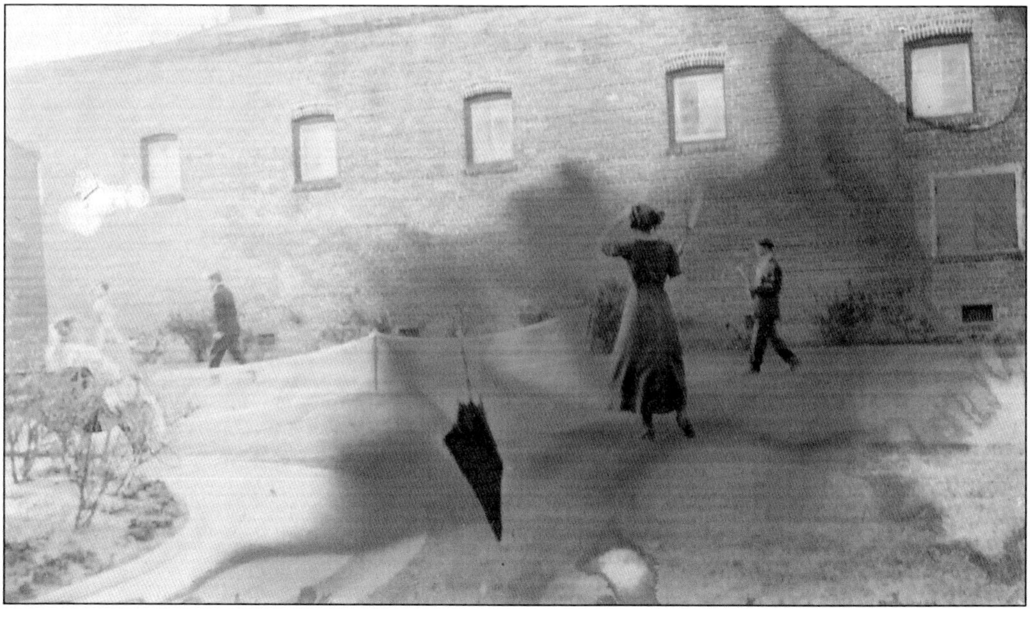

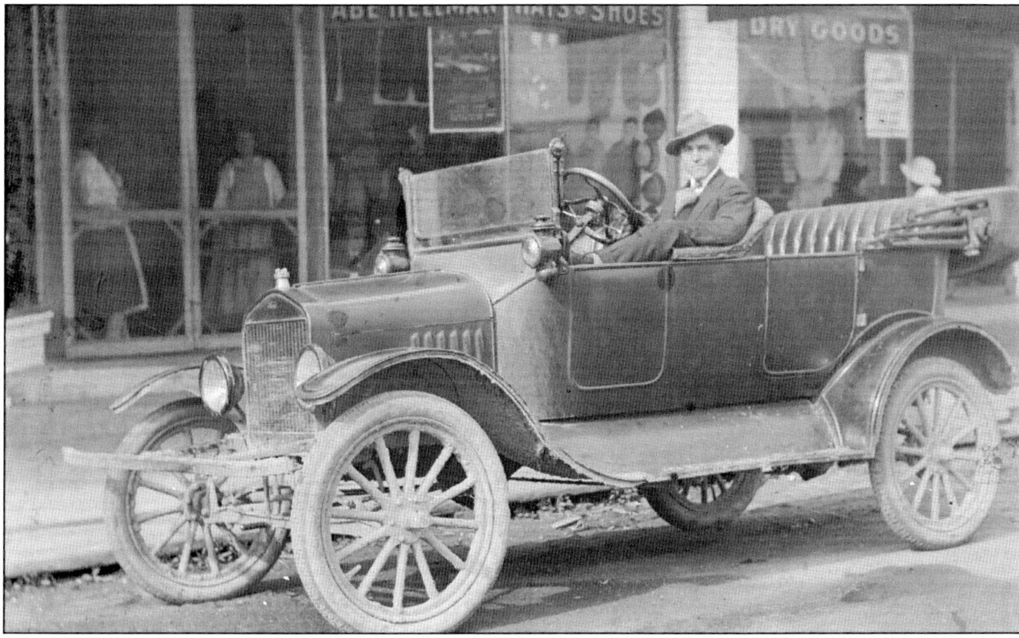

Abe Hellman's Department Store was on Plaquemine Street in Charles N. Roth's second building, built in 1904 between Railroad Avenue and Eden Street. The store opened in the early 1900s. Pictured around 1909 is an early automobile parked in front of Hellman's. The driver is Sam Tatar, a first-generation Polish immigrant who worked for the store. This building was eventually demolished.

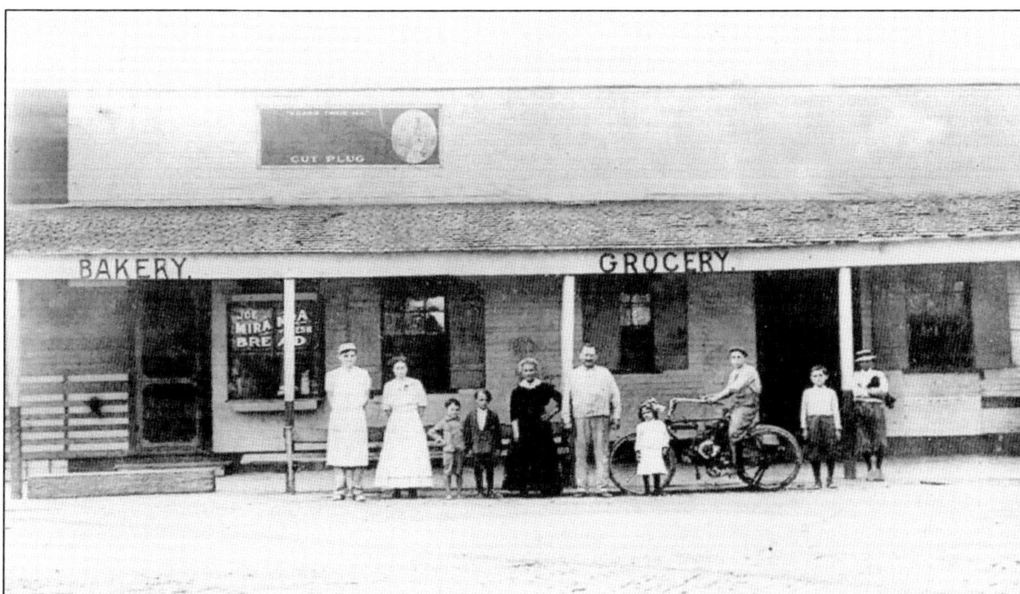

Joseph Miranda and Mary Quartana moved to Plaquemine from Palermo, Sicily, around 1900 with their five children. Upon arrival, they opened Miranda Bakery and Grocery Store on Plaquemine Street. This c. 1909 photograph includes (from left to right) T.J. "Chick" Guido, Bernadine, Anthony, James, Mary Quartana, Joseph, Corinne, Pietro Miranda, and two unidentified. They sold the store in 1919 and moved to Baton Rouge, opening a new store there.

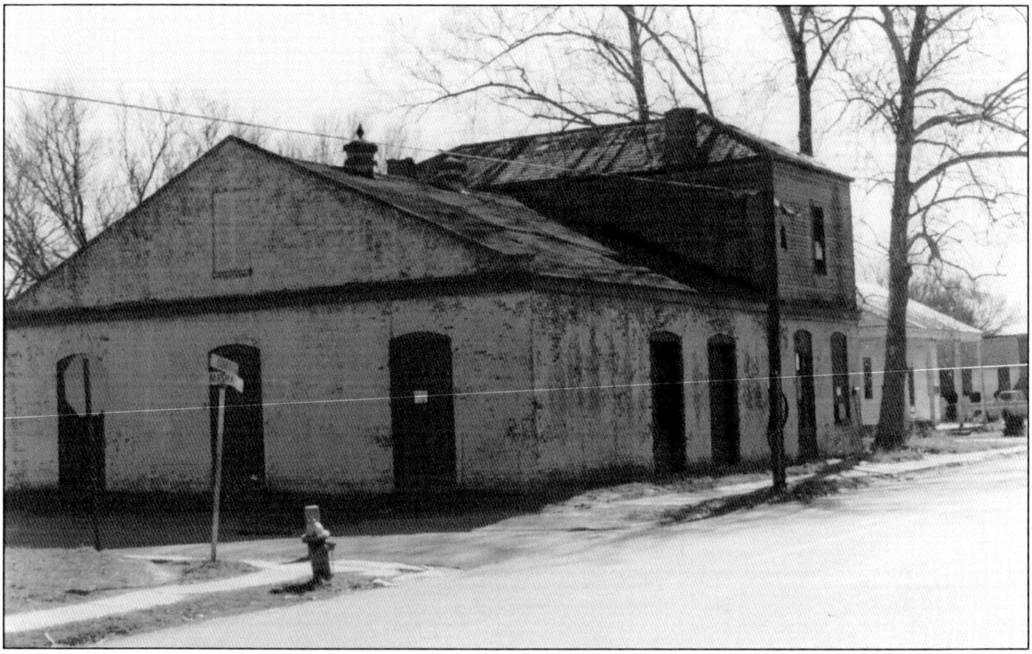

The Desobry building is considered the oldest commercial building in Plaquemine. It is named for its founder, Louis Desobry, a prosperous merchant and planter. The building dates to 1822 and was initially at the corner of Main and Bank Streets. Plaquemine's first post office opened in the building at this time. In 1850, major foundational changes were made to the building, and in 1875, the second story was added. In 1882, the building was moved, brick by brick, to its current location at Marshall and Court Streets to protect it from frequent levee cave-ins. Over the years, it has been home to numerous commercial businesses as well as a residence. It was listed in the National Register of Historic Places in 1986. These photographs were taken by Robert Mooney around 1982.

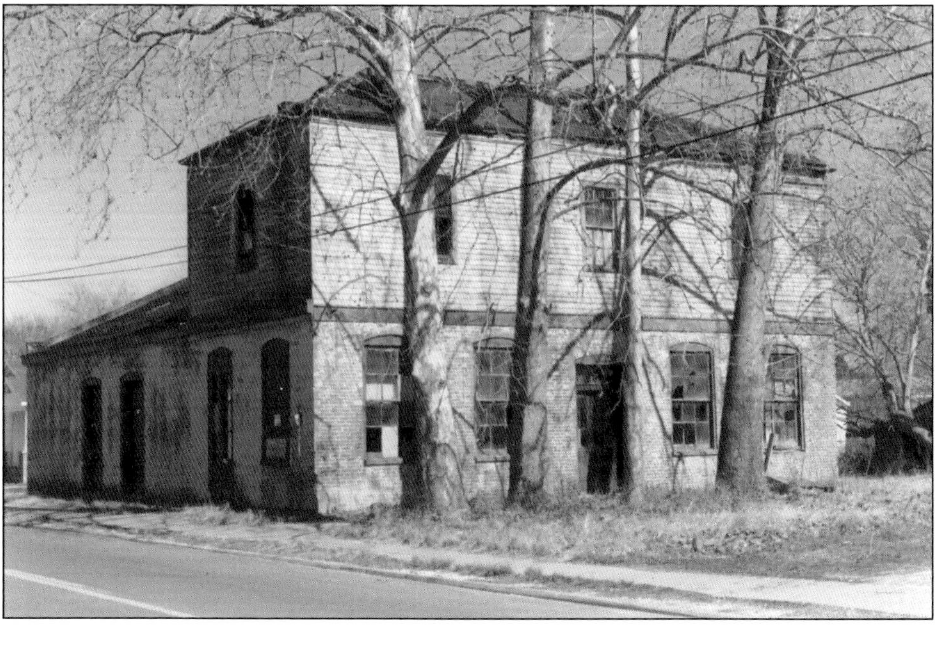

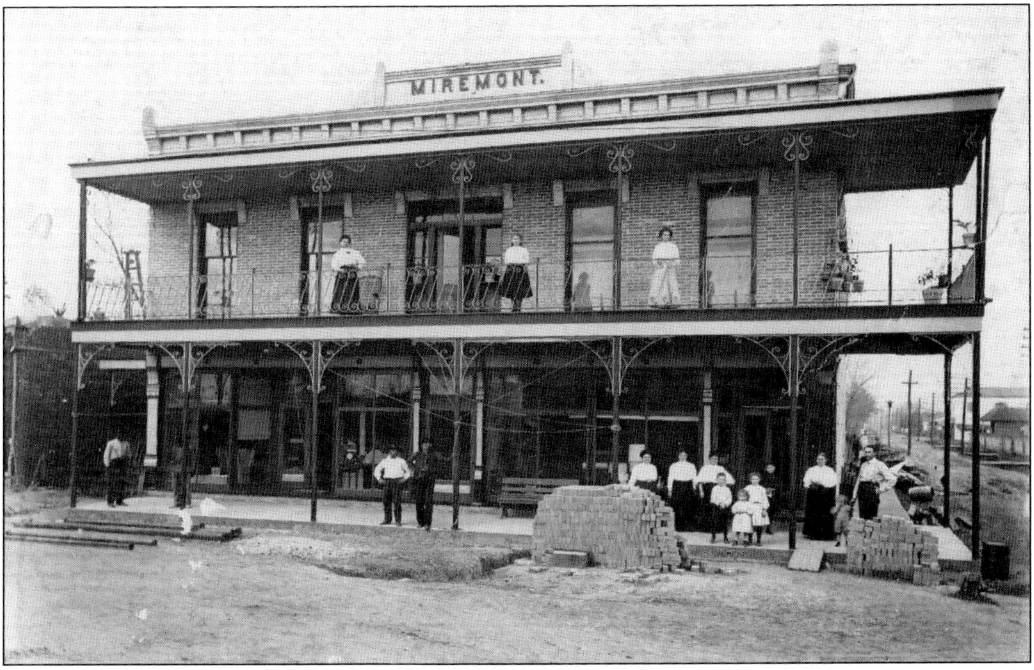

The Miremont General Store, pictured here in 1909, opened in 1907 at the foot of Court Street near Bayou Plaquemine. James Edward Miremont, the store owner, also operated two paddle-wheel boats that delivered goods to customers down Bayou Plaquemine. In 1917, the family sold the store and moved to New York. The building eventually reopened as the Colonial House and is remembered for its ice-cream sodas.

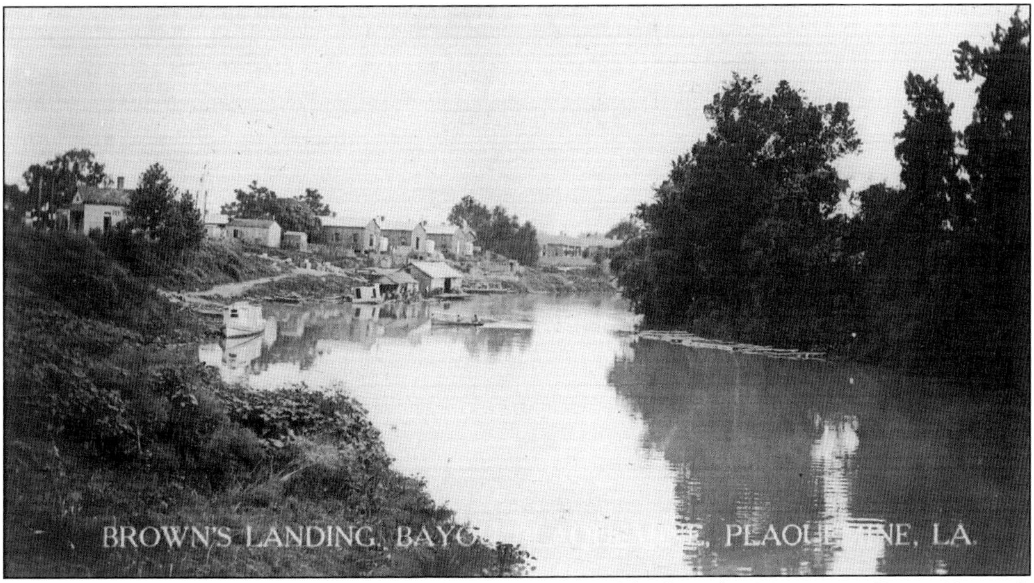

Between 1868 and 1909, when Bayou Plaquemine was diked at the Mississippi River, Brown's Landing was the last stop on Bayou Plaquemine, as the water became too shallow and crowded with logs and overgrowth. It was at the foot of Plaquemine Street on Bayou Plaquemine and was used as a boat launch for steamers and smaller boats traveling into the Atchafalaya Basin. (Photograph by William Stadeker, courtesy of IPL.)

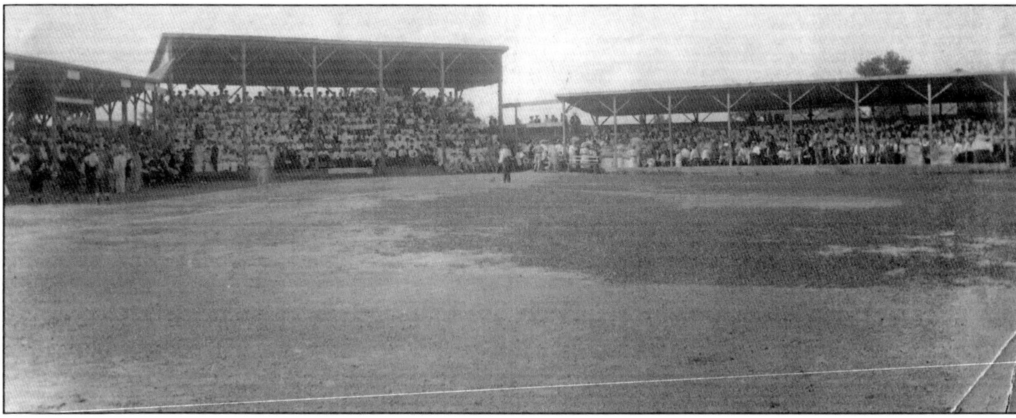

Pictured above is Plaquemine Park on August 3, 1914. This was one of Plaquemine's many baseball parks, opening around 1900 on Meriam Street. The field belonged to the Plaquemine Maroons baseball club, which was organized around 1900. One of the town's first baseball parks opened in 1883 for the Viguets club. In 1894, the Viguets were renamed the Plaquemine Greys, and a new park opened in 1898 for baseball and horse races. On the 1916 Sanborn Fire Insurance map below, another baseball park is shown on Haase Street in the Dupont Annex for the black community. (Below, courtesy of Library of Congress.)

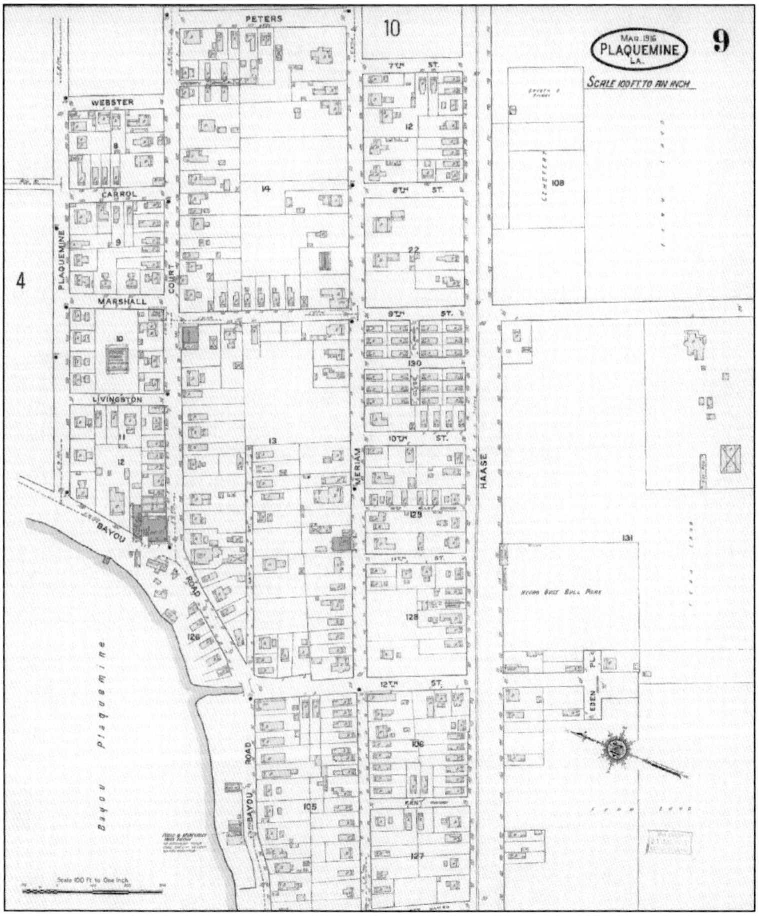

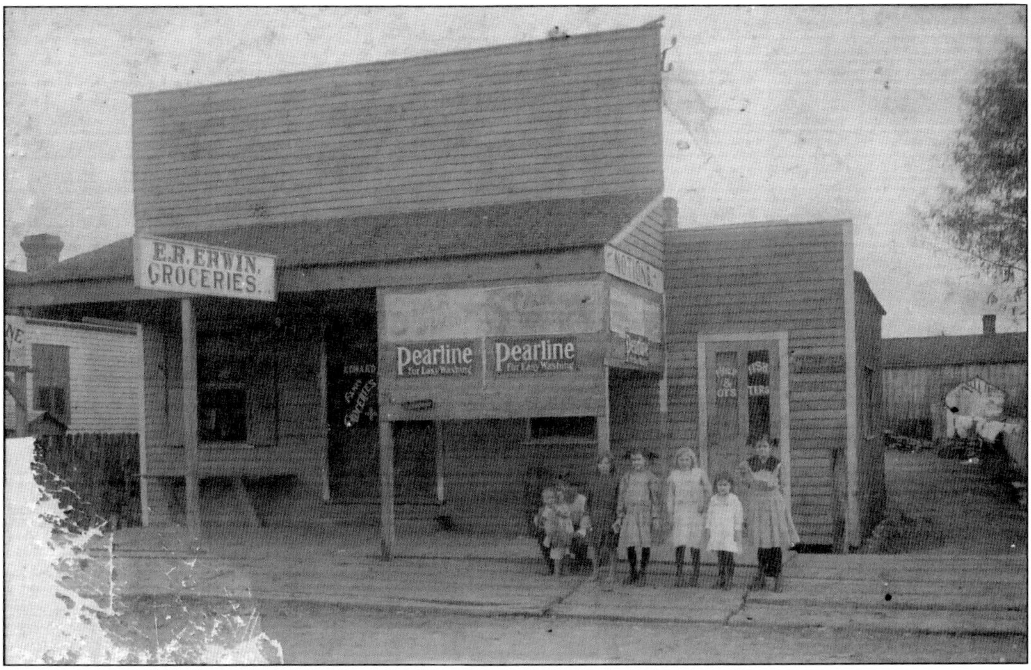

Edward Roger Erwin opened E.R. Groceries and Bakery in the early 1900s. He trained under Gillis A. Daigle, who owned Daigle Steam Bakery on Church Street before opening his shop on Meriam Street in Haaseville. The above c. 1913 photograph shows the storefront. In front of the shop, from left to right, are Edward R. Erwin Sr. holding Edward R. Erwin Jr., Irene Erwin, unidentified, Leona Erwin, and two unidentified. The bakery with steam ovens was behind the shop. Its interior is pictured below. Erwin became known locally for his cinnamon rolls, but he also advertised fresh cakes and bread. (Both, courtesy of Rita Lynn Jackson.)

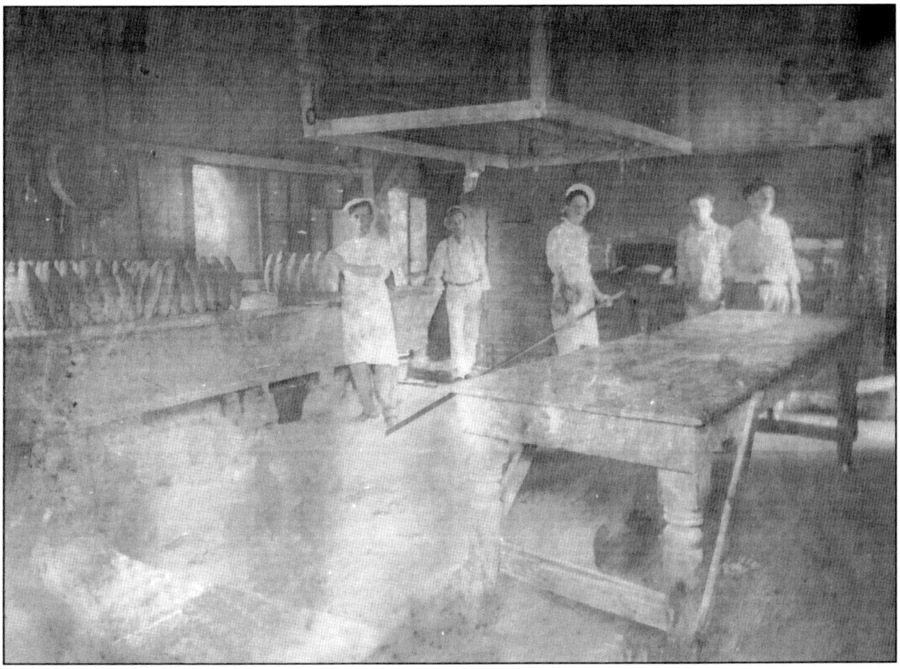

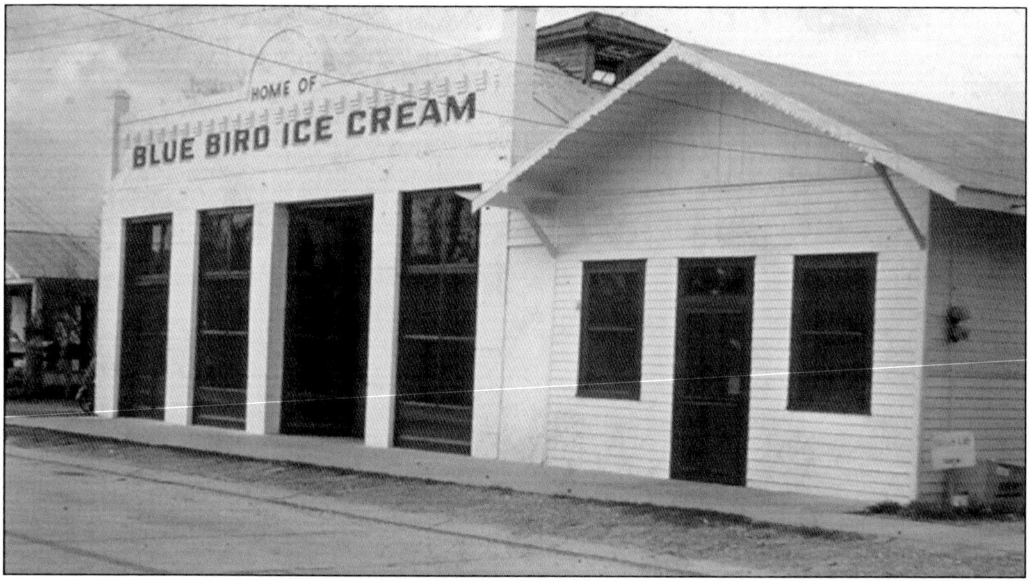

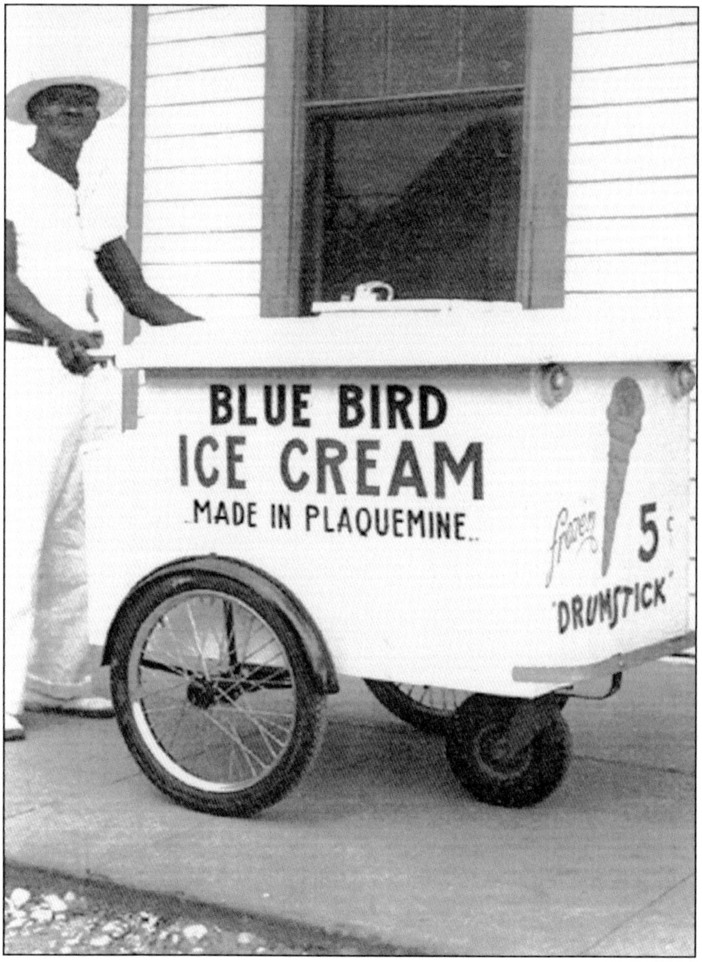

Albert Callais originally built this building on Meriam Street in 1909 as a grocery store, but in the early 1920s, it was transformed into the Plaquemine Ice Cream Company, the first ice-cream plant in Plaquemine. Later, Ben Cutrer of Baton Rouge purchased the company and changed the name to Blue Bird Ice Cream Company. He then commissioned Charles Dupont, who owned a blacksmith shop on Court Street, to put wheels from an old Model T on a small icebox that a peddler could push around town to sell ice cream on the street. Over the years, the plant changed hands a few times, but from 1943 to 1953, Anthony Fama owned and operated the business. He continued the ice-cream wagon tradition, hiring Jim Wallace, pictured at left, as its driver. (Both, courtesy of Tony Fama.)

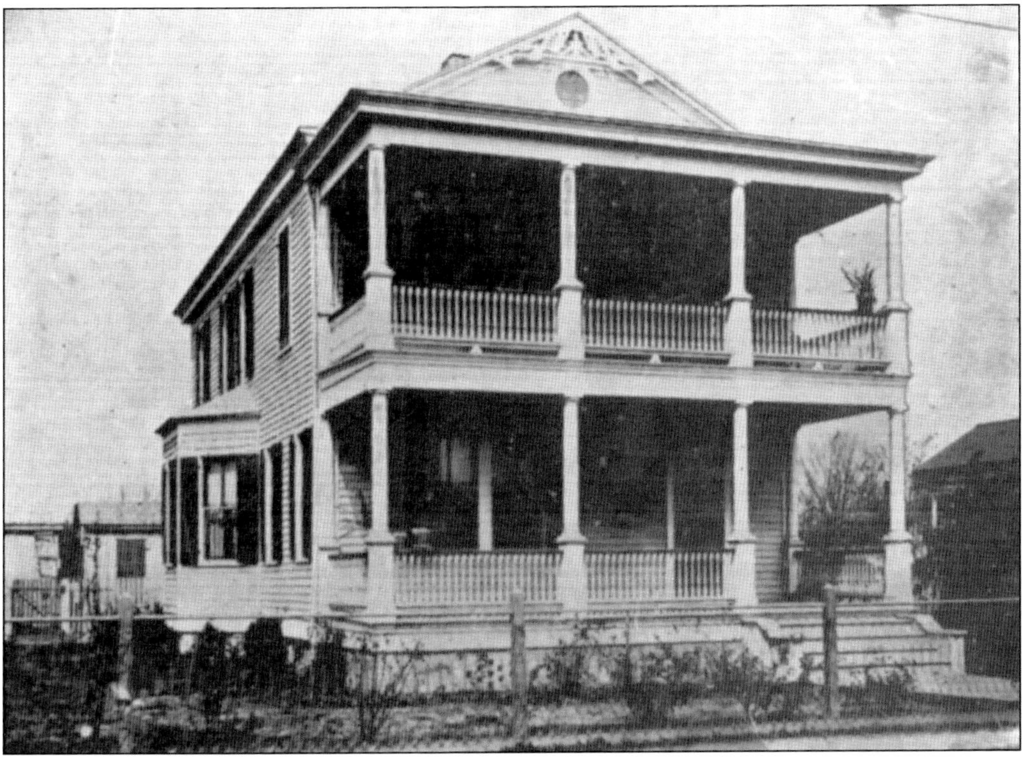

Philip Smith Postell IV, son of Dr. P.S. Postell, built this house on Meriam Street near Federal Street in 1904. Shortly after constructing the home, Postell moved his family to California, and the house was sold in the estate sale of his mother, Margaret P. Logan, in 1911. Here it is pictured around 1906. It eventually became the home of Grover and Kelli Harrison.

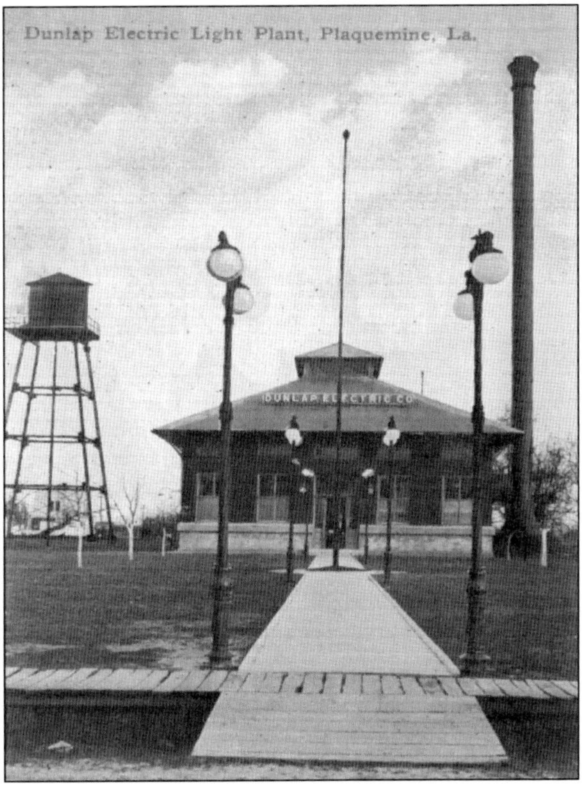

Across the street from the Postell house was the Dunlap Electric Company. James E. Dunlap founded this company in 1909 after a devastating fire destroyed the first electric plant owned by Electric Light and Power Company. Dunlap opened this plant on Meriam Street, pictured here around 1910. It closed around 1923.

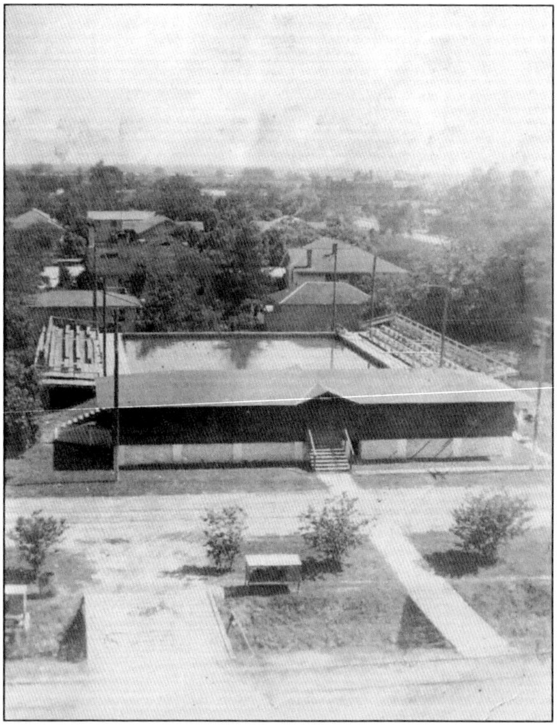

The first public pool in Plaquemine opened in the 1940s for the white community. It was on Haase Street, later known as Capt. T.T. Harris Street, near Ferdinand Street. In 1955, a new pool opened at Ferdinand and Sherburne Streets, and in 1957, a pool for the black community opened on Bayou Road. The pools were later integrated, but all had closed by the end of the 20th century.

The Lozano House on Eden Street at Haase Street was built between 1896 and 1900 by a local builder, P.W. Briggs, in the Free Classic Queen Anne style. Louis S. Lozano owned the home for a short period before his untimely death in 1904. The house was later owned by Edward Grace and Robert and Helen Rhorer. In 2019, it was purchased and restored by Dan and JoAnn Bucholtz. (Courtesy of Paul Bouy.)

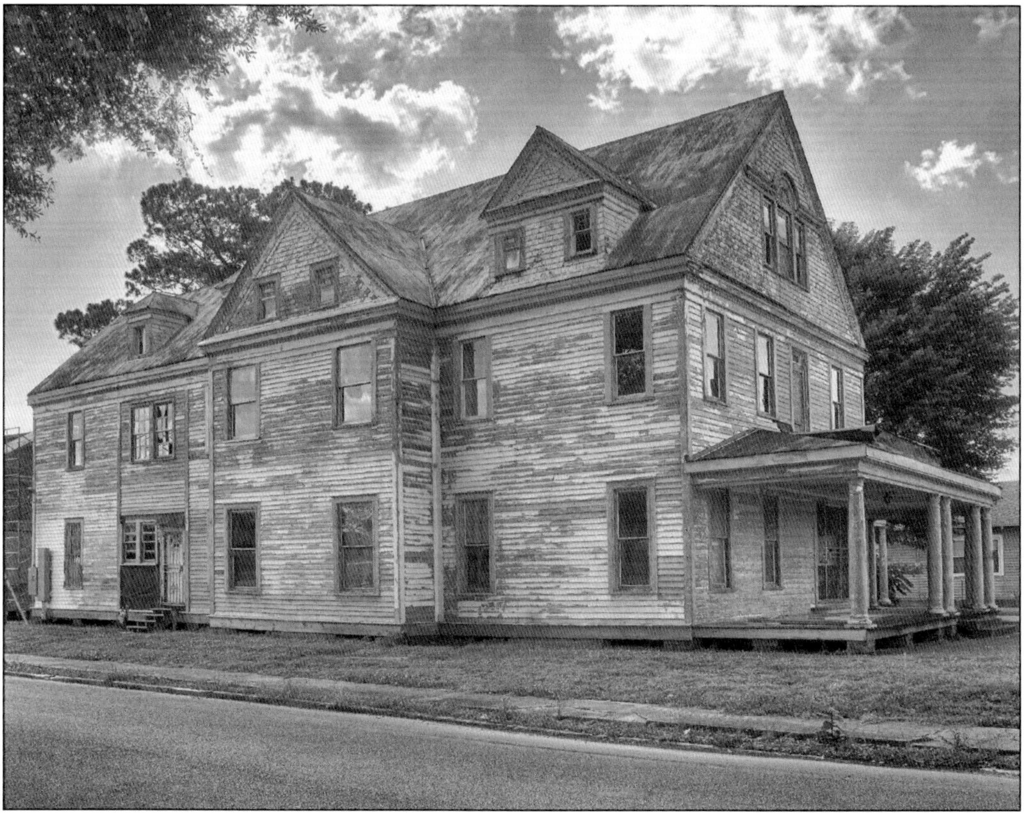

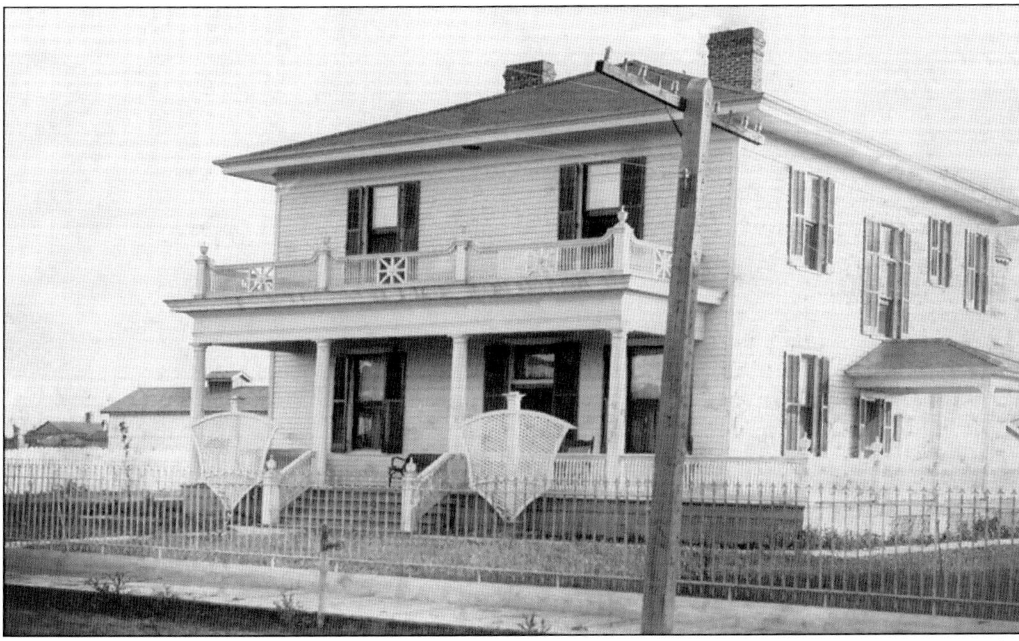

Edward B. Schwing built this house for his bride, Sarah Jane Hickman, in 1899. It is on Eden Street near Martin Street, which was part of the Labauve Addition. Pictured above is the house around 1906. When constructed, it had seven bedrooms and a sleeping porch. The sunroom shown below was added around the 1930s. After Schwing died in 1950, Hickman made plans to donate the family home to the parish library. The first library in Plaquemine dated to 1850 at the *Southern Sentinel* newspaper's office on Main Street. The E.B. Schwing Memorial Library opened in 1958 and served as the parish library until the 1980s, when a new building was built on Belleview Drive. The building was then converted back to a private residence and eventually purchased by Joseph and Courtney Lewis. (Above, courtesy of Tony Fama; below, courtesy of the State Library of Louisiana.)

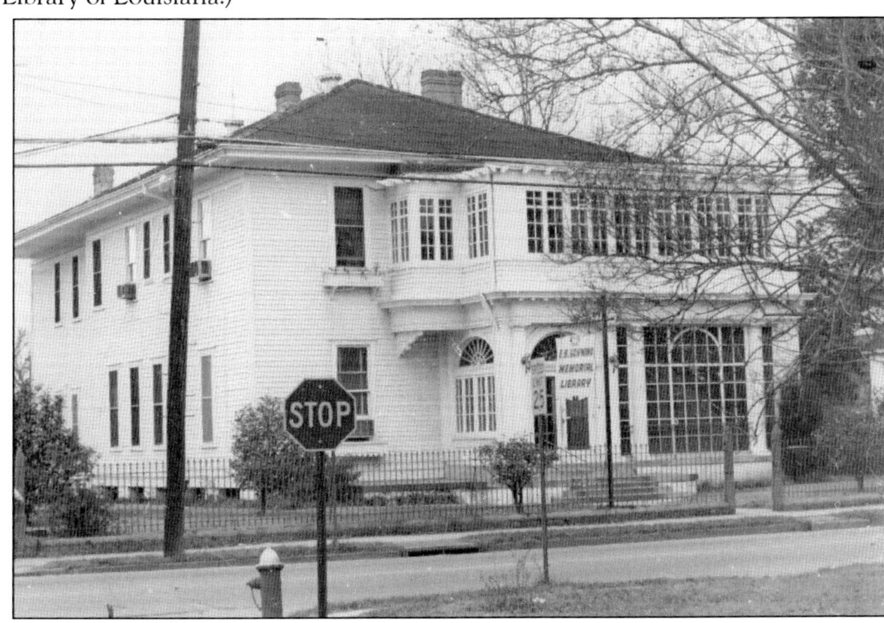

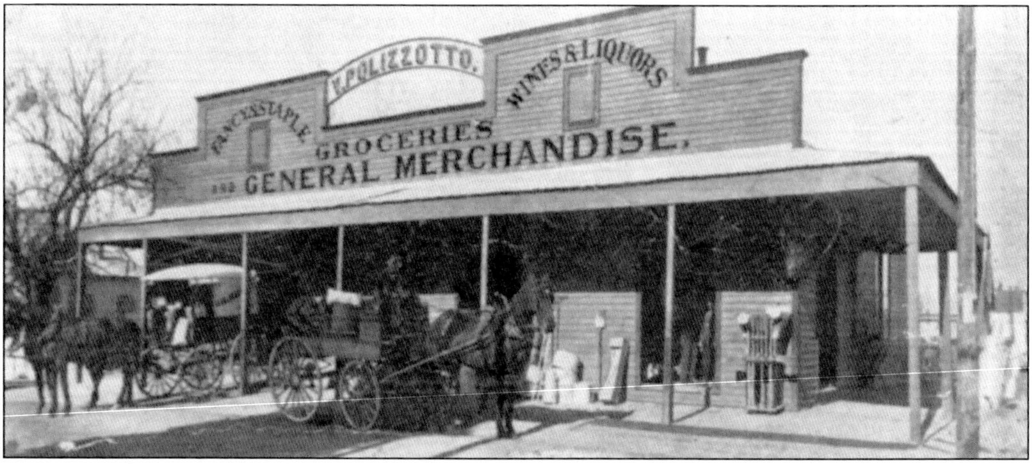

Vincent Polizzotto opened a grocery and general merchandise store, V. Polizzotto & Sons, in Plaquemine around 1890, speaking only Italian at the time. It soon became the largest grocery store in Plaquemine, located in Fortville at Fort and Church Streets. After Polizzotto's death, his sons took over the business, and it eventually moved to Railroad Avenue before finally closing. The store is pictured here around 1906.

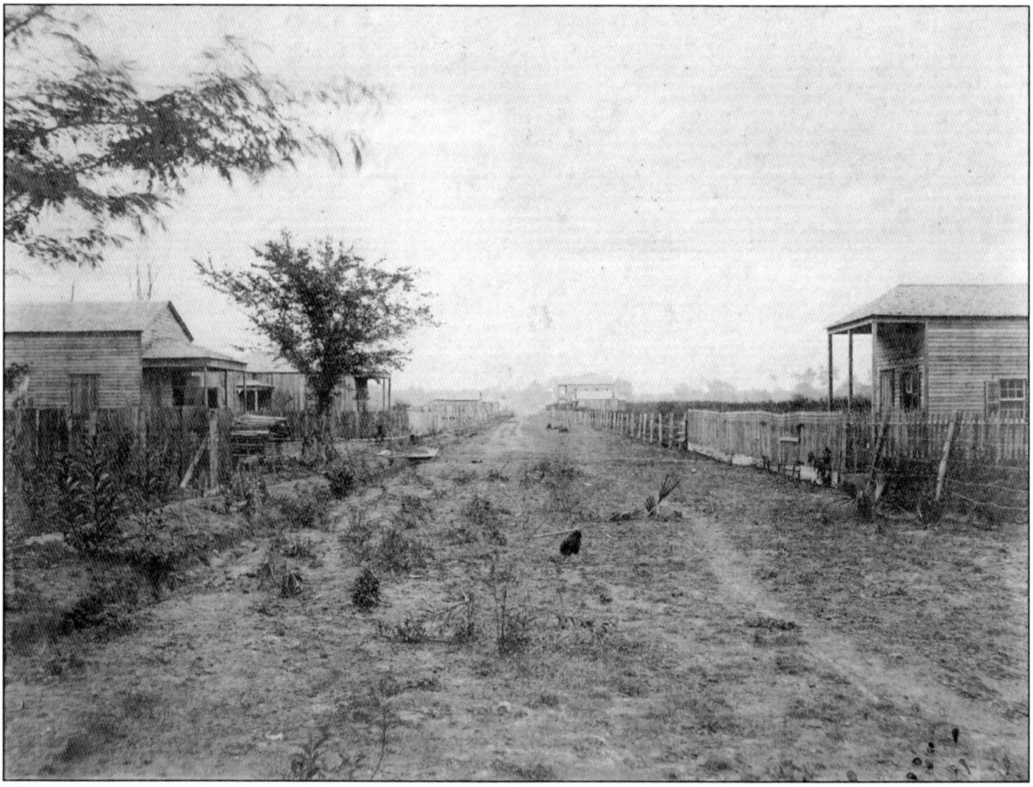

This c. 1902 photograph shows Patureau Lane in Crescent along Bayou Plaquemine. The road is named after the Patureau family. Dr. Vincent M. Patureau was a veterinarian in Plaquemine with a horse hospital near his home on Bayou Plaquemine. He also had a headquarters at People's Drug Store and Bailey's Drug Store. At right is the Star Club, a community hall. (Courtesy of Ralph Stassi.)

Six

Railroad Avenue

Before 1881, the only way to travel to and from Plaquemine was by boat or horse carriage. The nearest railroad was the New Orleans Pacific Railroad Company in White Castle, which connected with New Orleans. In 1878, the company made plans to extend its rails through Plaquemine and Baton Rouge, sending its chief engineer to Plaquemine to get permission to build tracks through town. Most of the city council did not want the railroad to pass through downtown. However, they eventually conceded after learning the alternate plan was to build the tracks about a mile outside city limits. Fearing this would destroy the commerce of Plaquemine, as a new village would spring up where the railroad constructed the depot, the city council passed an ordinance in March 1879 allowing the railroad to pass through the middle of town on Canal Street. Finally, in June 1881, the railway was completed, and Plaquemine opened its first railroad depot.

Upon the railroad's opening, downtown Plaquemine boomed as freight and passenger trains visited the town daily. Locals soon began referring to Canal Street as Railroad Avenue, and several wholesale companies opened along the railroad. Additionally, spurs were added to reach the mills and factories outside city limits. In 1888, a branch line was built down Haase and Osage Streets and traveled to Indian Village near Grand River. Presently, daily freight trains still pass through Plaquemine, but the last passenger train in town stopped on December 17, 1969.

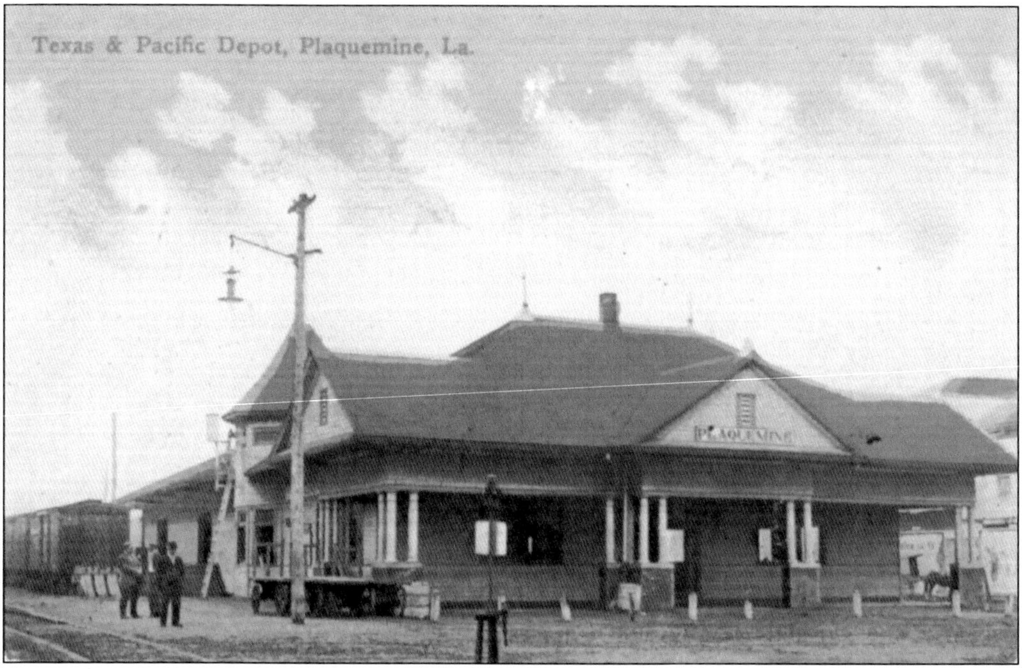

Pictured is a c. 1906 postcard of the second railroad depot in Plaquemine, which opened in 1902. It was built in the same location as the first, at the foot of Canal and Main Streets. The front entrance on Main Street opened into a large waiting room and ticket booth.

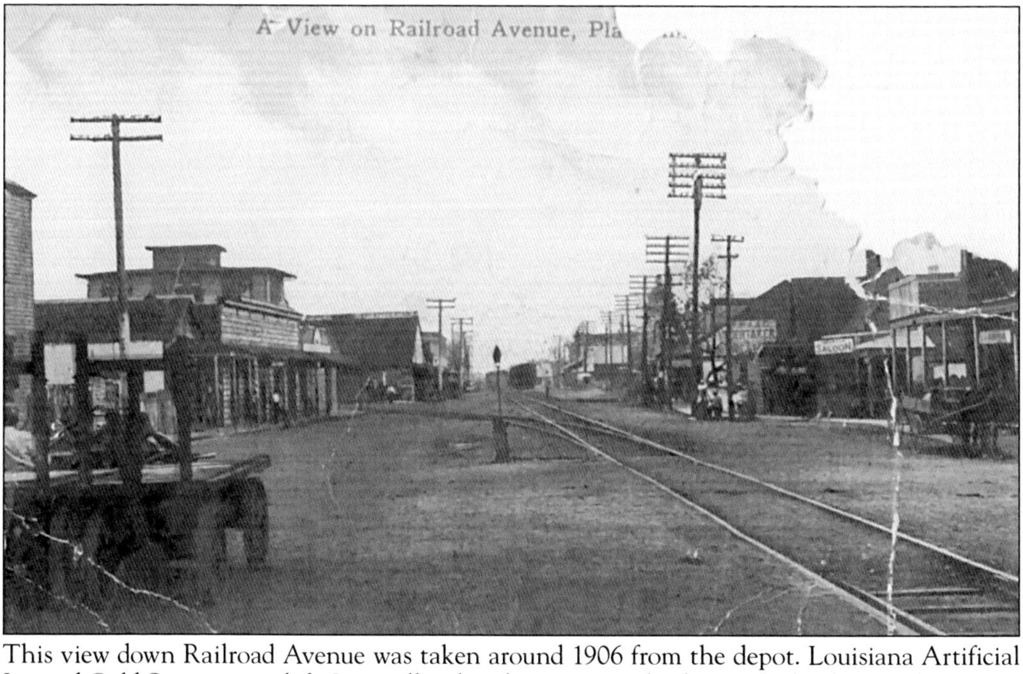

This view down Railroad Avenue was taken around 1906 from the depot. Louisiana Artificial Ice and Cold Storage is at left. Its small railroad spur is seen leading to its loading dock. On the right are signs for an undertaker and saloon, presumably the Four Jacks Saloon owned by Jack Rosso, or Charles Martin's saloon and barroom. At one point, there were nine saloons within a stone's throw of the depot.

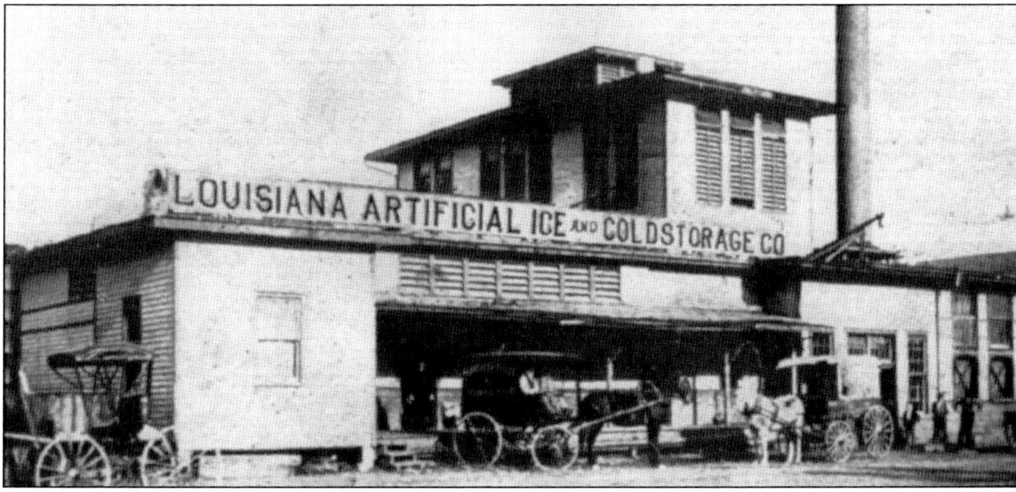

Louisiana Artificial Ice and Cold Storage Company opened in 1891. It was owned by the Anheuser-Busch Brewing Company of St. Louis. In 1896, it opened the building pictured here on Railroad Avenue in Plaquemine. The *Iberville South* in 1901 stated that Louisiana Artificial Ice and Cold Storage Company were "the people to supply fuel for your refrigerator." The company closed around 1914.

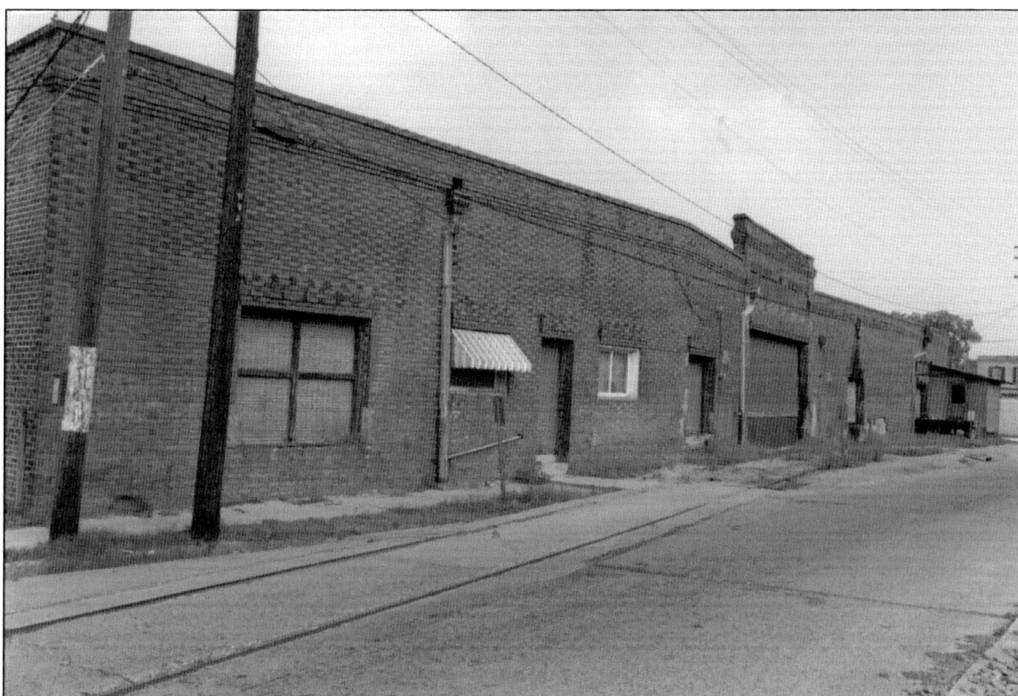

In 1915, Iberville Wholesale Grocery Company purchased the lot and built a new brick building, seen here around 1981. Victor Kurzweg and Henry N. Sherburne founded Iberville Wholesale, later known as Consolidated Companies, around 1904 as a general wholesale grocery business for Plaquemine and adjoining towns. The building was torn down in 1988. (Photograph by Robert Mooney.)

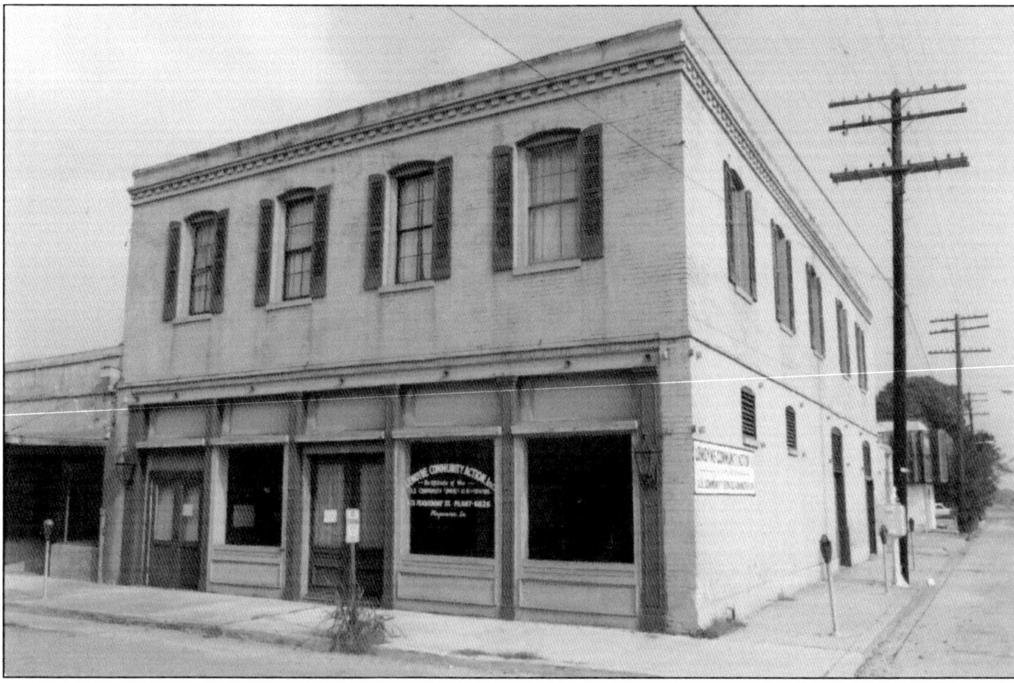

Prior to his work with Kurzweg, Sherburne founded Sherburne-Schlater and Company in 1899 with T. Weisinger Schlater. It was also a grocery firm and was located in the two-story brick building on the corner of Plaquemine Street and Railroad Avenue, pictured above around 1981. In 1904, Schlater sold his shares, prompting Sherburne to go into business with Kurzweg, who worked as a bookkeeper for Sherburne since he was 15. They operated at this location for several years before building the new building up the block in 1915. In 1918, Kinberger Grocery Company opened there and operated for many years. (Above, photograph by Robert Mooney; below, courtesy of IPL.)

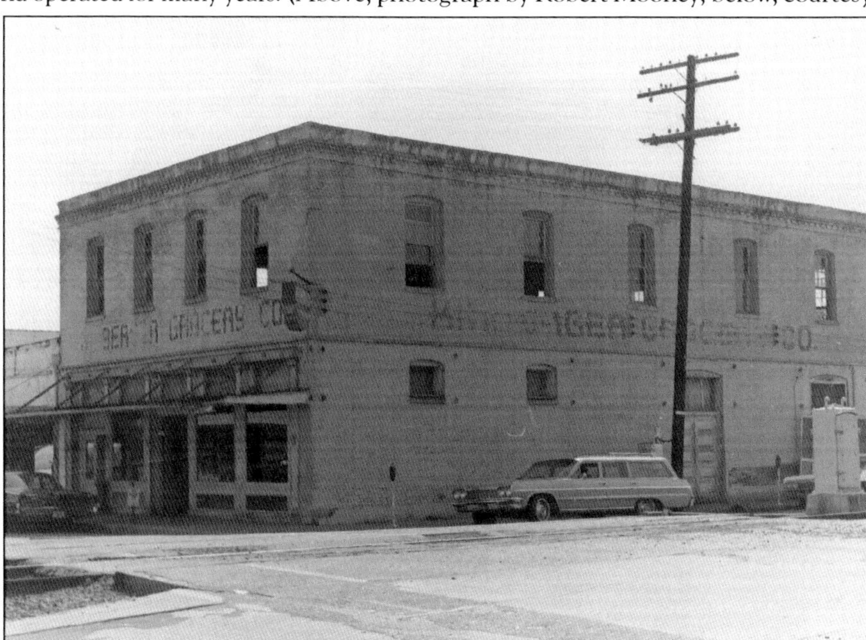

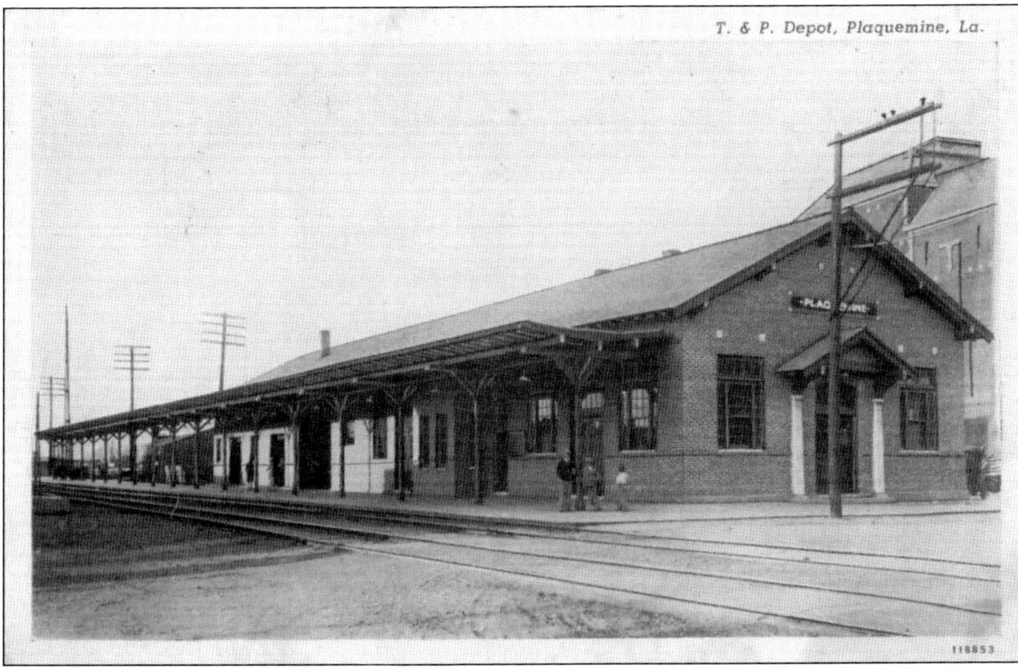

In October 1926, Plaquemine opened its third railroad depot built by Arthur Babb. It cost $60,000 and was constructed with the help of the Louisiana Public Service Commission (PSC). Town officials requested assistance from the PSC after the Texas & Pacific Railroad Company refused to build a new station and freight depot for Plaquemine. Huey P. Long, future governor of Louisiana, was chairman of the PSC at the time of the dispute. The freight depot, which was demolished when Highway 1 was widened, was immediately north of Bayou Plaquemine in Turnerville. After the depot closed in 1969, the building was used as the Plaquemine Police Department, seen below around 1981. (Below, photograph by Robert Mooney.)

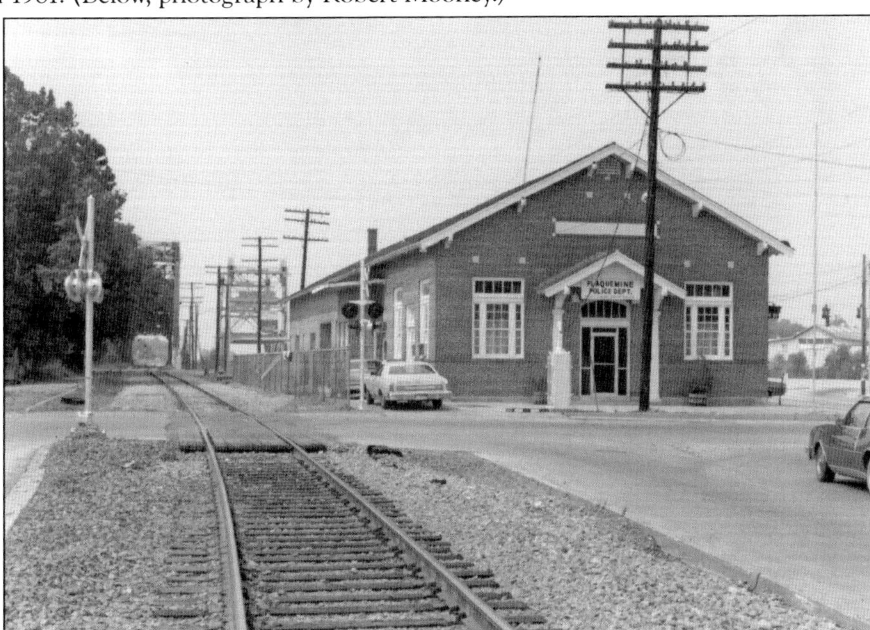

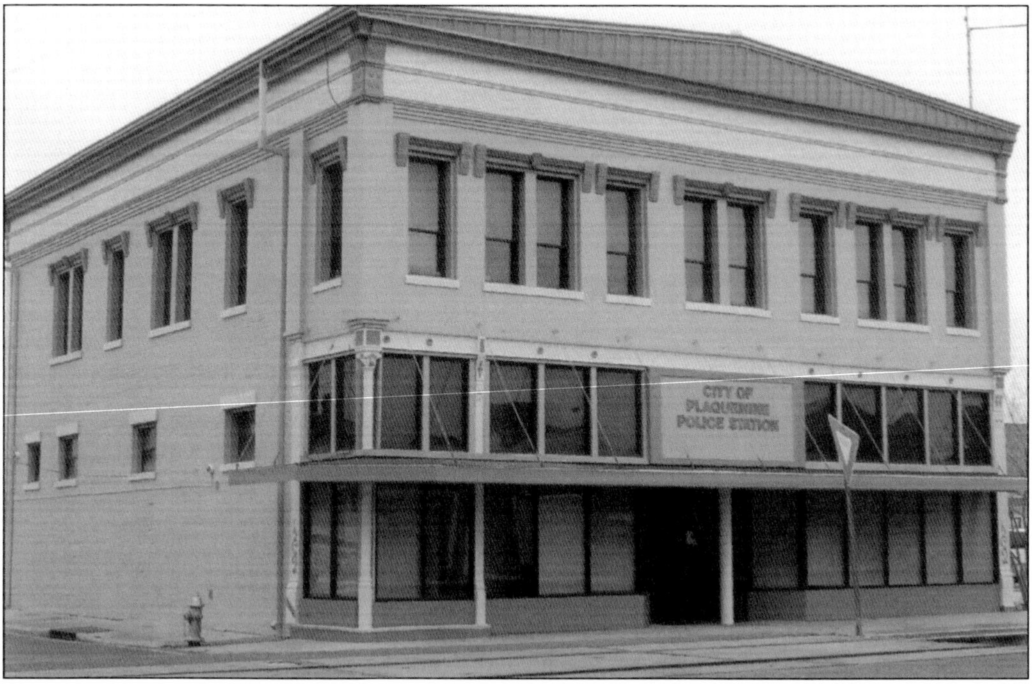

In 1906, Moise Levy, a parish judge, built the building pictured above around 2013 on the corner of Railroad Avenue and Court Street. It housed several different businesses, including the Plaquemine Post Office, several doctors' offices, and a grocery store. However, it is most remembered as Weill's department store, owned by Capt. Nicholas George Huth from Lafourche Parish. In the 1990s, attorney Barry Marionneaux donated the building to the City of Plaquemine, which restored it and turned it into the Plaquemine Police Department. Pictured below is an architectural drawing of the building from 1906 printed in the *Weekly Iberville South* before the building was completed.

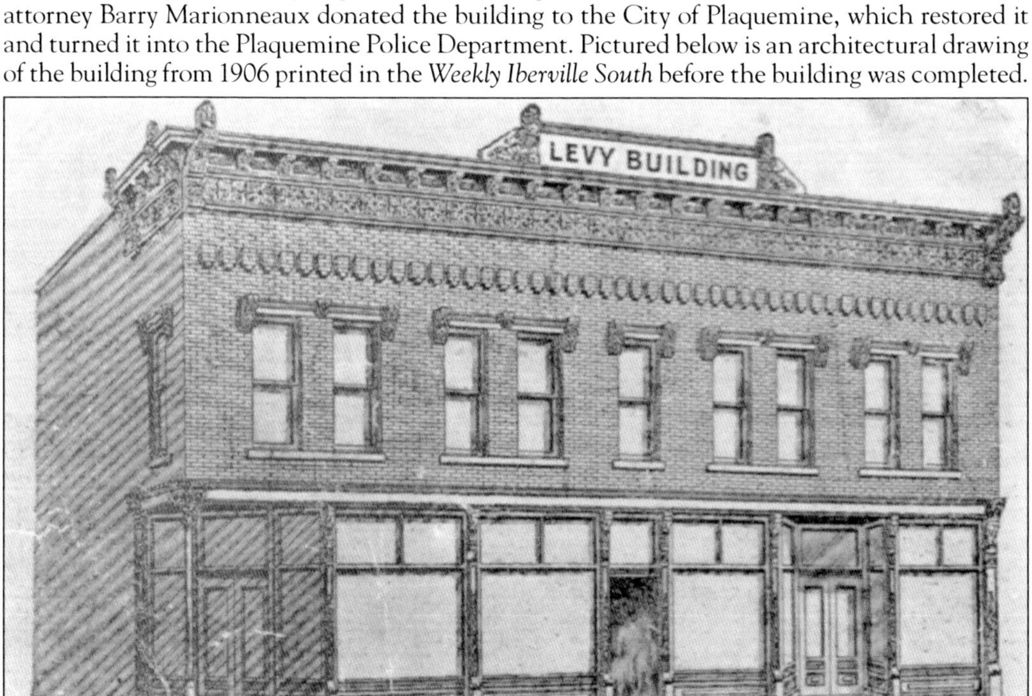

The Hirsch Building opened on the corner of Railroad Avenue and Barker's Alley in 1931. Mrs. Hirsch and Sons hired Butler and O'Donnell to build the brick building that became the new home to Heuman and Dampf's dry goods and clothing store. The Morgan and Lindsey five-and-dime store later moved into the building. It is pictured around 1981 before being renovated by Plaquemine Main Street. (Photograph by Robert Mooney.)

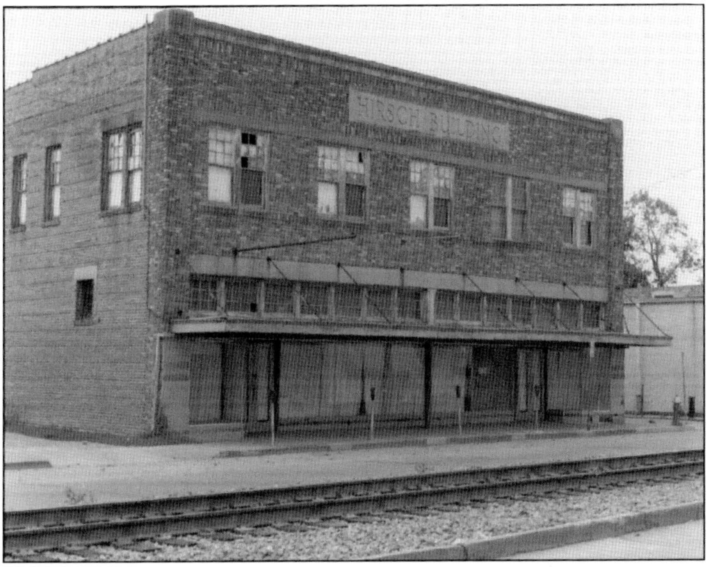

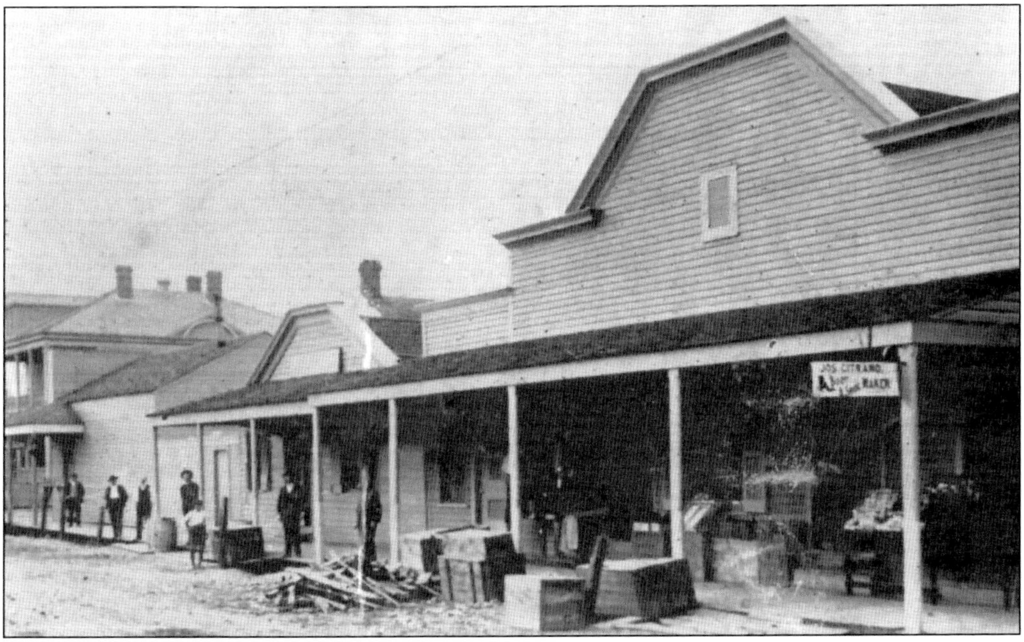

Joseph Adolphe Dupuy's mercantile store, pictured around 1906, opened in the late 1880s on Railroad Avenue near the northeast corner of Plaquemine Street. In 1890, Henry Contejean opened his watchmaking and jewelry store next door. By 1900, Contejean's shop was replaced by Joseph Citrano, an Italian lace maker. A sign for Citrano is visible in this photograph.

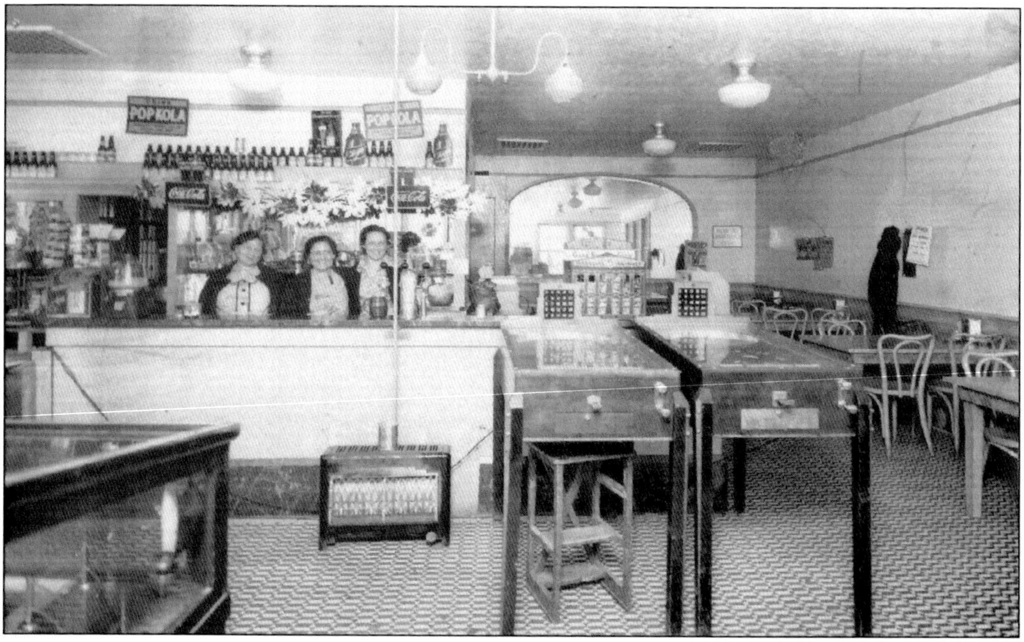

The Dew Drop Inn was opened in 1930 by Regger Rosso Fama (pictured at left above) at the corner of Railroad Avenue and Barker's Alley. She opened the restaurant in front of Star Bottling Works, owned by her father, Jack Rosso. Pictured below is a c. 1912 Star Bottling Works' Firemen's Parade float. The Dew Drop Inn is considered the first restaurant in Plaquemine to offer curbside service and often fed the students and teachers of Plaquemine Elementary two blocks away. It was known for its chicken spaghetti, prepared with a red gravy made from a family recipe and simmered for two days. The cafe closed in 1949 when Fama retired. (Both, courtesy of Tony Fama.)

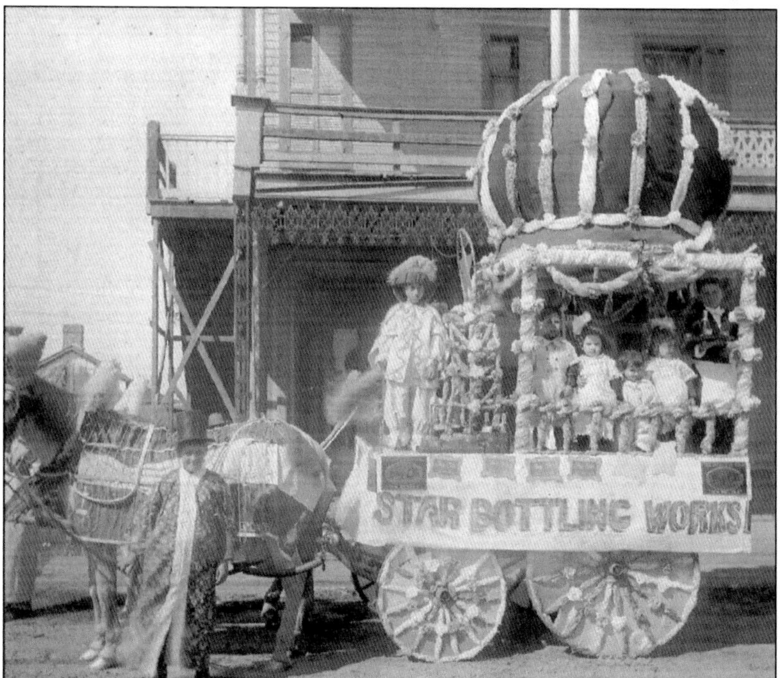

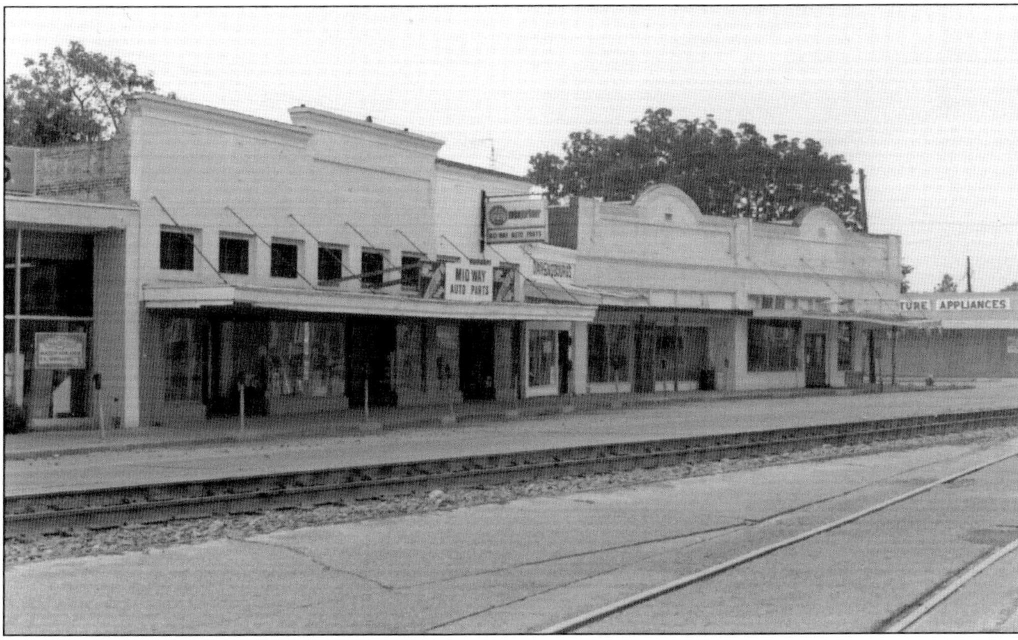

The Rosso Building (left) was completed in 1933. The lot was originally home to the Four Jack's Saloon, owned by Jack Rosso. When the saloon closed during Prohibition, the Rosso family demolished the original wood-frame structure and constructed a new brick building in its place. Over the years, it housed the Plaquemine Drug Store, Morgan and Lindsey's five and dime (pictured below during Christmas 1935), and Vandel's Clothing Store, which opened in the early 1950s and closed in the late 1970s. From left to right below are Vera Comeaux, Daisy Millet, Whitney Broussard, and John Miranda. (Above, photograph by Robert Mooney.)

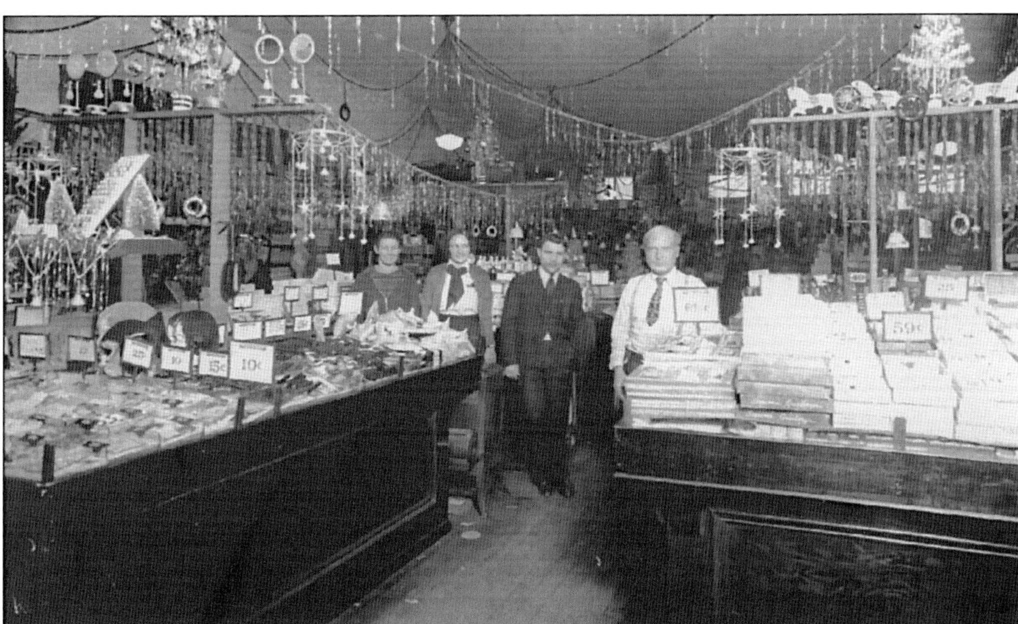

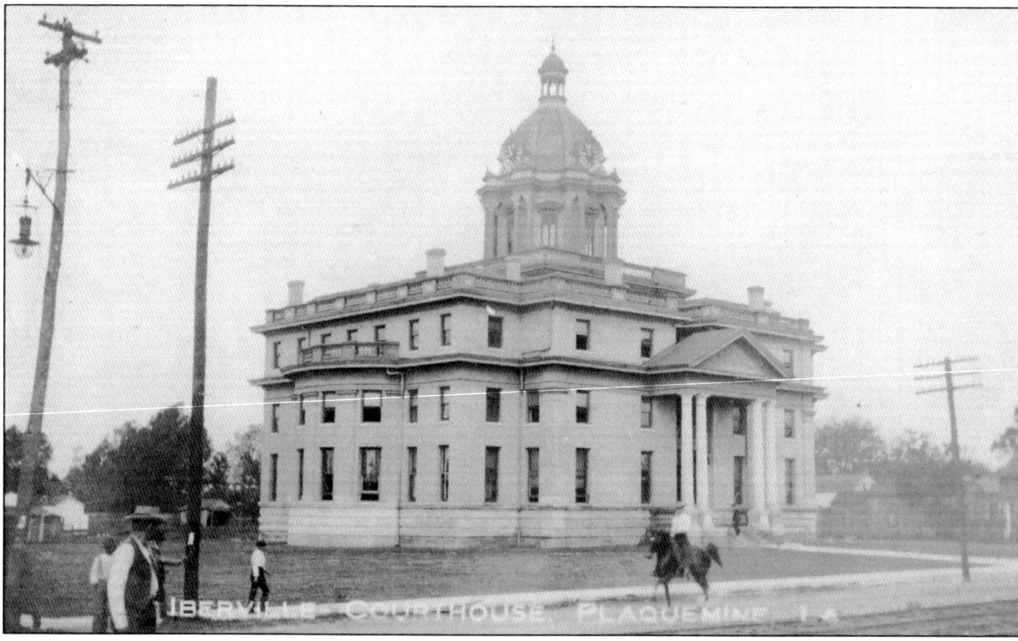

For years, the Iberville Parish Police Jury debated building a new courthouse and where it would be located. Several council members thought they should build on the existing lot. Another argued for a location on Eden Street. However, in June 1905, the police jury voted to build the new courthouse on Jacob McWilliams's property on the corner of Railroad Avenue and Meriam Street. In July 1905, Jacob McWilliams and John Arthur filed an injunction against the police jury, restraining them from building the new courthouse on the site selected. But the Louisiana Supreme Court in November 1905 sustained the police jury's right to build on the lot. Pictured below is the laying of the cornerstone on March 31, 1906. (Above, courtesy of Louisiana State University.)

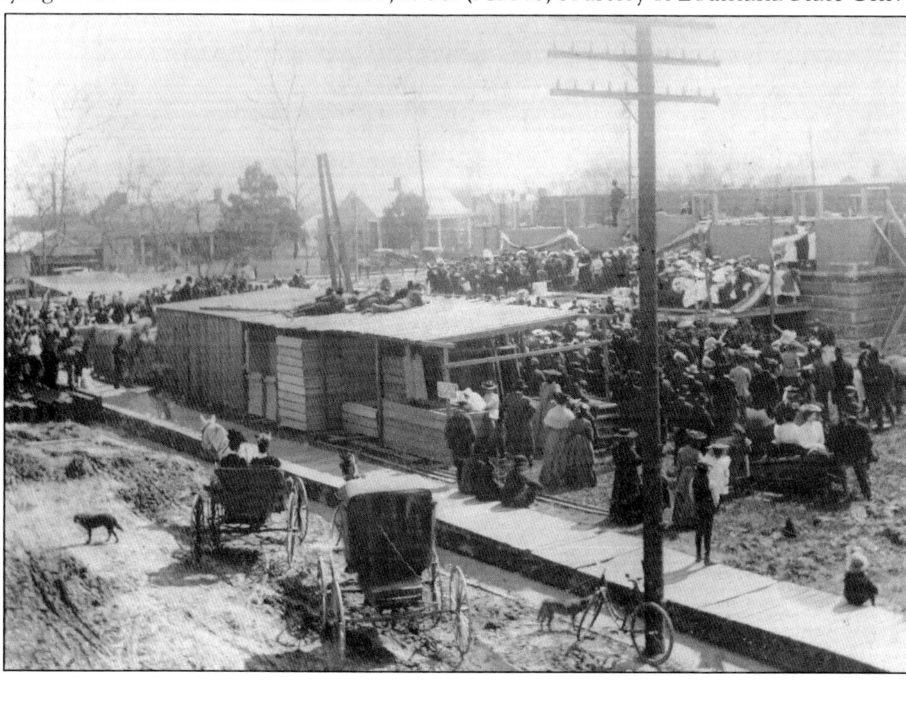

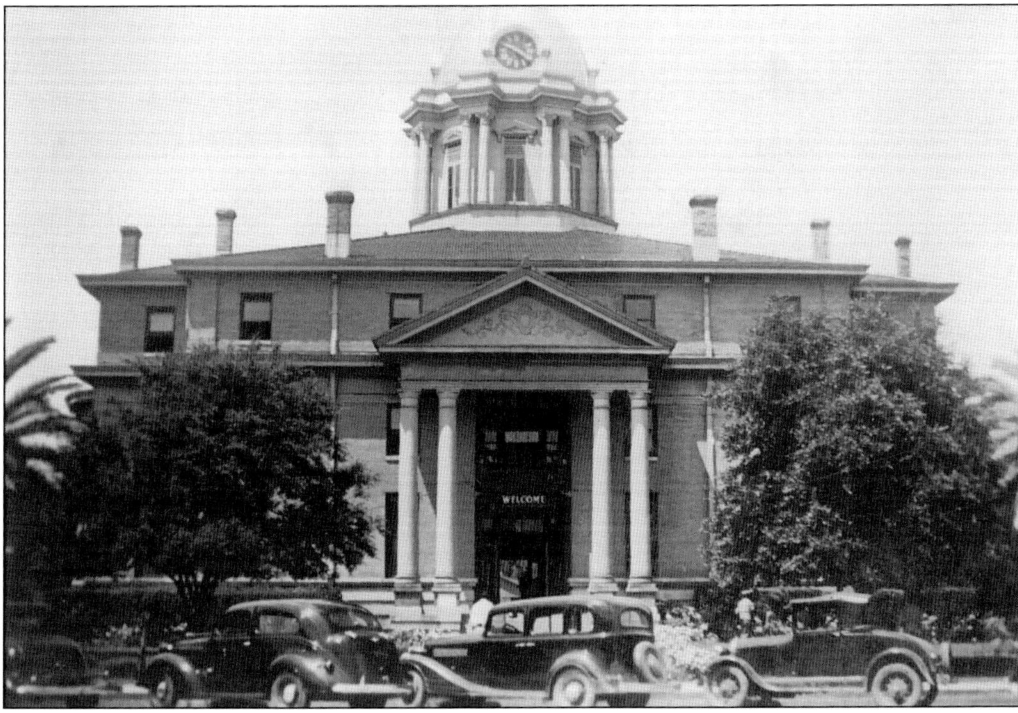

The courthouse was completed on November 21, 1906. It served the parish until 1985, when a fourth courthouse was built on Meriam Street on a lot that once housed the c. 1926 jail. After the new courthouse was completed, city hall took over the vacant courthouse on Railroad Avenue.

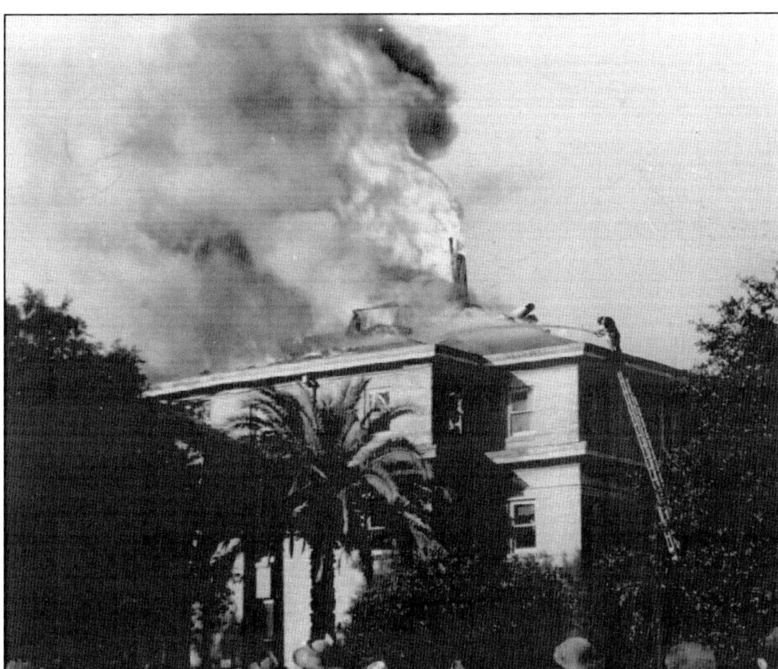

Pictured here is the courthouse fire that occurred on May 4, 1945. The fire department mostly controlled the fire, but it did ruin the building's handsome cupola. The roof was replaced in December 1948, but the clock tower was never rebuilt.

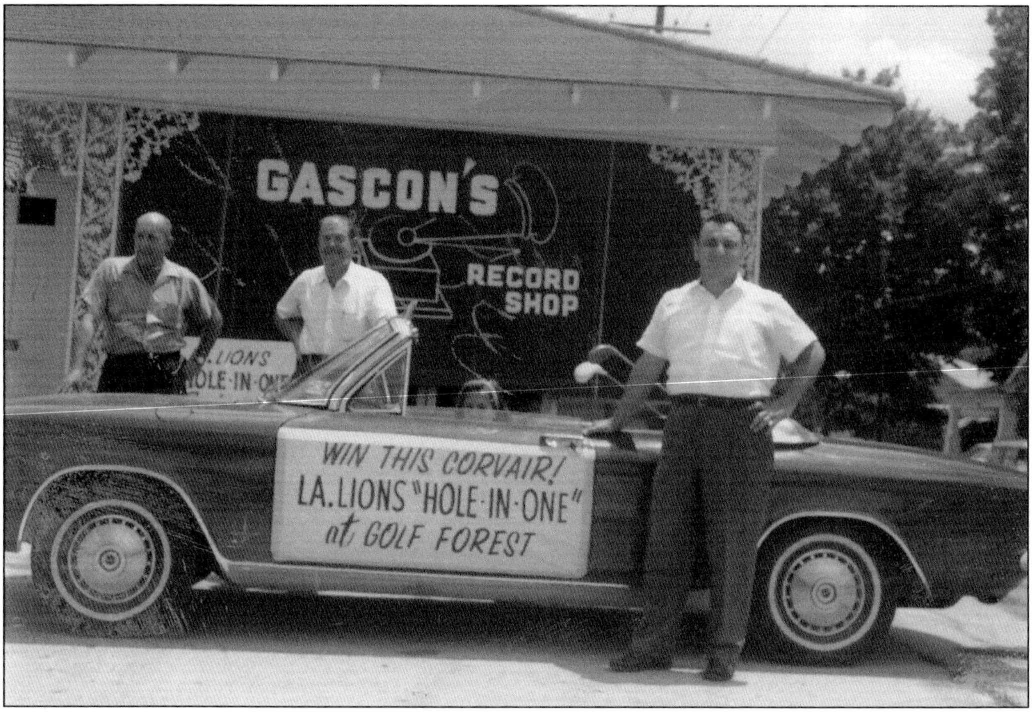

Gascon's Record Shop was opened by Houston C. Gascon (far left) in 1961 on Railroad Avenue and Haase Street. The building also housed Hammy Records recording studio and other offices. Charles V. Kirkland Sr., a local musician, supplied Hammy Records with his recording equipment, which was used to record dozens of local artists. Pictured below is the interior of the record shop. The store closed in 1987. (Both, courtesy of IPL.)

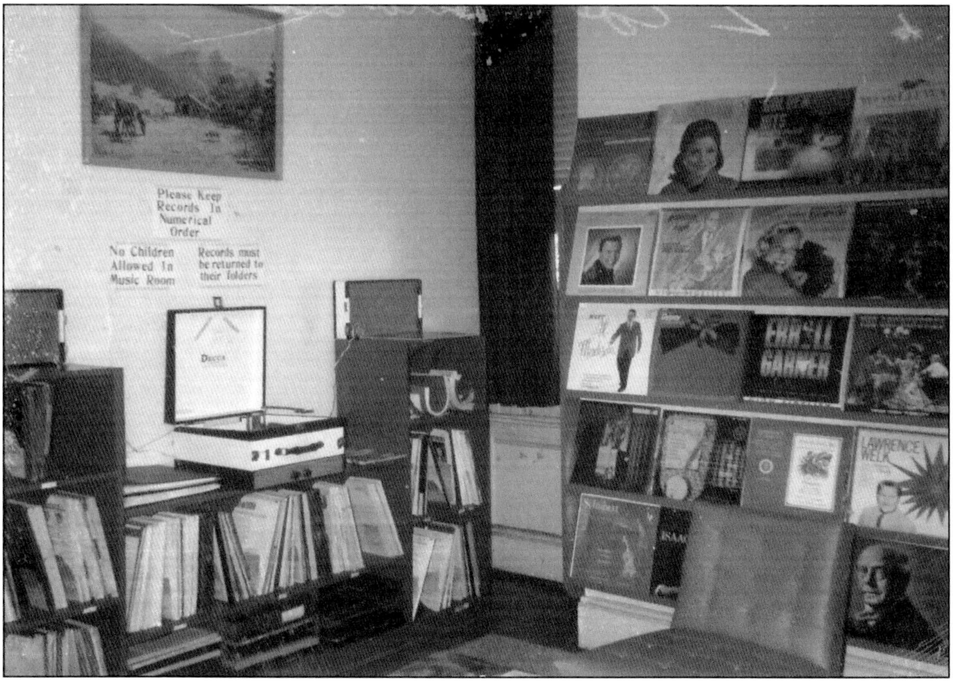

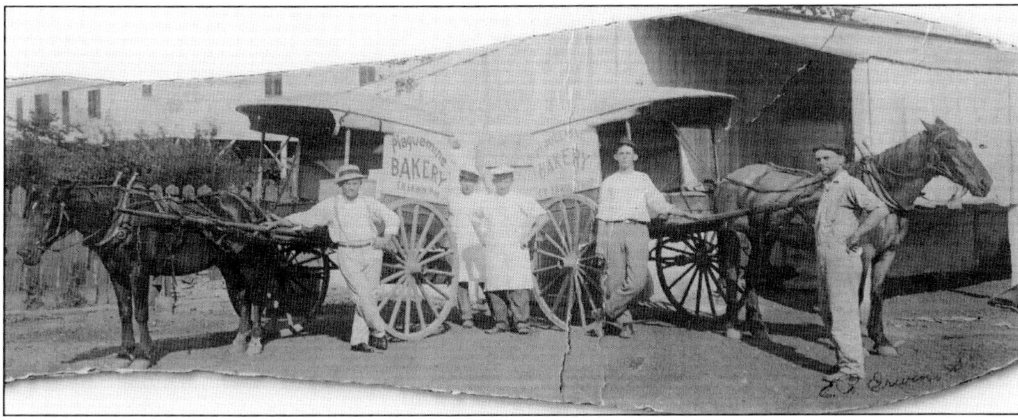

In the 1920s, Edward Roger Erwin (pictured above on the left) moved his bakery from Meriam Street to Railroad Avenue. Around 1938, Andrew Pirello purchased the bakery, renaming it Pirello's Quality Bakery. In 1958, Pirello sold the bakery to George Marionneaux, and it operated as George's for 12 years. Ronnie Dimm then purchased the building from Marionneaux and opened his own bakery in 1970. Dimm was known for his unique pastries and old-time French bread. He and his family lived upstairs above the bakery. The shop closed in the late 1990s. (Above, courtesy of Rita Lynn Jackson; below, photograph by Robert Mooney.)

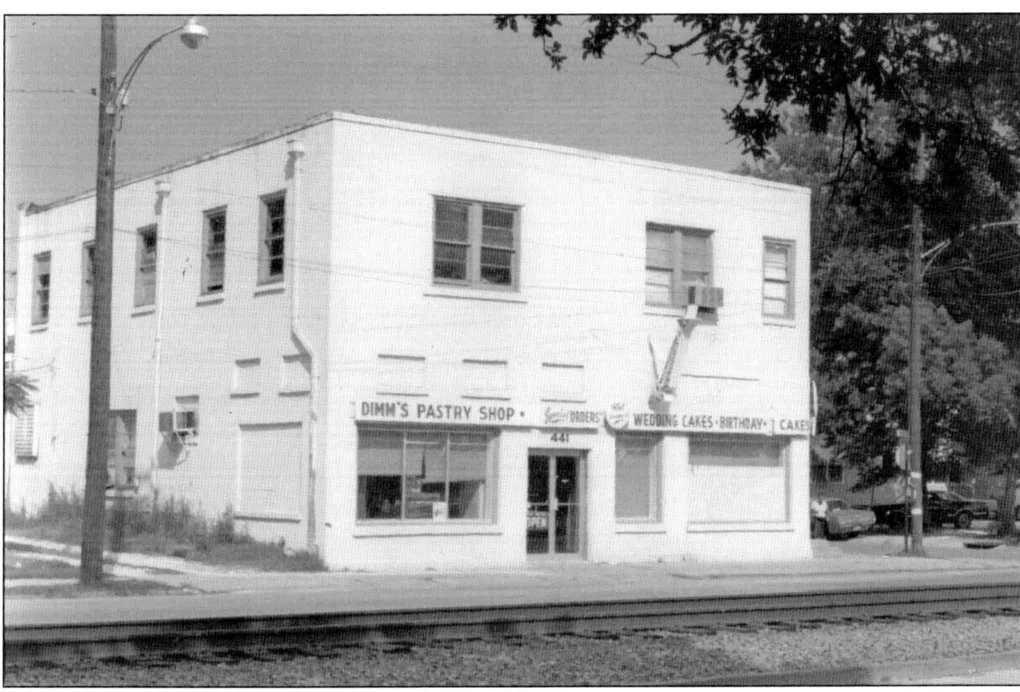

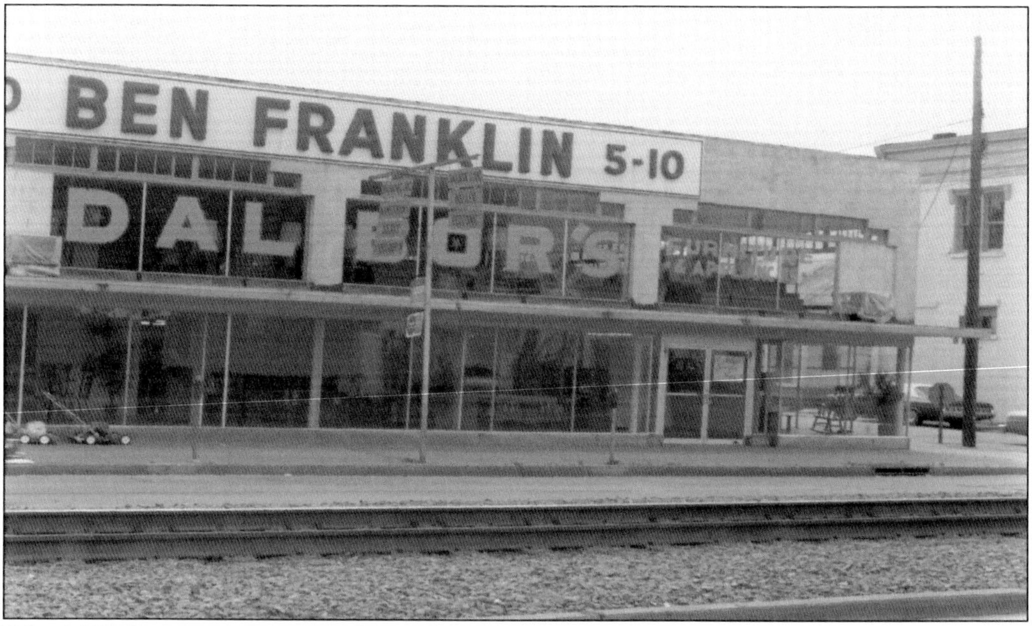

Felix J. D'Albor Sr. of Iberia Parish purchased property along Railroad Avenue at the southwest corner of Court Street in 1924 to open his furniture store. The wood-frame building on the corner that housed Bergeron Cleaners and Pressers was demolished, and the cleaners moved around the corner to Court Street. D'Albor then constructed his new building (pictured above around 1981). The furniture store officially opened on December 26, 1931, to a crowd of 6,000. Later, a five-and-dime store opened on the right side of the building. In 1980, the D'Albor family made plans to relocate to Belleview Drive, and the building was demolished around 1982. Below, a street performer is seen standing in front of the D'Albor building in about 1940. (Above, photograph by Robert Mooney.)

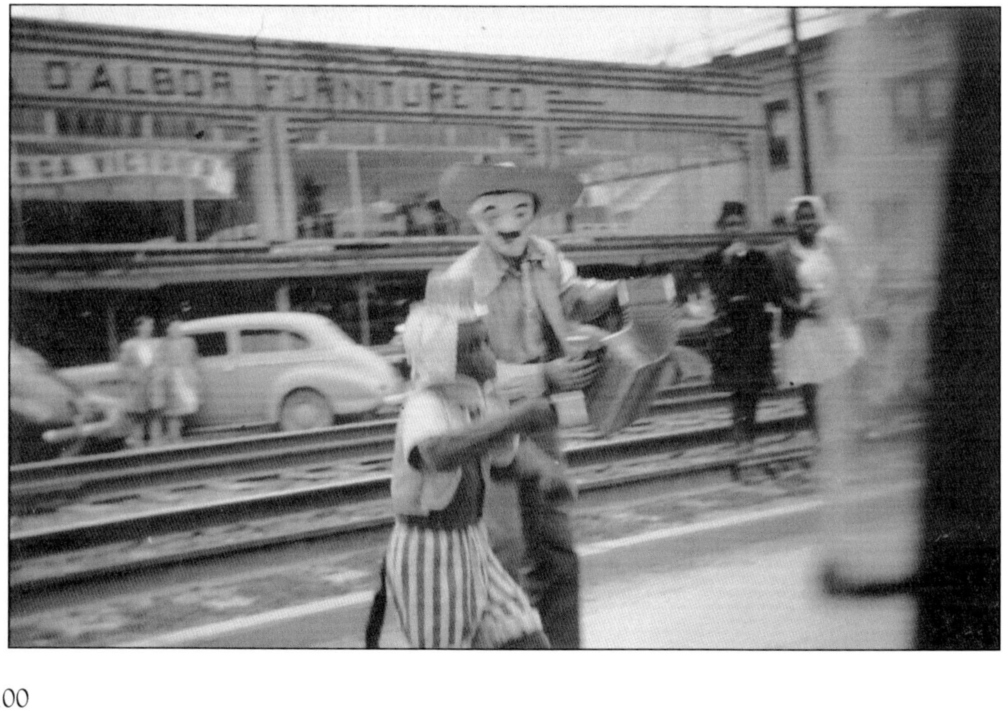

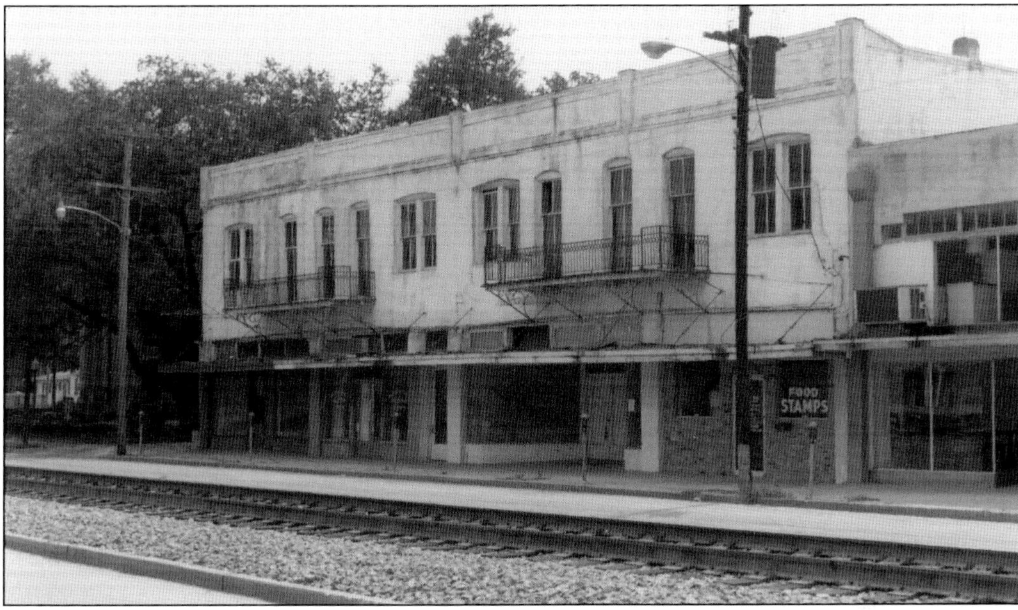

The D'Agostino Building was on Railroad Avenue between Meriam and Court Streets. Joseph D'Agostino bought the lot in August 1925 and contracted T. Reymond Hebert to construct a two-story brick building at the Old Scharff building. D'Agostino grocery opened in 1926 on the building's first floor, and the second was used as rented office spaces. Pictured here is the building in 1981 shortly before being demolished. (Photograph by Robert Mooney.)

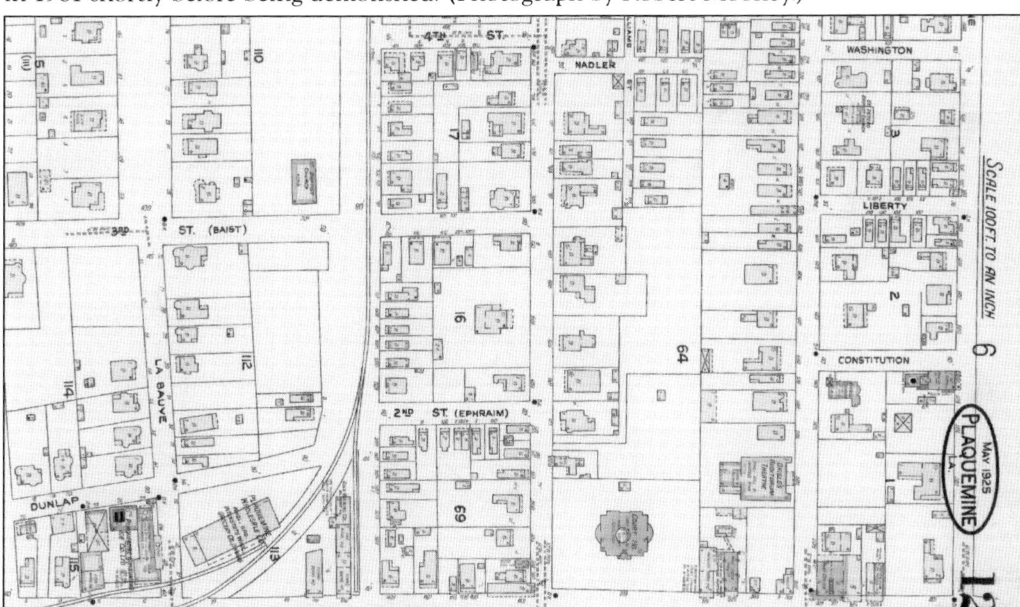

Daigle's Skating Rink opened around 1919 after G.A. Daigle purchased the rink from Minora Barker Hiriart. It was on Court Street behind the D'Agostino building. In 1924, Daigle tore down the rink's old wooden structure and built a new brick skating rink and auditorium that showed movies and road shows nightly. This 1925 Sanborn map of Plaquemine shows the rink's location near the corner of Court Street and Railroad Avenue. (Courtesy of the Library of Congress.)

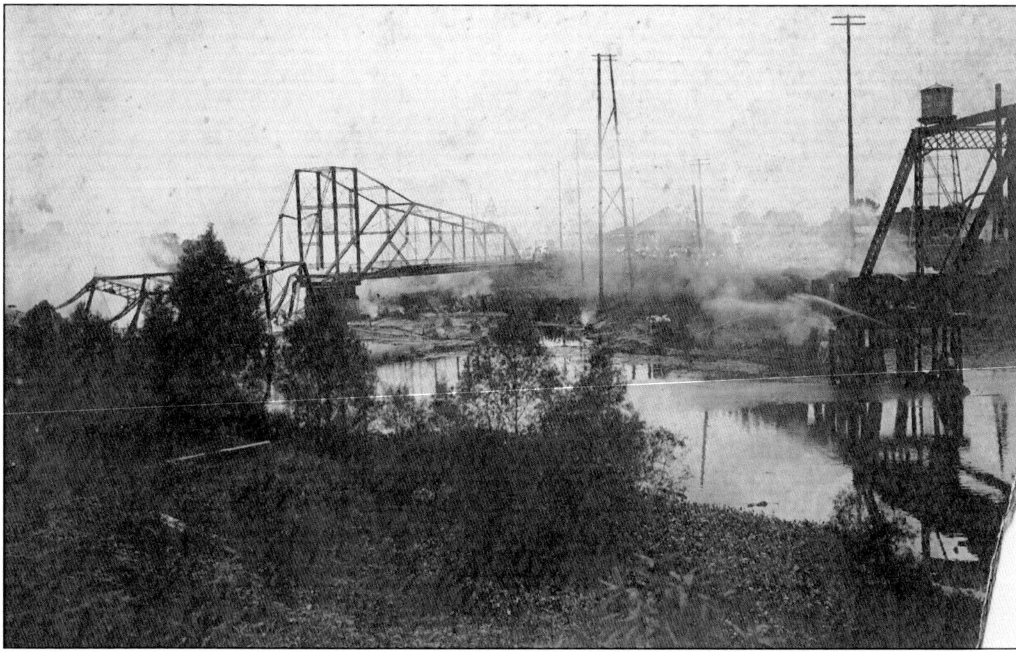

The first railroad bridge over Bayou Plaquemine opened in 1881. By 1898, the parish government built a public bridge over the bayou near the railroad that connected Plaquemine and Turnerville. On the morning of July 25, 1905, an oil fire on Bayou Plaquemine destroyed the parish's public bridge and damaged the railroad bridge. The aftermath of the fire is pictured above. It also destroyed several boats and boathouses belonging to Joe D'Agostino. Locals used a temporary pontoon bridge until a new public bridge opened in 1908. This bridge remained until 1950. The railroad bridge was repaired after the fire and was replaced in 1923. Pictured below is the first train crossing the new railroad bridge in August 1923. (Above, courtesy of IPL.)

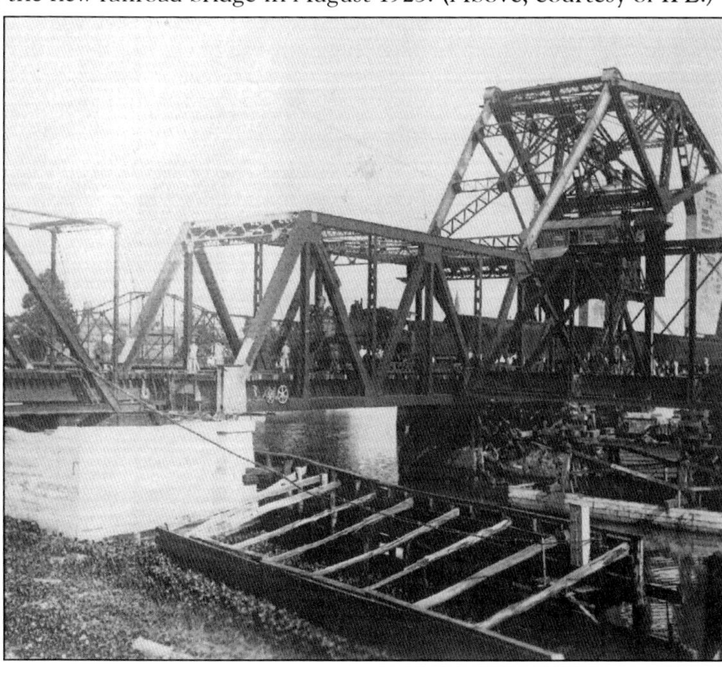

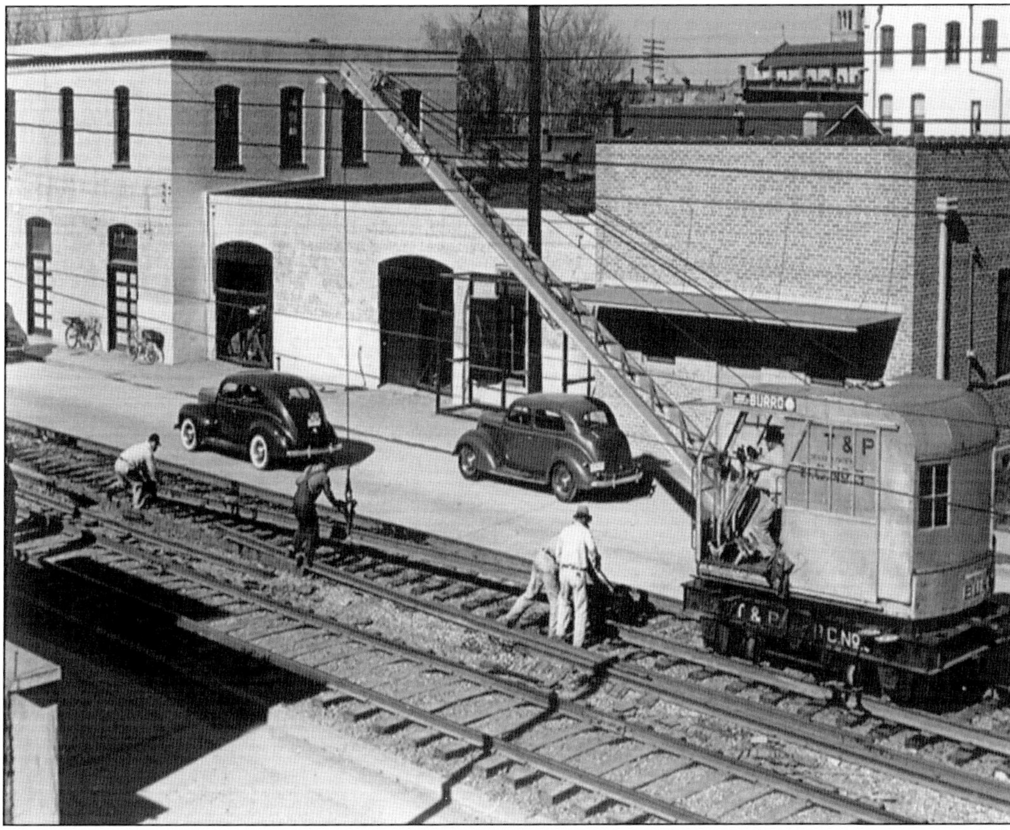

By 1941, railroad traffic in Plaquemine had increased significantly, with four passenger trains daily as well as a number of freight trains. As a result, the Texas & Pacific Railroad Company built a second track through Plaquemine. The construction of the new track is pictured here in front of the Kinberger Grocery Company. (Courtesy of Tony Fama.)

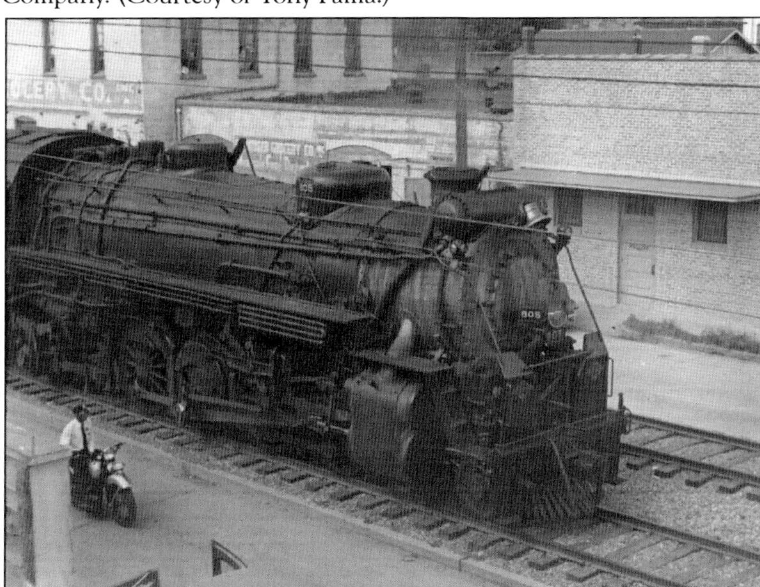

The popularity of passenger trains in Louisiana took a dive by the mid-20th century. On December 17, 1969, the last passenger train stopped in Plaquemine. Pictured here is Texas & Pacific locomotive No. 805 on Railroad Avenue in front of Kinberger Grocery Company around 1950.

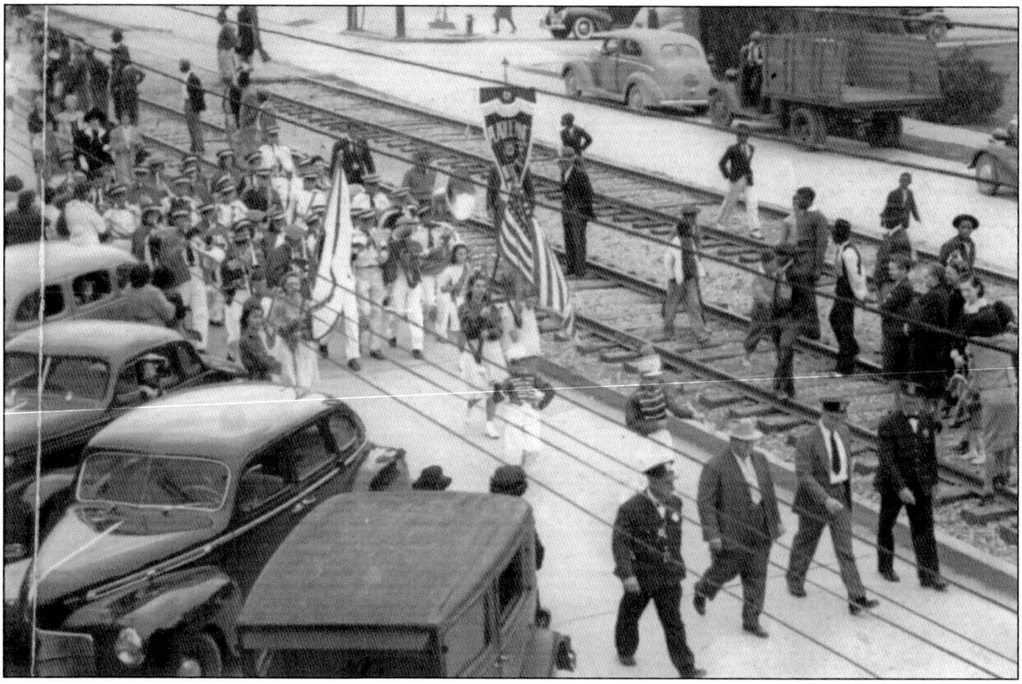

Over the years, Railroad Avenue remained at the heart of Plaquemine's culture and commerce. During the 20th century, trains would halt their schedules for townsfolk to host parades down the avenue. Pictured above is a 1940s Plaquemine High School Marching Band leading a parade on Railroad Avenue. The avenue was also home to the famous Grey Monkey Parade started by Plaquemine Elementary teacher Lolita Daigre in 1946, the Junior Deputy Parades, the Cub Scout Races Parade, and Plaquemine's Christmas Parade. Pictured below is a c. 1940s Christmas Parade float. (Below, photograph by Leana Boudreaux Brady.)

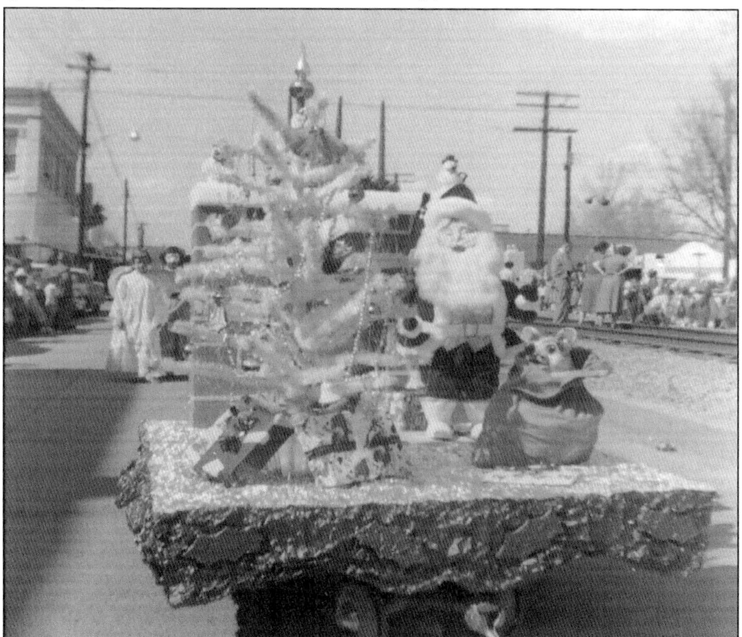

Seven

Churches and Schools

In many ways, Plaquemine's churches and schools developed hand in hand. Some of the first schools in town were started by a church. For example, the Plaquemine Female Seminary was incorporated in 1857 by the Presbyterian Church; Plaquemine College, a school for boys, was started in 1853 by the Catholic Church; and the Point Pleasant Baptist Church, a few miles south of Plaquemine, was founded in 1876 and used as a schoolhouse for both boys and girls. Other early private schools included Miss Fourrier's Academy, which aimed to prepare girls for the convent, and St. Augustin School for Black Children.

Public education in Plaquemine did not develop until the 1870s after Louisiana passed a law opening schools to all children regardless of race, color, or creed. By 1885, Plaquemine had two growing public schools separated by race. The white school was taught by Nellie E. Murphy and Lena Watson and had 90 students, while the school for black children had 288 students. It was under the leadership of J.L. Jones and six other teachers. However, their schoolhouse was notably overcrowded, requiring the school to rent the M.E.R. Church or a public hall on Marshall Street between Court and Plaquemine Streets. Access to public education continued to increase into the 20th century, and while many schools and churches shaped the community, this chapter will only highlight a few.

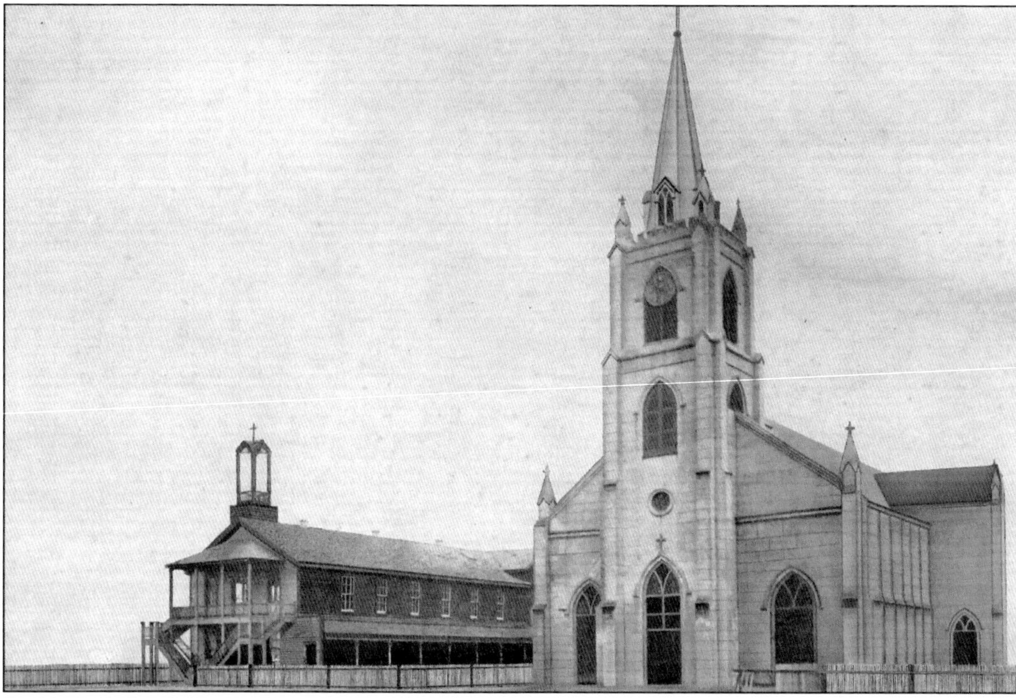

In 1840, Judge John Dulton donated land facing the public square for a Catholic church, the first in Plaquemine. St. John the Evangelist Church was finished in 1850 but destroyed in a fire eight years later. This print is from 1900 and shows the second building, completed in 1861. The building on the left is St. John's School for Boys, built in 1888.

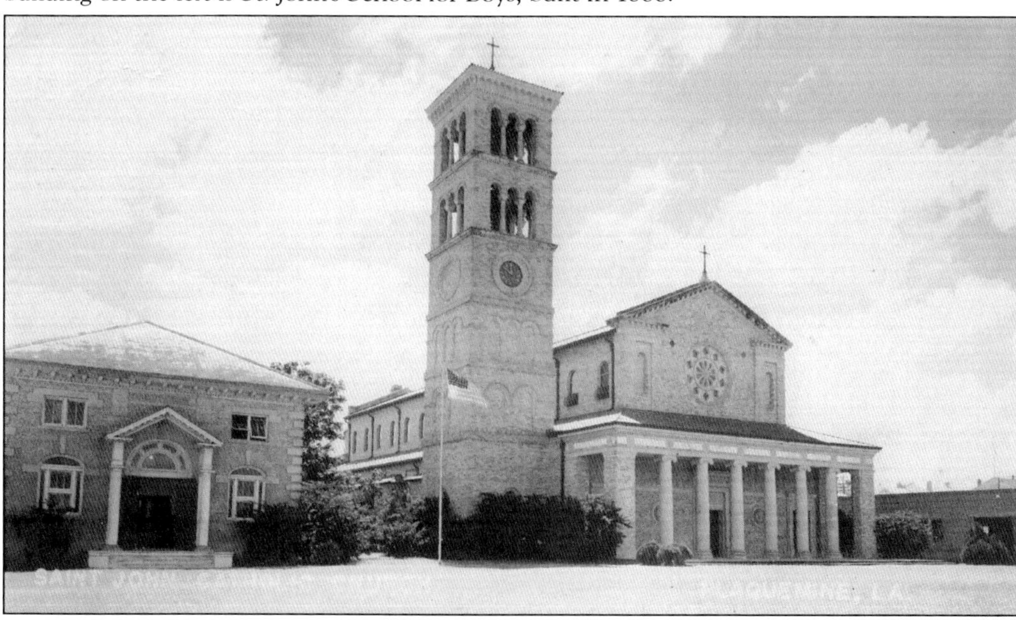

The school's building was destroyed in a fire on April 12, 1907. In 1910, a brick two-story building was built to replace it, and in 1949, a third story was added. The church was torn down in 1926 to build a larger cathedral. The construction was completed in October 1927 at a cost of $300,000. This postcard is from around 1942. (Courtesy of the Mooney family.)

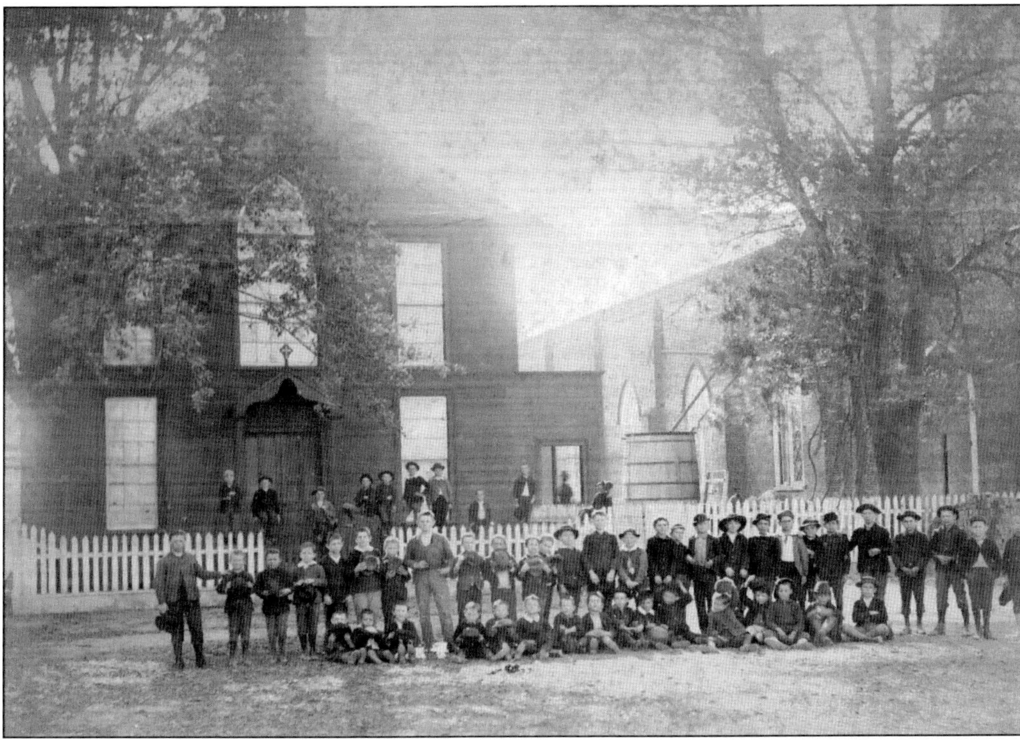

St. John's School for Boys was founded in 1886 by Rev. Mathurin Canon Harnais and was in the parish rectory at the corner of Plaquemine and Church Street. This photograph was taken shortly after the first schoolhouse was built in 1888.

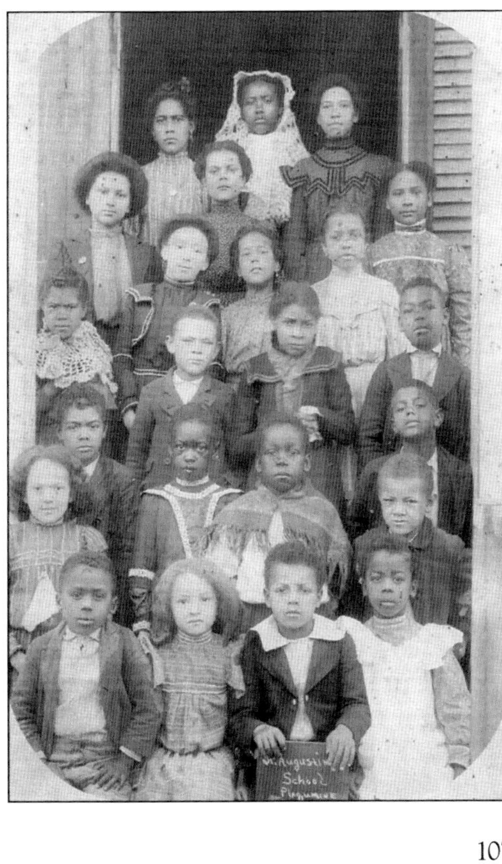

St. Augustin Catholic School was opened around the mid-1880s by the African American Sisters of the Holy Cross. It started in their segregated convent on Court street between Church and Eden Streets. Around 1891, a new school building was opened in the same location. Pictured here are students around 1903. The Church of the Immaculate Conception opened at the end of Main Street in 1939, shortly after the school closed, and operated a new black Catholic school in a nearby house. The church closed in the 1980s, and in 2006, it reopened as the Abundant Life Christian Church.

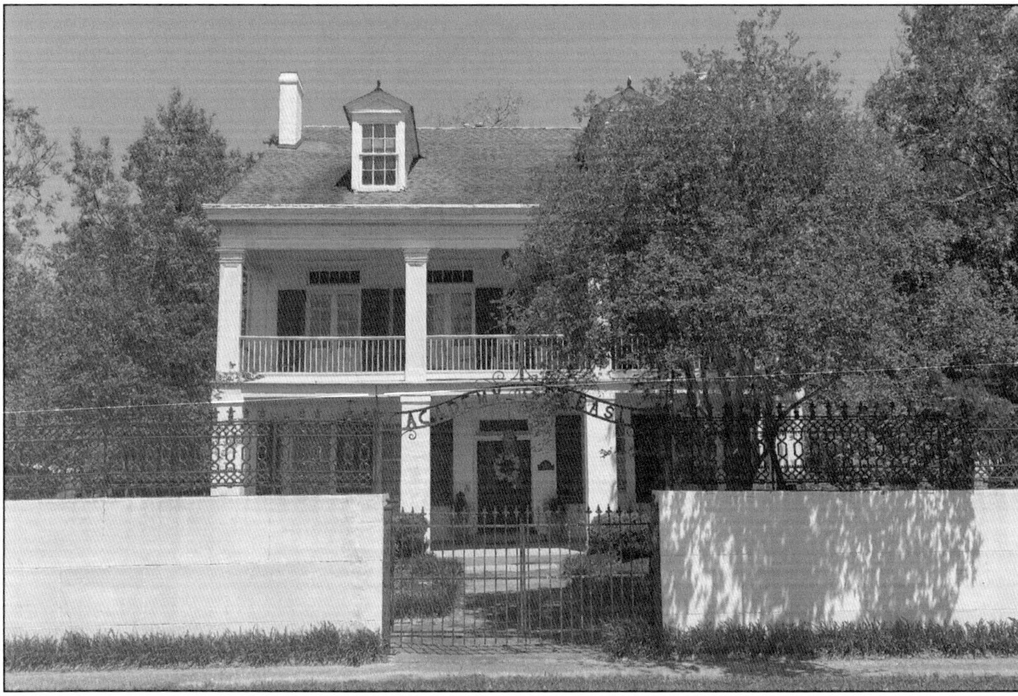

Dr. Edward Scratchley and Irma Elizabeth Labauve built this house on the corner of Church and Court Streets in 1850. In 1859, it was gifted to the Marianite Sisters of the Holy Cross to establish a girls' school. The school was named St. Basil's Academy after the founder of the Sisters of the Holy Cross. In 1862, the school and convent were used as a federal headquarters for the Union army. After the Civil War, in 1865, the sisters returned and continued teaching. In 1937, the school was merged with St. John's School, and the sisters remained in the convent until 1976. The photograph below is from 1912 and was taken from St. John's steeple. St. Basil's is on the right, and in the back center is the Presbyterian church.

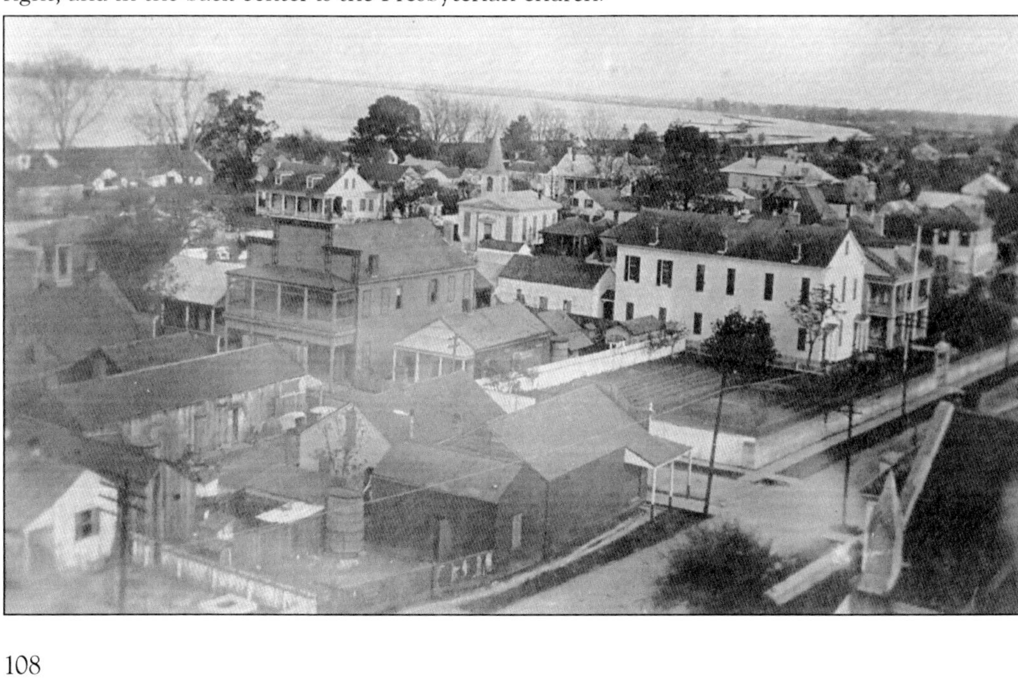

A Presbyterian church was opened in 1828 in Plaquemine by David Dunmore Chesnut. After he died in 1837, the congregation quieted until 1841, when records show they joined with the Methodists and Episcopalians in a meeting hall at Church and Court Streets. In the 1850s, they built this church on a lot at Court and Seminary Streets. It was torn down in 1942 after being vacant for several years. This photograph is from 1906.

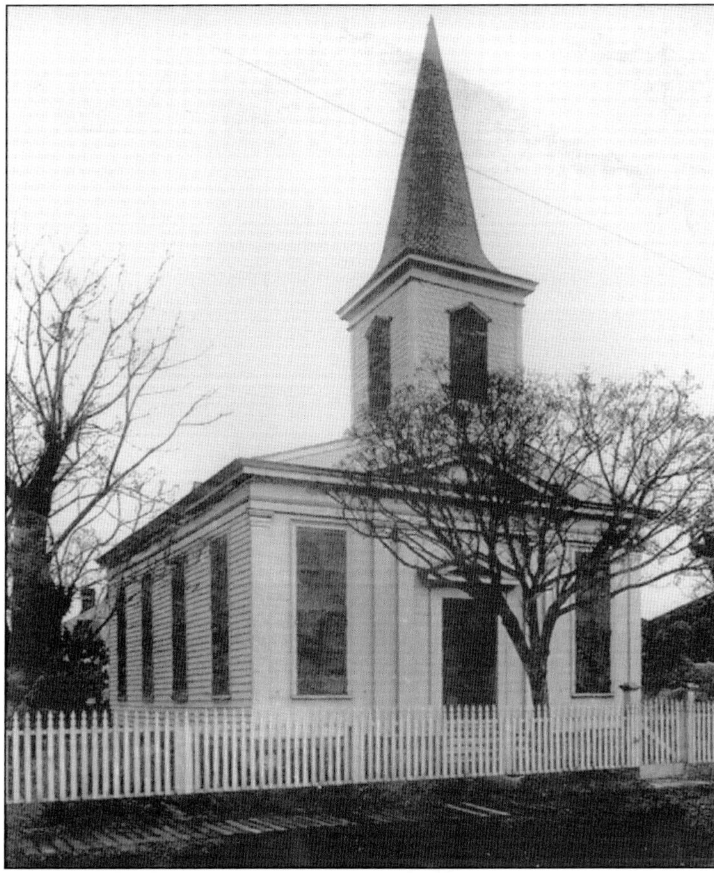

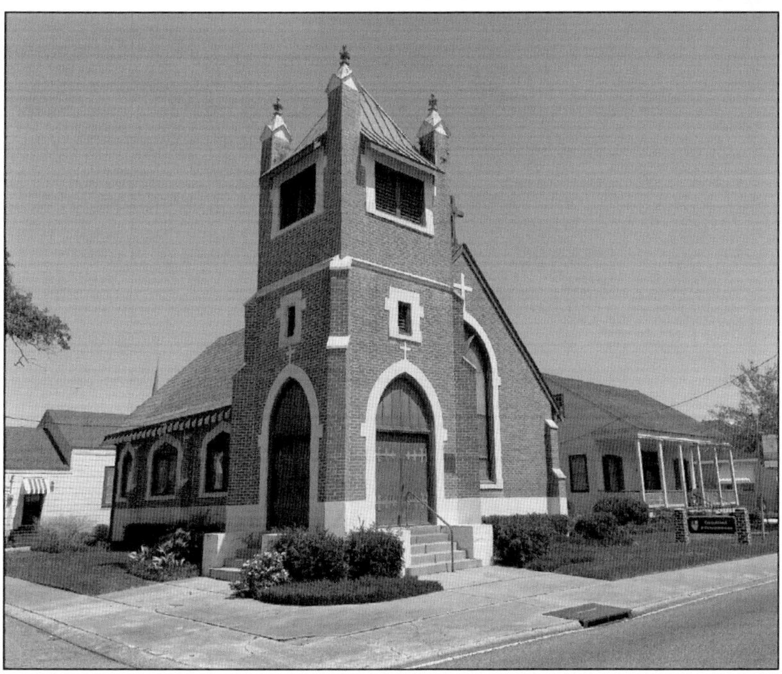

The Episcopal Church of the Holy Communion was founded in 1886 after receiving land on the southeast corner of Court and Constitution Streets to build a church. The original church burned down in February 1913, and a second building was completed in November 1913. (Photograph by Meghan C. Sylvester.)

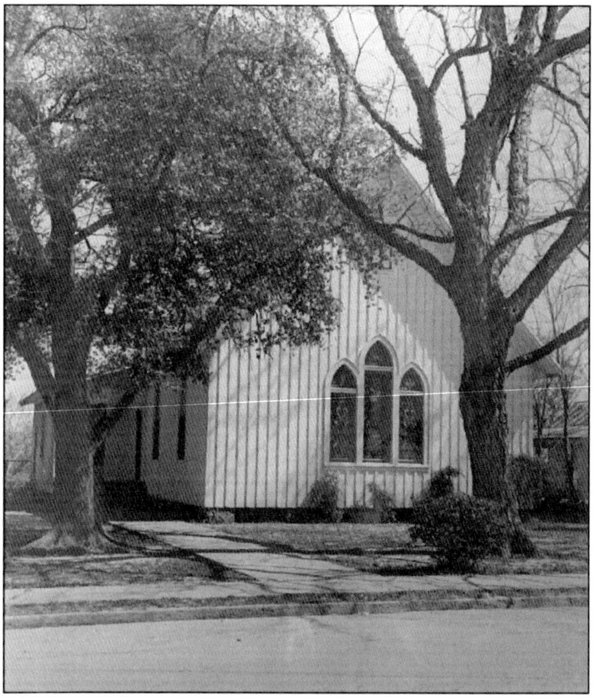

The Methodist-Episcopalian church in Plaquemine began as a joint Protestant church known as Union Church. It opened in 1841 on the corner of Church and Court Streets and was used by the Methodists, Presbyterians, and Episcopalians. A fire in 1873 destroyed the building, and a public school opened there shortly after. By 1884, the Methodist church was rebuilt next to the schoolhouse. In 1953, the building was remodeled, and the church was renamed the First United Methodist Church in 1968. (Both, courtesy of the First United Methodist Church.)

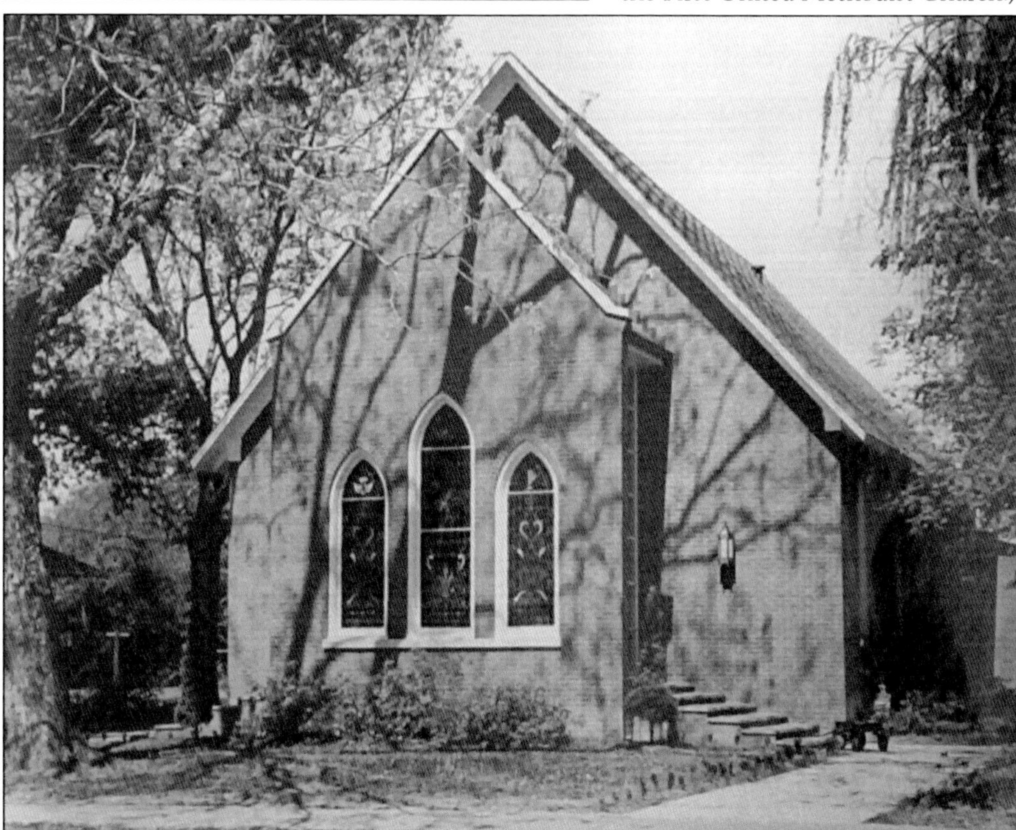

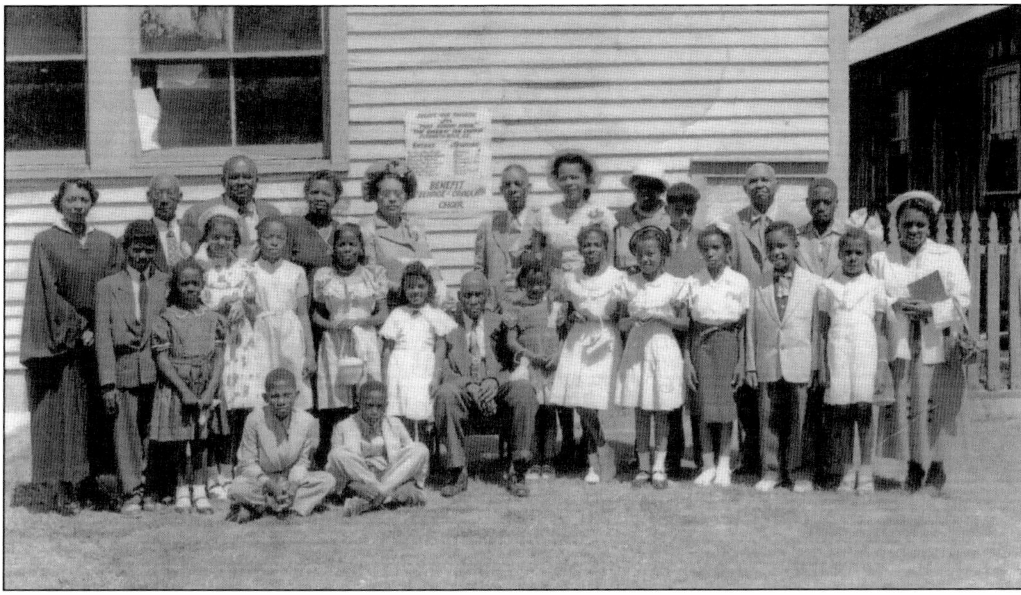

Plymouth Rock Baptist Church was founded by Rev. Ambrose Hubbs Sr. in 1894. The church was at Court and Union Streets. During the 1960s, it was nicknamed "Freedom Rock" for its role in the civil rights movement. In 1974, a new church was built on Iron Farm Road, and the original building was eventually torn down. This c. 1956 photograph shows a baptism class.

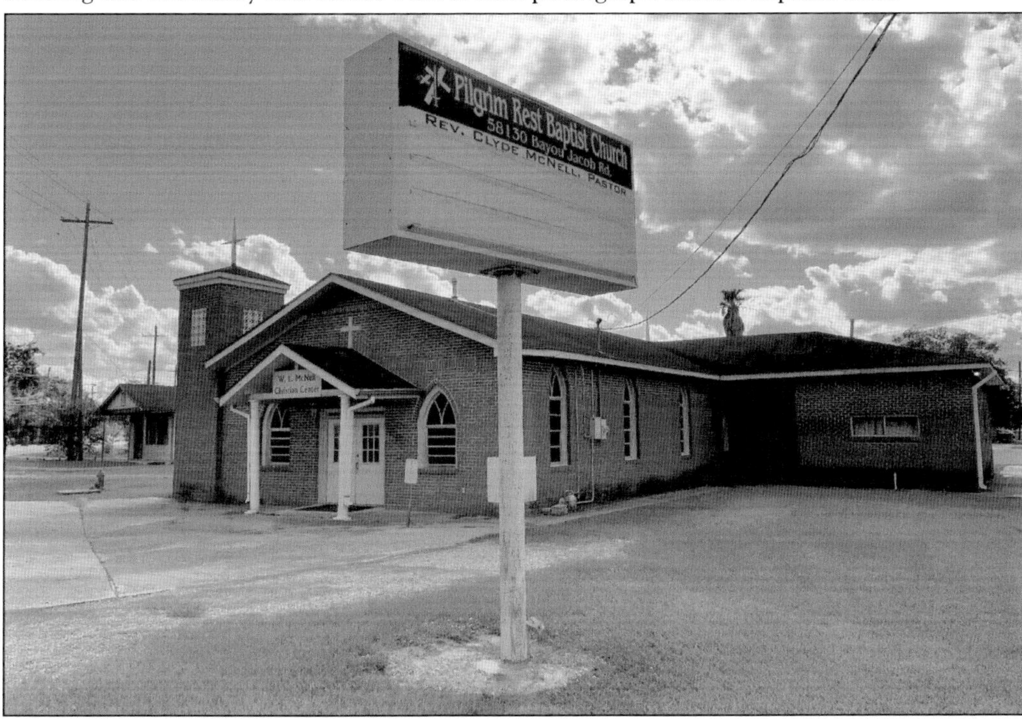

The Pilgrim Rest Baptist Church was founded in 1875 by Rev. G. Palmer and a contingent of former slaves. They built a church and cemetery, and established a Sunday school and a public school, where children on the surrounding plantations could learn to read and write. Today, it sits on the corner of Bayou Jacob Road and Talbot Drive. (Photograph by Meghan C. Sylvester.)

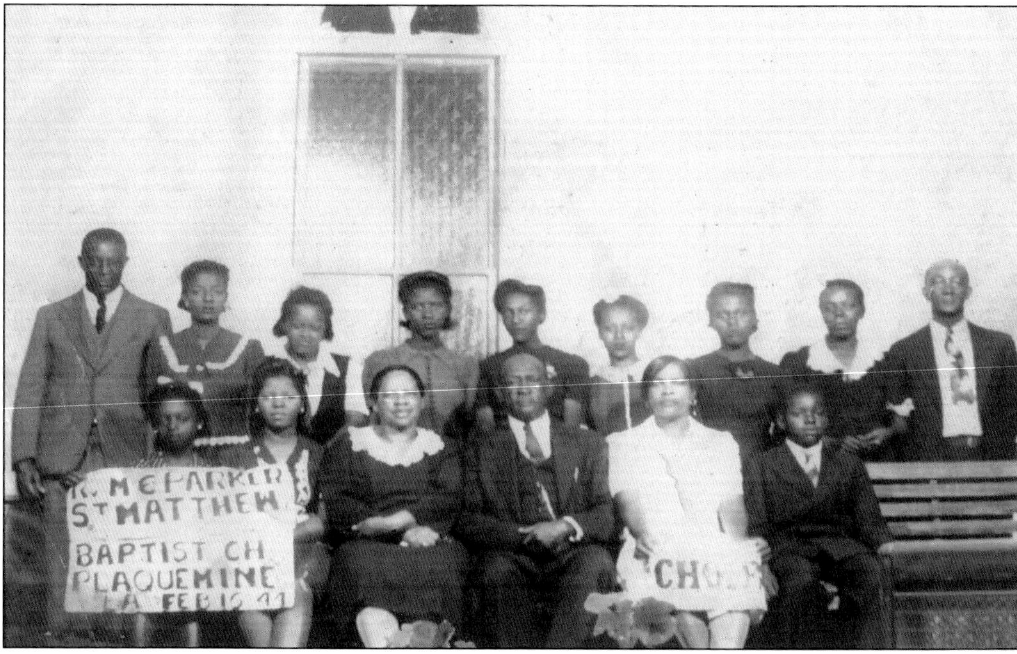

St. Matthews Baptist Church (pictured below) was founded on Myrtle Grove Plantation in 1874. Rev. Matthew Dunlap was ordained as its first pastor. In 1884, a storm destroyed the church, but the community rebuilt in Turnerville, near its present site. Levee construction in 1927 again required its parishioners to rebuild. Today, it stands on the corner of Government and Warren Streets. The above photograph was taken on February 16, 1944, of the church's choir. At center in the first row are pastor Matthew E. Parker and his wife, Sophronia Parker. Sophronia Parker was a devoted school teacher. In 1923, she opened a school in Turnerville for the local black youth known as Turnerville Private School. The elementary school was located behind her house on Jacob Street and included grades first through fourth. In 1957, Parker retired, closing her school. (Below, photograph by Meghan C. Sylvester.)

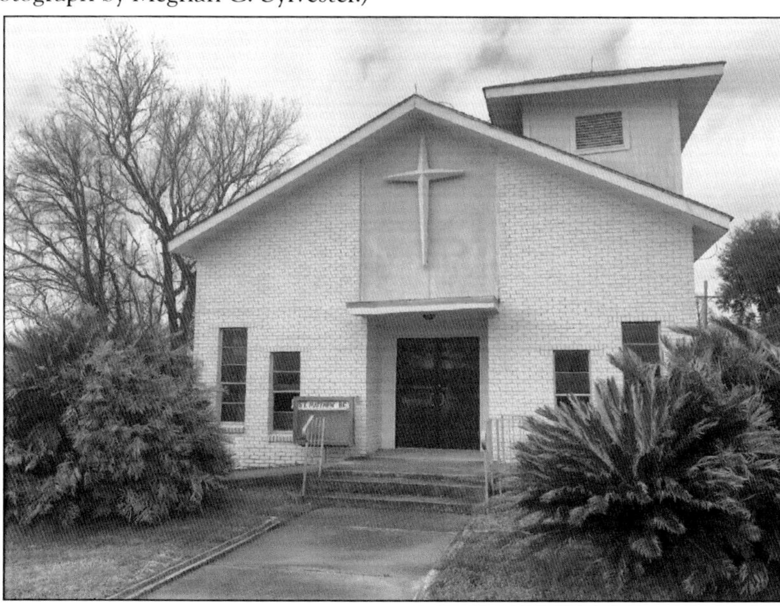

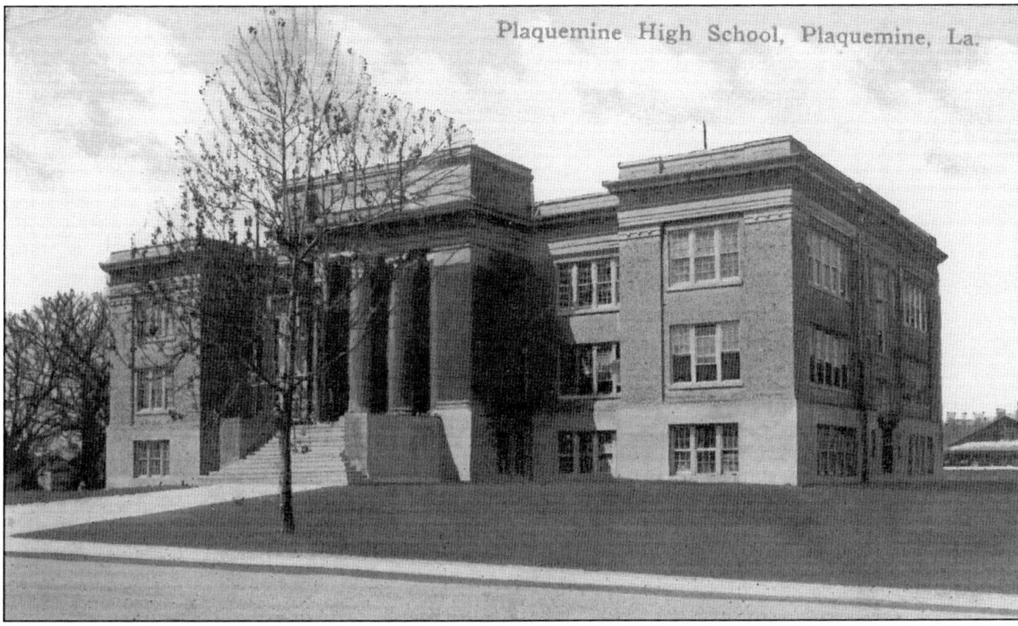

The first public high school in Plaquemine opened for the 1894–1895 school year. The school board rented the Slack building, a two-story wooden structure on Plaquemine Street near present-day Constitution Street. In 1910, a special school tax was passed to construct a new high school, and in 1911, the second school building, which was erected at that same location, opened. This postcard was produced around 1912.

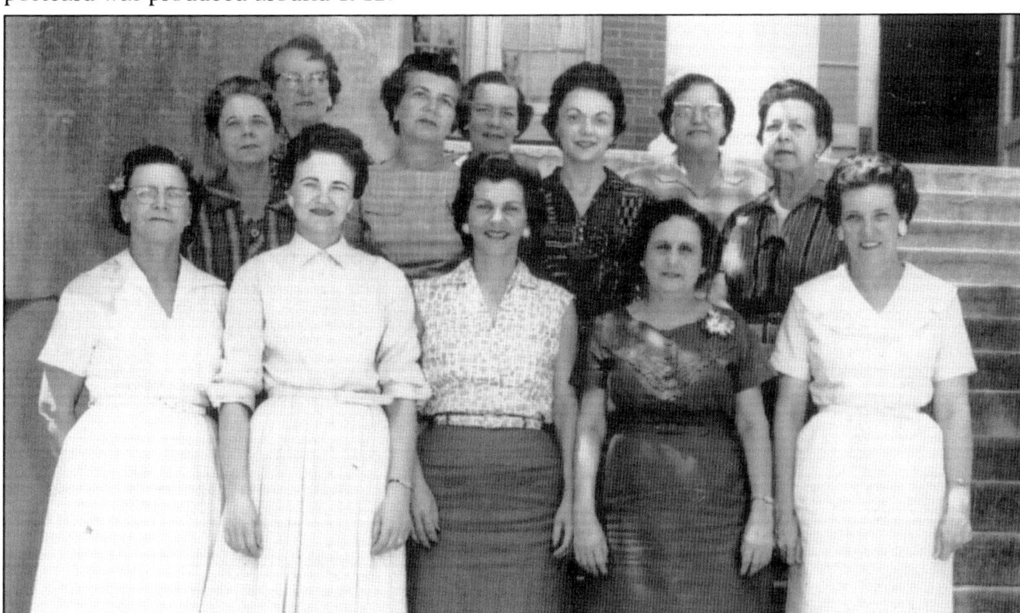

By 1931, a third Plaquemine High School building was opened on Ferdinand Street, turning the second building into Plaquemine Elementary. Pictured here are teachers at the elementary school in 1959. From left to right are (first row) Pauline Becnel, Norma Jean Dupont, Audrey Bickham, Ruby Saurez, and Sis Kinberger; (second row) Lolita Daigre, Lena Hebert, Ruth Bourgeois, Ruth Robertson, unidentified, Mary Brown, and Zeta Patureau. (Courtesy of Tony Fama.)

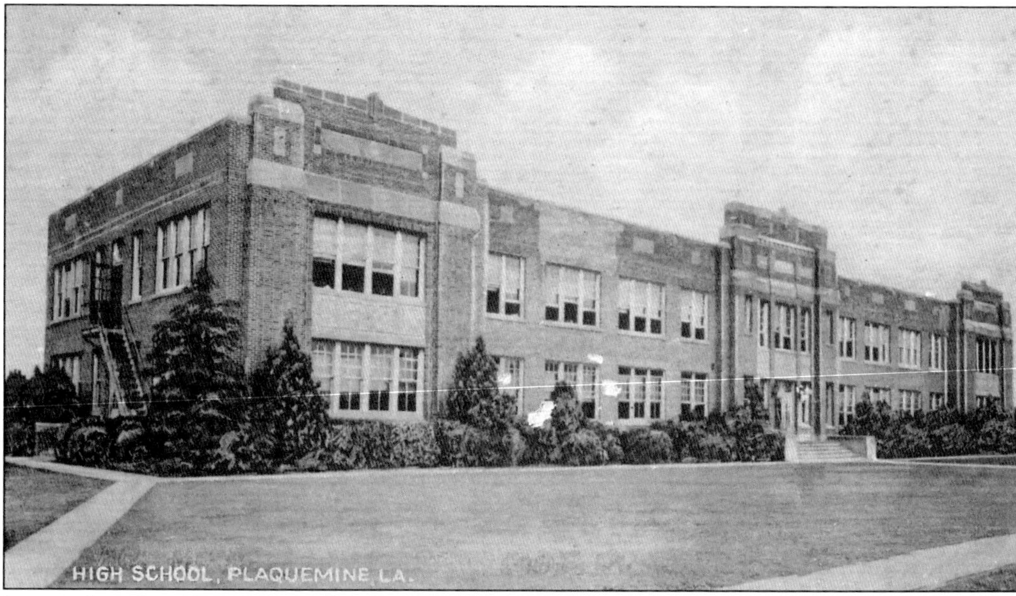

Pictured on this 1940s postcard is the Plaquemine High School on Ferdinand Street. This school was eventually integrated at the end of the 1960s, and in 1974, a fourth Plaquemine High School building was erected on Belleview Drive.

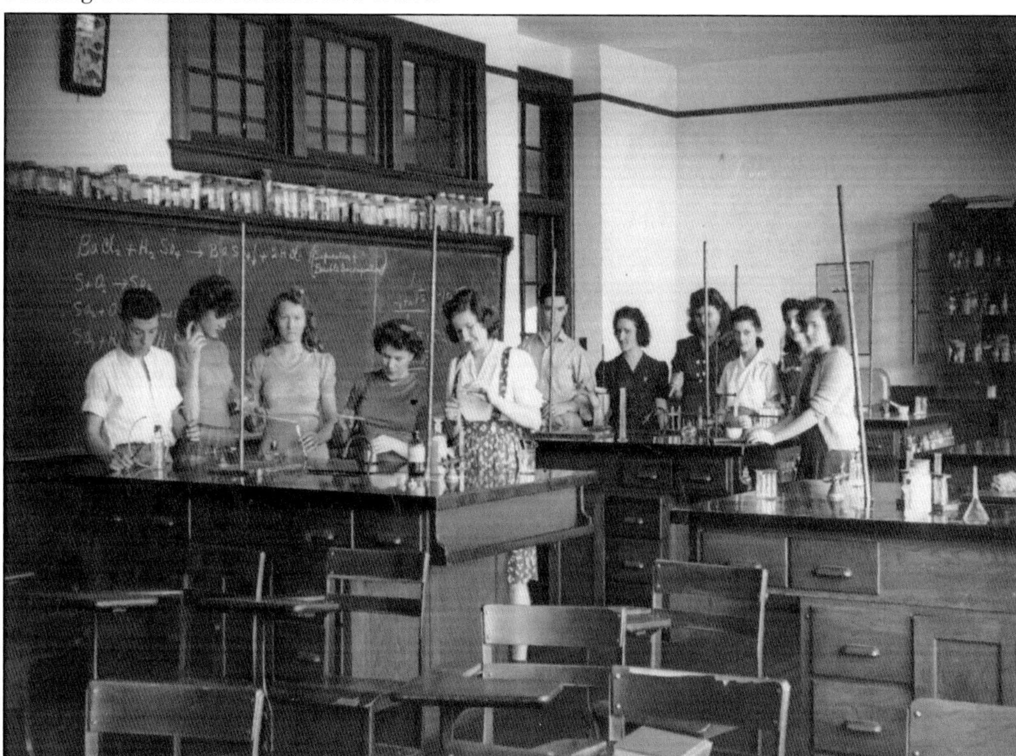

This 1940s photograph shows a chemistry class at Plaquemine High School and was taken by the Plaquemine High Camera Club. It also shows off the beautiful interior of the old school building, which is currently owned by the City of Plaquemine and used to house its activity center.

The Works Progress Administration (WPA) was founded in 1935 to combat unemployment during the Great Depression. One of its many projects was the building of Plaquemine High School's athletic field and gymnasium. This photograph is dated August 21, 1936, and shows WPA workers digging the gym's foundation. (Courtesy of the State Library of Louisiana.)

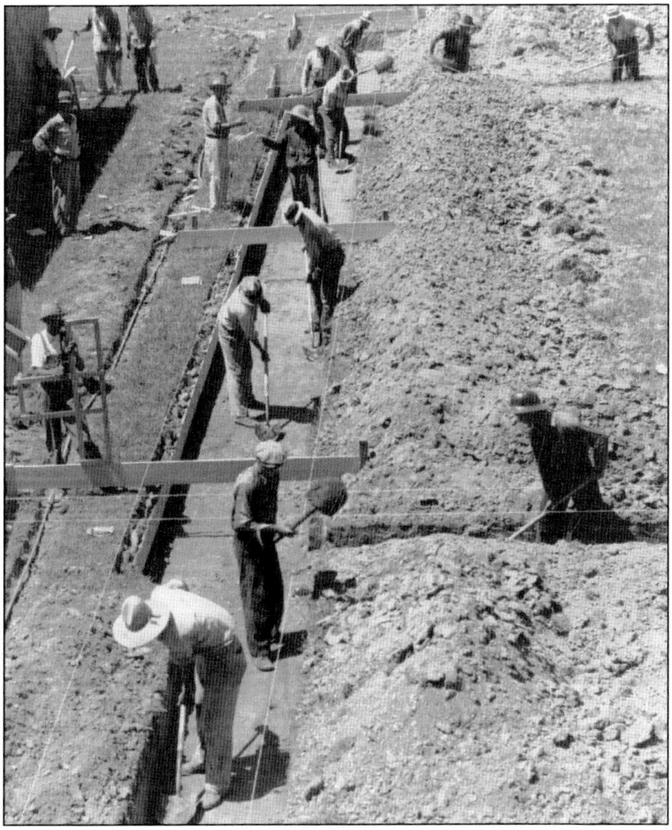

This is the completed athletic field for Plaquemine High School around 1937. The field's bleachers were added in the decades that followed. This photograph was taken from the school and gymnasium and looked in the direction of Calvin and Fort Streets. (Courtesy of the State Library of Louisiana.)

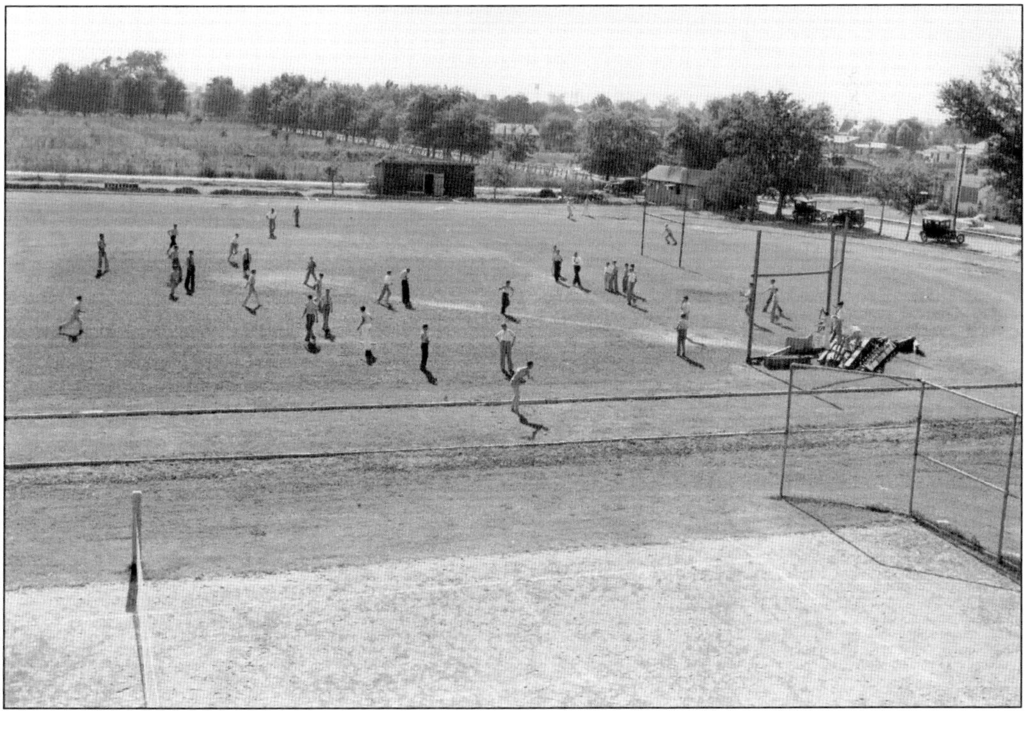

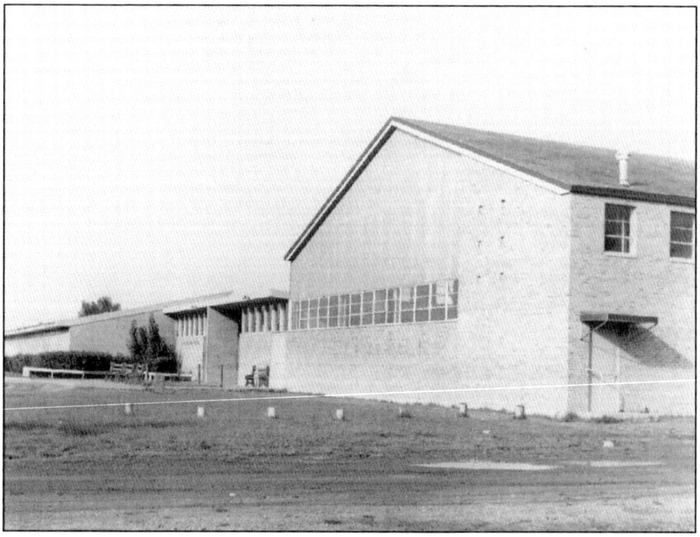

Iberville High School opened on Iron Farm Road in 1935 as a black public school in Plaquemine. Wendell O. Williams, a local educator, started as an English teacher and assistant principal in 1935. He was the principal from 1942 until its closure in 1969. During the 1960s, Iberville High's students played a crucial role in the local civil rights movement, advocating for equality and access to education and jobs in the parish.

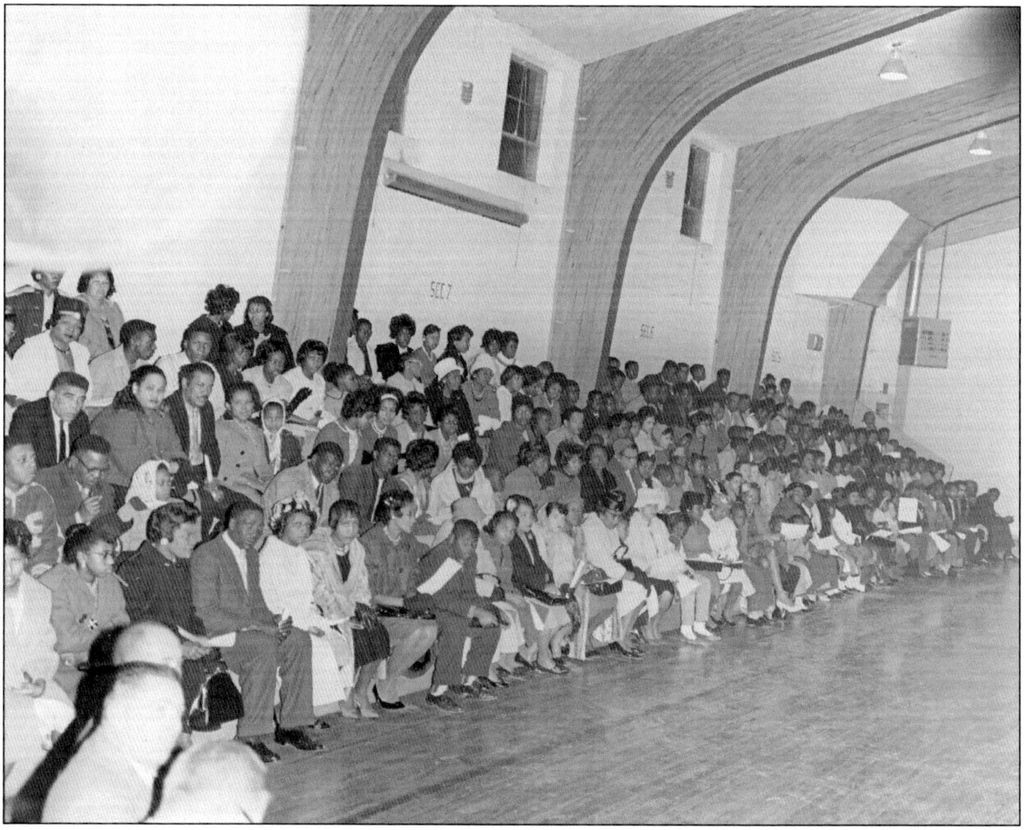

The original Iberville High campus consisted of over two acres and featured a two-story academic building with 12 rooms, two trade school buildings, and a shower house. However, the school was destroyed in an electrical fire in April 1940. It soon was rebuilt, and after its closure in 1969 following desegregation, it became Iberville Elementary. This c. 1961 photograph captures a Parent-Teacher Association workshop in the gymnasium.

Eight

Plaquemine and the Civil Rights Movement

During the summer of 1963, Plaquemine was chosen by the Congress of Racial Equality (CORE) as a headquarters while it worked to increase black voter registration across the state's sugar parishes. Local teacher William W. Harleaux wrote a letter inviting Ronnie Moore, CORE field secretary, and Gordon Carey, CORE's national program director, to Plaquemine. Harleaux requested their aid in increasing voter registration in the parish. His letter explained that no black person in Iberville had successfully registered to vote since 1958.

Upon CORE's arrival to town in mid-July, Moore set up a 10-day interracial training program. It taught participants how to lead voter registration drives and practice non-violent tactics. The training ended on July 24, and teams rolled out from Plaquemine to reach the more rural surrounding area. However, the movement in Plaquemine was just beginning. In early July, activists began picketing two stores in Plaquemine, Food Town near Plaquemine High School, and West Brothers on Eden Street. The demonstrations were led by local CORE task force workers Capt. Tolbert Harris, Rev. Jetson Davis, Spivey Gordon, and Ronnie Moore. The picketers wore shirts that read "Freedom Now" and asked for equal access to jobs at these locations.

City officials worked to curb these actions by passing 15 new ordinances that, for example, made it illegal for more than two people to picket and required one person to obtain a permit from the mayor and city council to conduct a parade. But the local civil rights leaders continued their fight for equality.

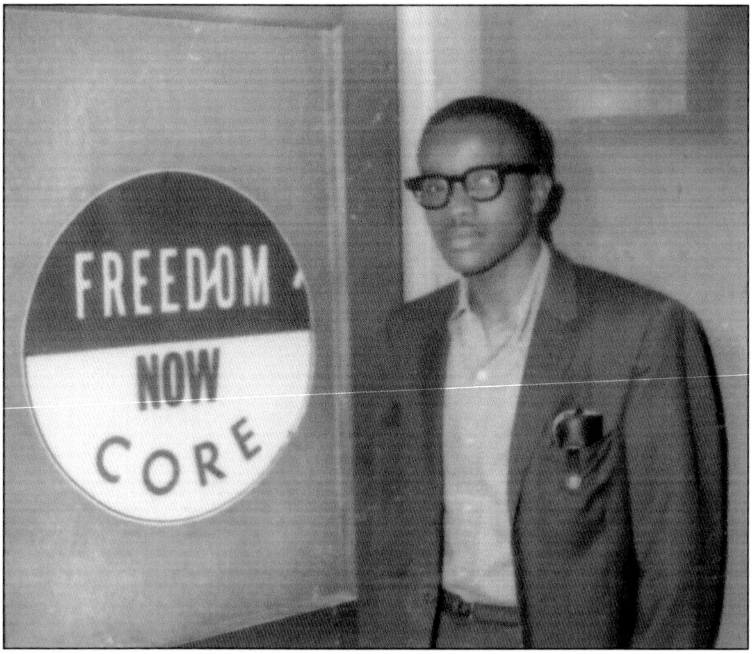

Ronnie Moore (pictured) was the field secretary for CORE between 1961 and 1965. During this time, he established voter registration initiatives in Louisiana and other parts of the South. He and other activists registered and motivated African Americans to vote and develop local CORE chapters in their communities. Spiver Gordon became Plaquemine's full-time field secretary. (Courtesy of Amistad Research Center.)

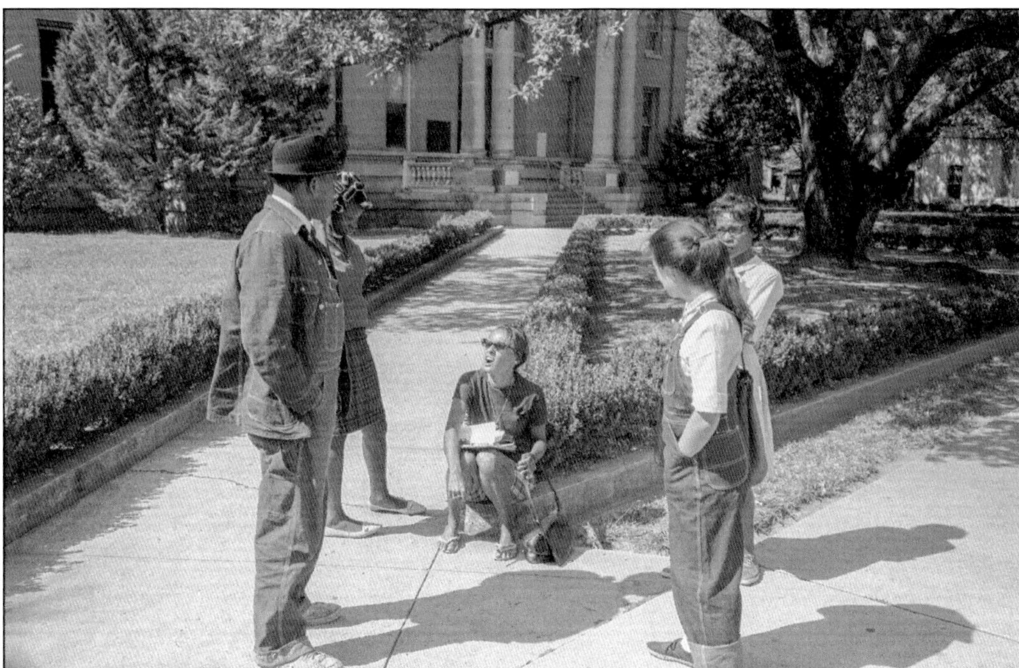

Pictured are CORE task workers in front of the Iberville Parish Courthouse to prepare a voter registration drive during the summer of 1963. Moore had suggested they bring an interracial group of both locals and people from across the United States. The woman standing at front right is Miriam Feingold, a college student from Brooklyn, New York, who was later arrested during protests in Plaquemine. While in the Port Allen Jail, she wrote a six-foot-long letter on toilet paper detailing her experiences in Plaquemine. (Photograph by Bob Adelman, courtesy of Bob Adelman estate.)

On August 13, twenty-five CORE workers traveling to New Orleans on their day off were arrested on the Plaquemine ferry after refusing to segregate themselves. The following evening, a march of about 150 people led by Capt. Tolbert Harris and Rev. Jetson Davis left Plymouth Rock Baptist Church on Court Street and walked to the courthouse (pictured below). Upon arrival, they sang the gospel song, "We Shall Overcome," and said a prayer for those in the parish jail and then returned to the church silently. The task force workers were released the following day, as parish leaders agreed that they had been wrongfully arrested. Moore declared this their first win and motivated others to keep fighting for equality. (Right, photograph by Bob Adelman; courtesy of Bob Adelman estate; below, photograph by Robert Mooney.)

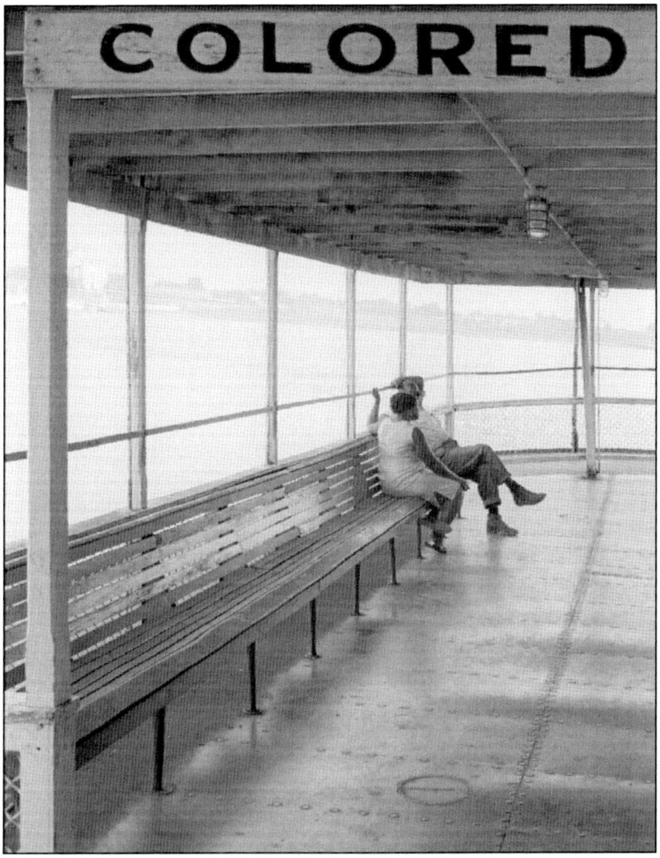

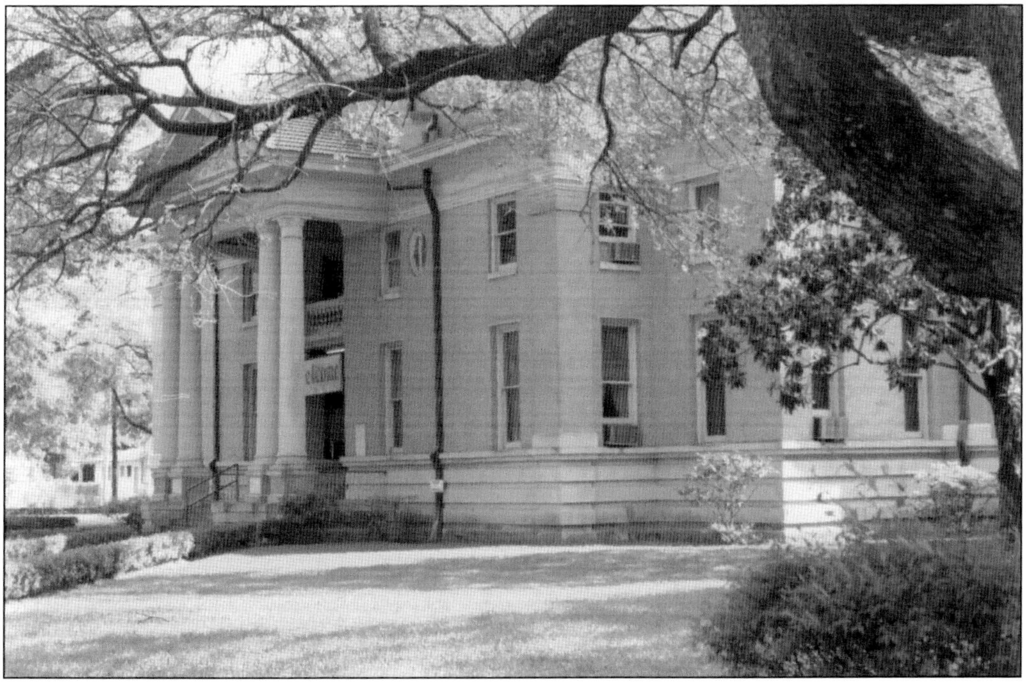

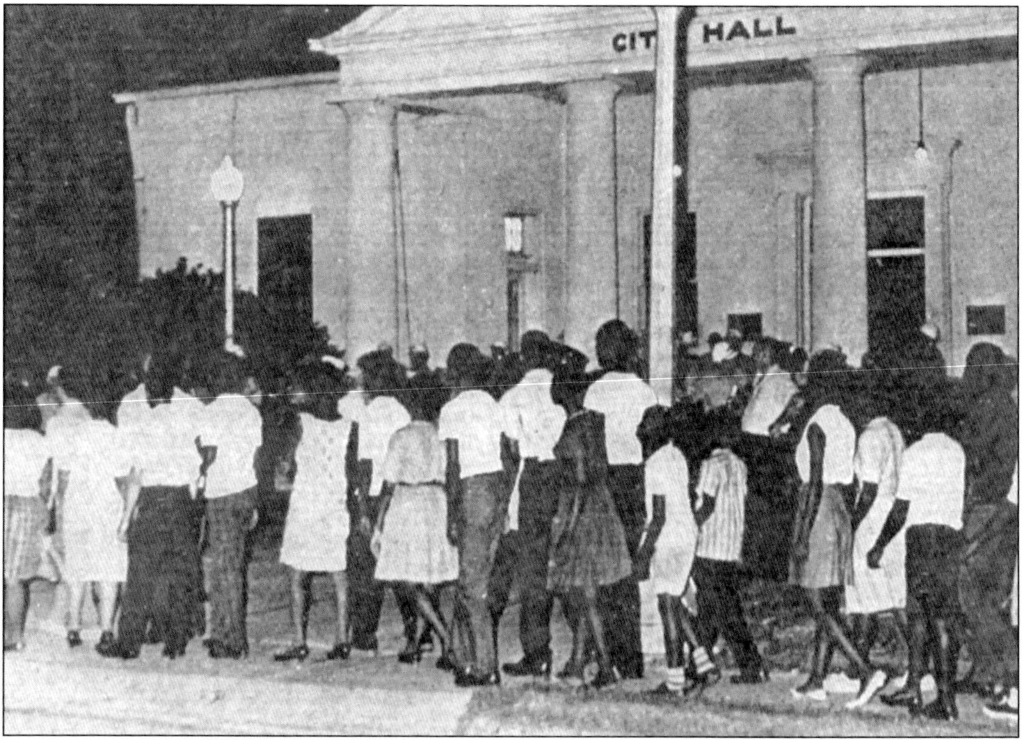

James Farmer, the national director of CORE, arrived in Plaquemine on August 19 with the intent of only staying in the state for three days. He spoke at Plymouth Rock Baptist Church to 500 people and then, along with Dr. Bertrand Tyson, William W. Harleaux, Rev. Jetson Davis, and Ronnie Moore, led a march on Plaquemine City Hall. The crowd walked in silence to city hall and was greeted by deputies on horseback asking them to leave. When the protestors began singing, the police teargassed them and arrested the leaders. Below, police with cattle prods chase a man in front of St. John school. Over the next few days, some 232 arrests were made, filling up the parish jail, requiring many to be sent to neighboring parishes. (Below, courtesy of Bettmann, Gettyimages.)

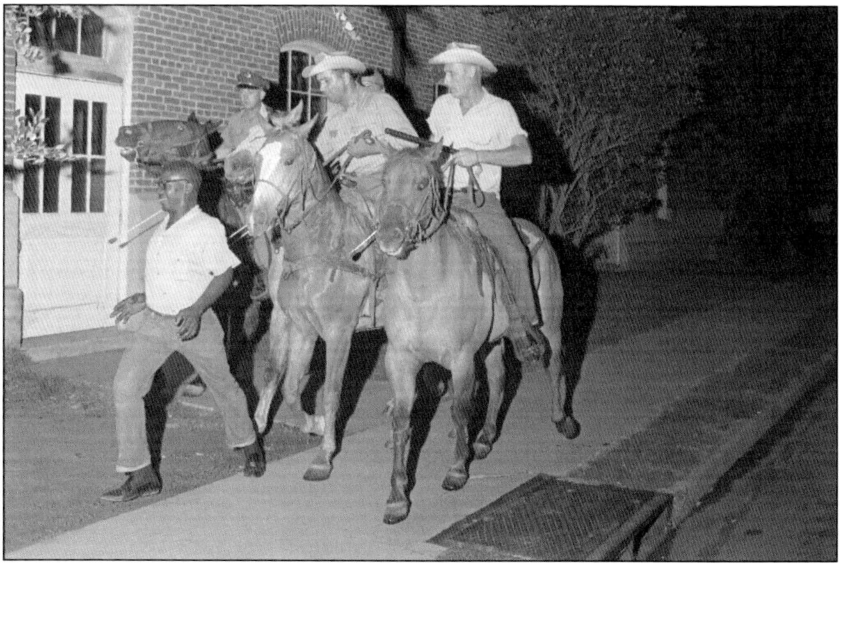

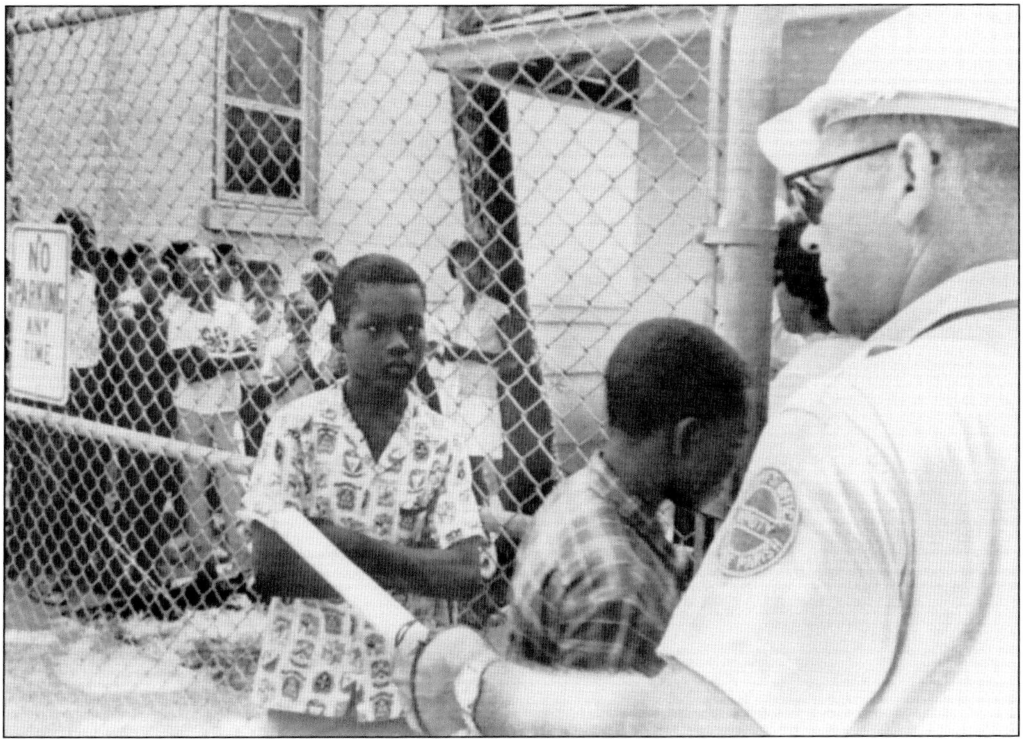

Activists worked to keep the movement going over the next few weeks. Many of the demonstrations were conducted by young students. Here, a deputy sheriff motions for a child to enter the compound at the courthouse after students stood around the fences and sang freedom songs on August 21, 1963. This demonstration was in protest of the parish's segregated school system. (Photograph by Jim Bourdier, courtesy of Associated Press.)

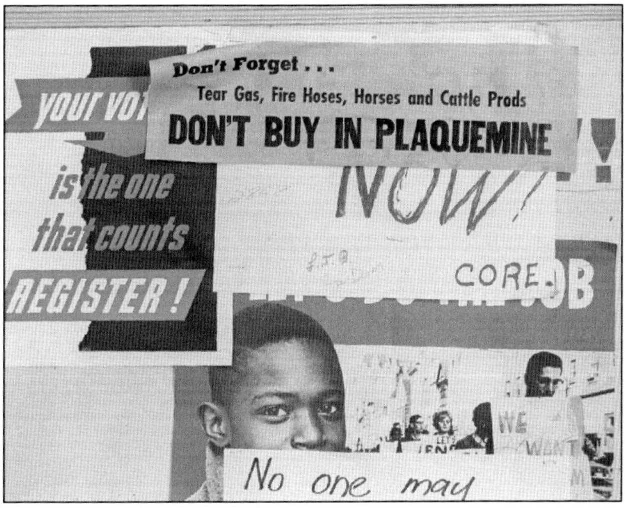

The boycotts of Plaquemine's stores also continued, as two local black neighborhoods, Dupont Annex and Seymourville, remained gerrymandered. Plaquemine's city limits completely surrounded Dupont Annex, but the neighborhood remained unincorporated, providing the community with no sewer lines, pavement, or street lights. Activists felt that if they could not be a part of Plaquemine, they would not shop in Plaquemine. (Photograph by Bob Adelman, courtesy of Bob Adelman estate.)

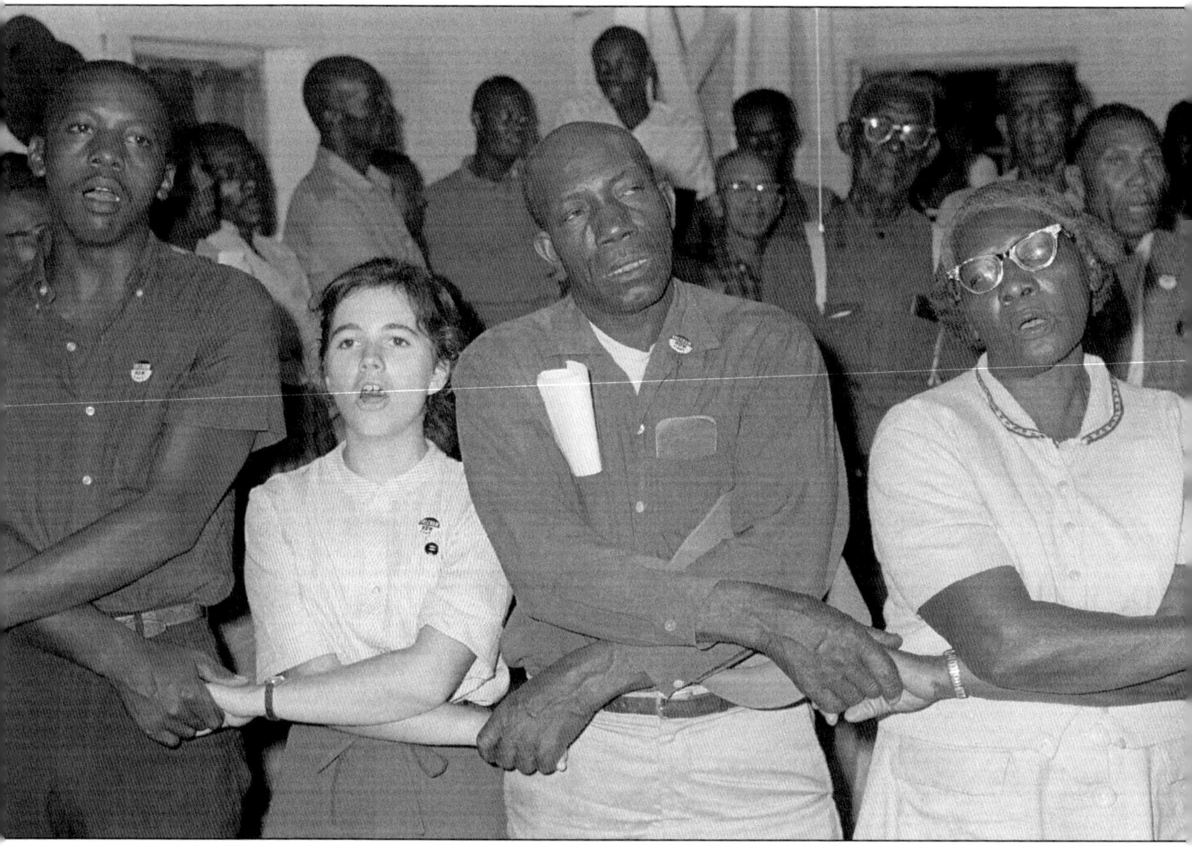

For 10 days, CORE's leaders sat in the Donaldsonville jail, including James Farmer. He was supposed to join Martin Luther King Jr. in Washington, DC, for the historic march on Washington. However, Farmer felt determined to remain with the people in Plaquemine. After most made bail, he and local leaders began organizing Plaquemine's largest demonstration, despite CORE being served a restraining order. On September 1, 1963, some 500 people left Plymouth Rock Baptist Church, proceeded to the courthouse square, and were met by police officers. They continued in silence back to the church, where they regrouped for another march, this time without James Farmer, as he feared his presence would provoke unnecessary hostility. But when the marchers arrived at the courthouse for the second time, mounted state troopers forced them to return to the church. Protesters then began throwing rocks and bricks, and what started as a non-violent demonstration for freedom quickly became a frenzied riot. Pictured here, members of CORE unite while singing freedom songs inside a church. (Photograph by Bob Adelman, courtesy of Bob Adelman estate.)

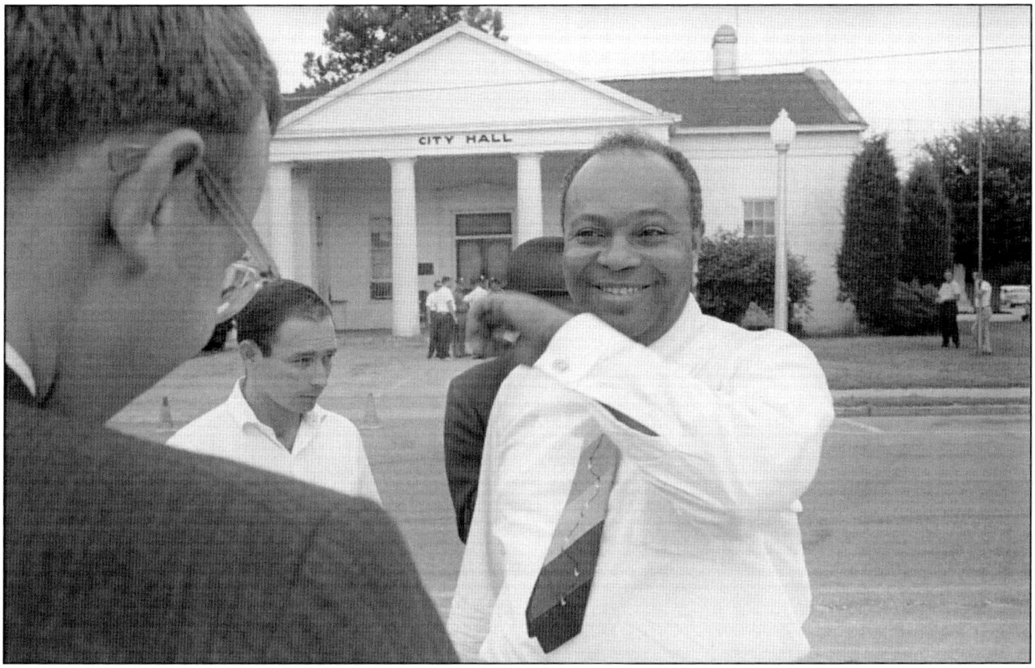

Officers used tear gas canisters and high-pressure water hoses to force protestors out of the church and went door to door searching for James Farmer. Out of fear for Farmer's safety, local citizens loaded him into a hearse belonging to Good Citizens Funeral Home on Plaquemine Street and sent him to New Orleans. Pictured above is Farmer on September 3 after returning to Plaquemine for his trial in the municipal court for charges from the August 19 demonstrations. Below, Capt. Tolbert Harris, CORE task force leader and retired US Army officer, is arrested after leaving the same hearing at city hall, accused of hitting a police officer with a brick during the demonstration. Behind him is the Plaquemine Youth Center on Main Street. Both Farmer and Harris were found guilty of disturbing the peace. (Both, courtesy of Associated Press.)

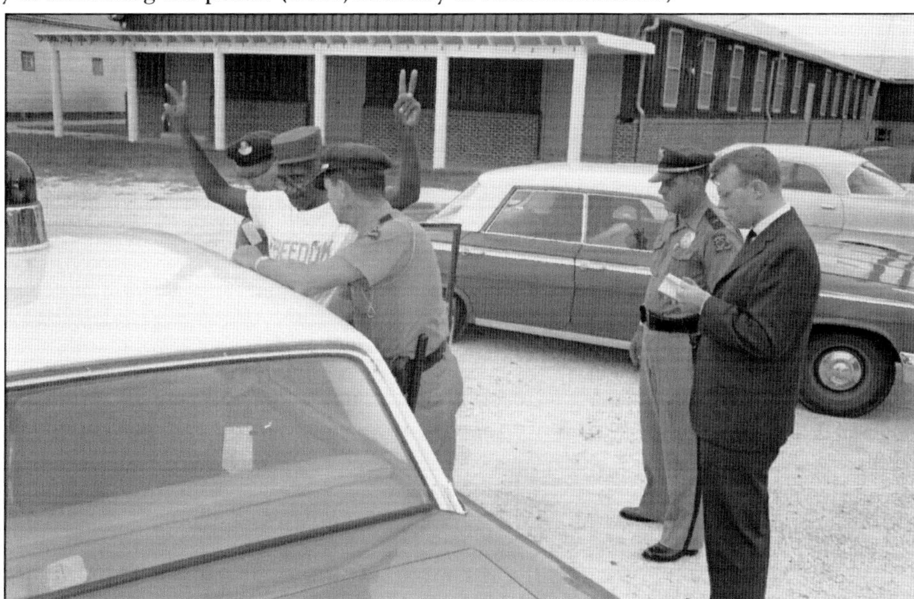

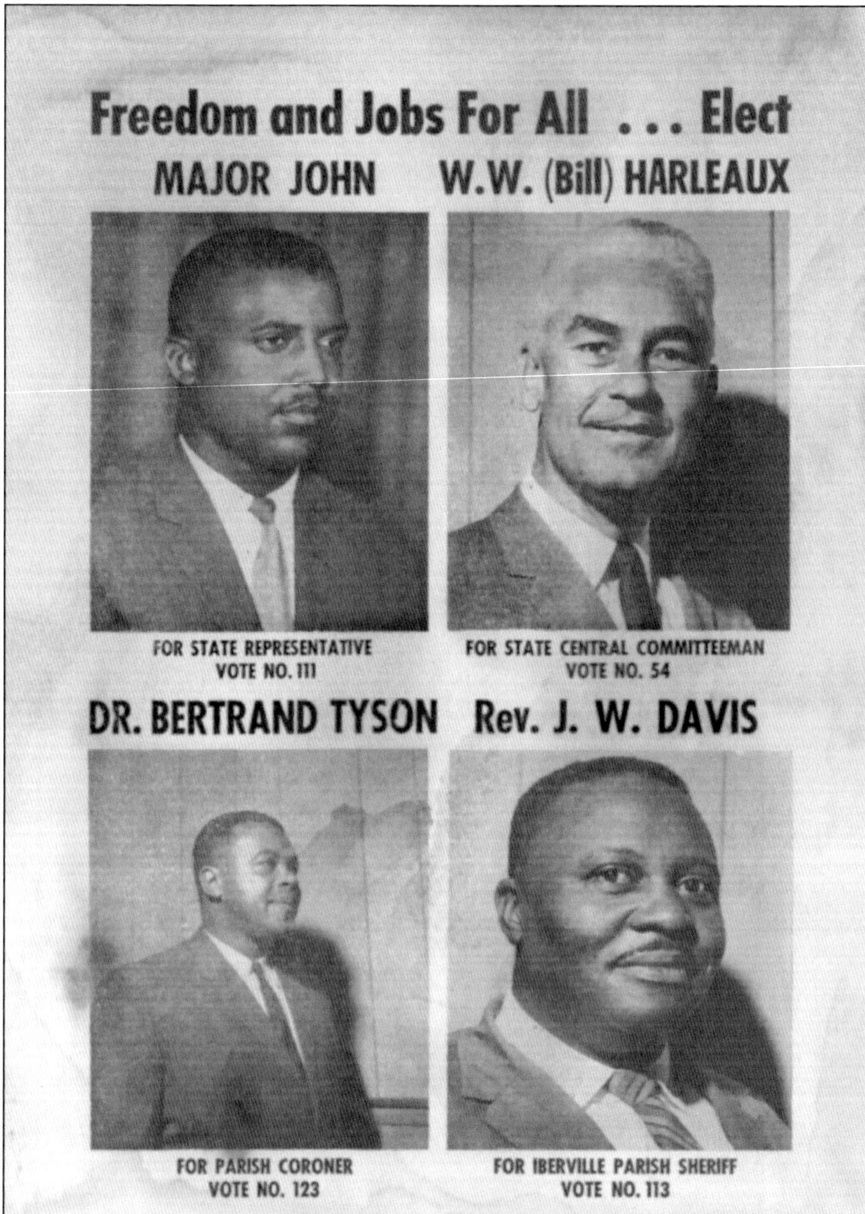

By the end of September 1963, a total of 11 black men in the parish qualified for the Iberville Parish Democratic primary election on December 7. Pictured on this election poster is Major Johns running for state representative. Johns was a native of Plaquemine and valedictorian of Iberville High, and his campaign focused on bettering the school system and providing more job opportunities. William W. Harleaux was a school teacher and principal. He ran for the state central committee. Dr. Bertrand Tyson was a medical doctor in Plaquemine, performing one of the first open-heart surgeries at the Plaquemine Sanitarium, and ran for parish coroner. Rev. Jetson W. Davis, the pastor of Plymouth Rock Baptist Church, announced his run for Iberville Parish sheriff in October 1963, stating he could "bring about a closer relationship among all people regardless of race, creed, or color." Others who ran for office were Herman Wilkerson and Spiver Gordon.

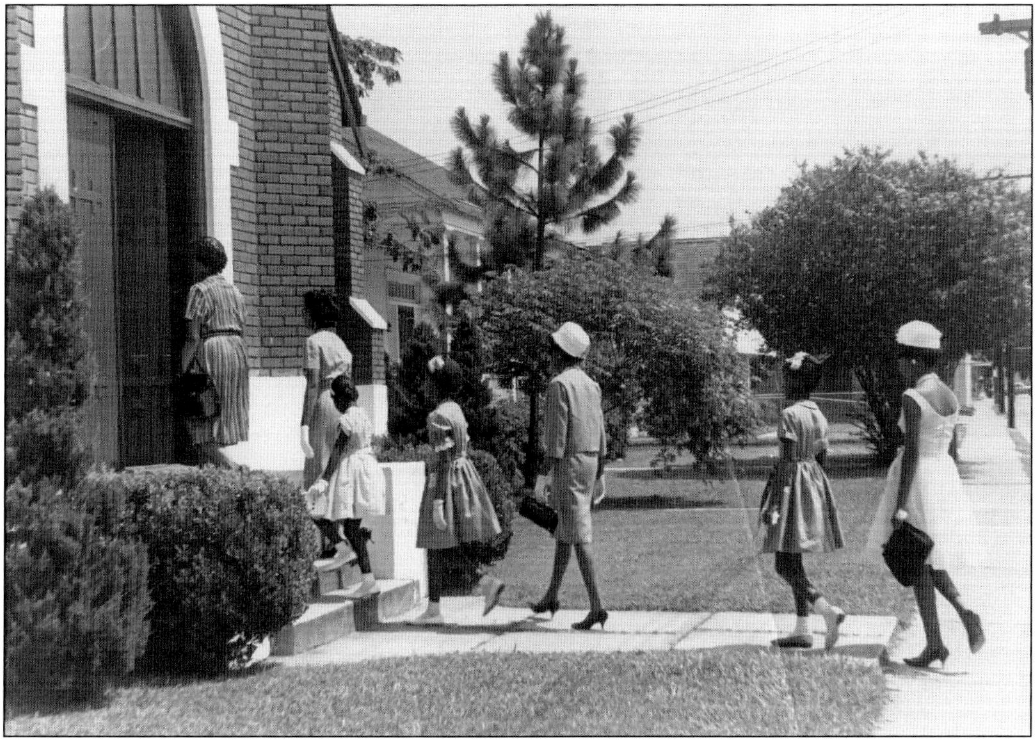

Besides some unrest in October at Iberville High School, overall, demonstrations in Plaquemine remained peaceful and organized. Activists led a march to city hall following the Birmingham church bombing, and (pictured here) demonstrators integrated the Episcopal Church in Plaquemine. They were also able to join the Catholic church and the Northside Baptist Church but were denied by the Methodist church and the First Baptist Church in Plaquemine. (Courtesy of IPL.)

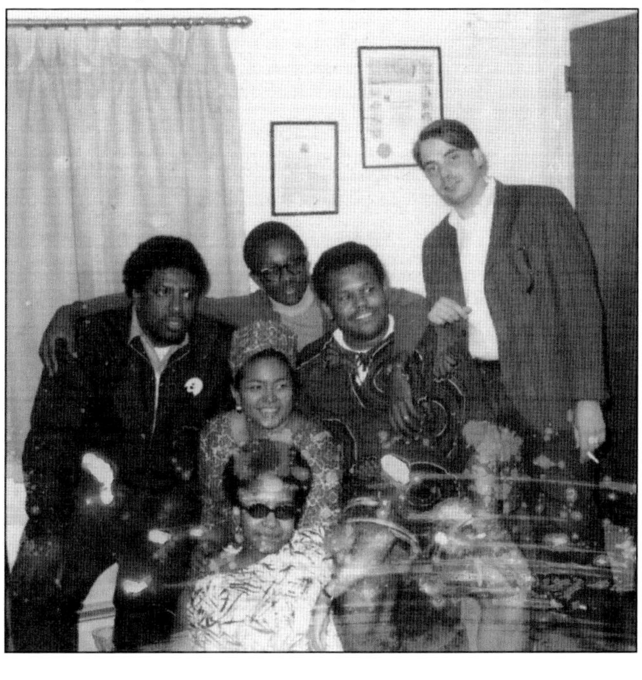

While some felt CORE's presence put unnecessary pressure on the community, their work in helping locals organize did support positive change. In 1965, when Pres. Lyndon B. Johnson signed the Voting Rights Act, Iberville Parish saw an 83.4 percent increase of black voter registrations, one of the three largest increases in Louisiana. Pictured from left to right are CORE officials Al Culpepper, Maria LeBlanc, Ronnie Moore, Spiver Gordon, unidentified, and LaRee Smith (front) in New York City in 1963.

Bibliography

Bernard, Shane K. *Teche: A History of Louisiana's Most Famous Bayou.* Jackson, MS: University Press of Mississippi, 2016.

Consolidated Companies Inc. *Round the Bend to Another 50 Years . . .*. Self-published, 1951.

Fairclough, Adam. *Race and Democracy: The Civil Rights Struggle in Louisiana 1915–1972.* Athens, GA: University of Georgia Press, 1995.

Fama, Anthony P. *Plaquemine: A Glimpse of the Early Years.* Self-published, 2004.

———. *Plaquemine: A Long, Long Time Ago.* Self-published, 2004.

Farmer, James. *Louisiana Story: 1963.* New York, NY: Congress of Racial Equality, 1963.

Follett, Richard. *The Sugar Masters: Planters and Slaves in Louisiana's Cane World, 1820–1860.* Baton Rouge, LA: Louisiana State University Press, 2005.

Grandchamp, Robert. *A Connecticut Yankee at War: The Life and Letters of George Lee Gaskell.* Gretna, LA: Pelican Publishing Company, 2015.

Riffel, Judy, ed. *Iberville Parish Cemeteries.* Baton Rouge, LA: Le Comité des Archives de la Louisiane, 1989.

———. *Iberville Parish History.* Baton Rouge, LA: Le Comité des Archives de la Louisiane, 1985.

About the Organization

The Iberville Museum Association is a nonprofit community organization in downtown Plaquemine dedicated to preserving and promoting Iberville Parish's heritage and culture. It is housed in the 1848 courthouse, which later became Plaquemine's city hall. The building was listed in the National Register of Historic Places in 1980 and is still owned by the City of Plaquemine.

In the late 1980s, with a group of dedicated citizens, the city led a major restoration project on the building. However, the building's final purpose was not yet clear. The Iberville Museum Association was founded in 1998 by Louis J. Nicolosi, Winifred Boudreaux, Brenda Blanchard, David Nicolosi, Zoe Spedale, Denise Murrell, Imogene Marionneaux, Jan Drinkwater, and Cindy E. Dickerson. The building's restoration was completed in 1999, and the city agreed to lease it to the museum for $1 for 10 years. In June 2000, the museum officially opened its doors to the public.

Over the next 20 years, the museum made it its mission to collect, preserve, and interpret the rich history of Iberville Parish. It houses over 2,000 objects and photographs in its collections and features exhibits on the history and culture of the Atchafalaya Basin, Plaquemine archaeology, Iberville Parish veterans, the Louisiana High School Boxing Hall of Fame, and more.

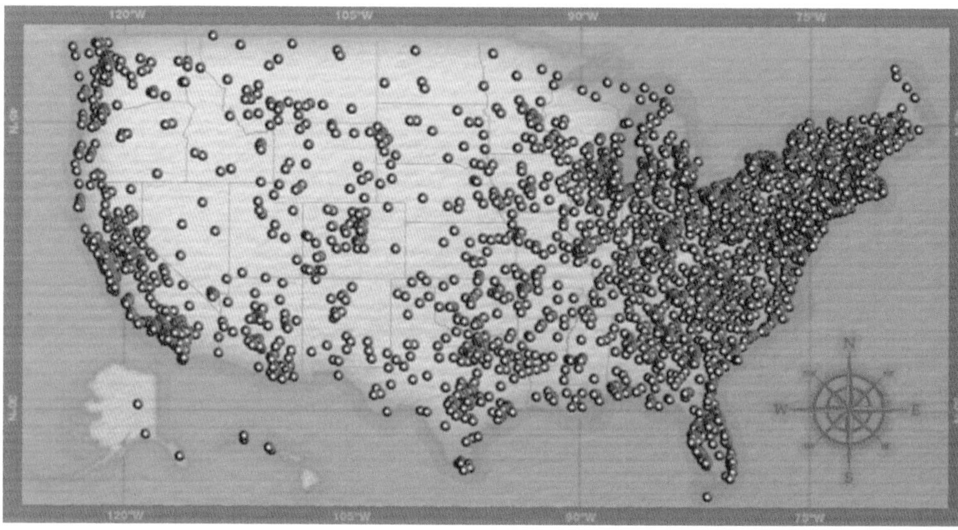